NEW
SUCCESS
at
FIRST
CERTIFICATE

ROBERT O'NEILL
Michael Duckworth & Kathy Gude

Oxford University Press

Oxford University Press, Great Clarendon Street,
Oxford OX2 6DP

Oxford New York
Athenes Auckland Bangkok Bogota Buenos Aires
Calcutta Cape Town Chennai Dar es Salaam
Delhi Florence Hong Kong Istanbul Karachi
Kuala Lumpur Madrid Melbourne Mexico City
Mumbai Nairobi Paris Sao Paulo Shanghai Singapore
Taipei Tokyo Toronto Warsaw
and associated companies in
Berlin Ibadan

OXFORD and OXFORD ENGLISH
are trade marks of Oxford University Press

ISBN 0 19 453332 8

© Oxford University Press 1997

First published 1997

Sixth Impression 2000

No unauthorized photocopying

Typeset by Oxford University Press

Printed in Dubai

Acknowledgements

**The authors and publisher would like to thank the
following for permission to reproduce copyright
material:**

The Daily Telegraph for extracts from the following
articles: 'Fear turns crime-free suburb into fortress' by
Kathy Marks; 'Pentagon spent £13m on psychic spies,
says CIA' by Hugh Davies; 'Head to head with a 3-D
world'; 'Child violence is linked to computer games';
'Bright ideas up for sale'; 'In the swing' all by
Christine McGourty; 'Mice put memory drug to maze
test' by Roger Highfield; 'Patient says thanks to her
flying doctors' by Sean O'Neill and 'Surgery at 33,000
ft with a coat hanger, scissors and brandy' by Michael
Smith, © Telegraph Group Limited, London, 1995

Anna Damski for an extract from 'Travels with Sir
David Attenborough'

First Choice Holidays for extracts from First Choice
Holiday brochure, Summer '96, Second Edition

The Press On-Line at www.press.co.nz for extracts
from 'Hero tells of dramatic rescue at sea' by Diane
Keenan

Illustrations by:

Veronica Bailey, Stefan Chabluk, Alison Everitt,
Robin Harris, Stephanie Hawken, Mike Ritchie,
Simon Roulstone, Martin Sanders, Technical
Graphics Dept., OUP, David Williams

Location photography by Bill Osment

**The publisher would like to thank the following for
their permission to use photographs:**

Ace Photo Library: 148; Allsport: 76 top left;
Associated Press: 42 top right, 134; Barnabys Picture
Library: 92 bottom left; Catherine Blackie:
59, 74 centre, 92 bottom right, 106, 118; British
Tourist Authority: 90 top right; Camera Press:
113, 140 top; Collections: 92 centre right, 101 top left;
Dee Conway: 21 bottom; Robert Harding Picture
Library: 34 top right; Hulton Getty: 94; Hutchison
Library: 76 top right, 76 centre left, 76 bottom right,
97, 157; Image Bank: 5, 10 right; Kobal Collection:
44 top; Magnum: 42 top left (photo Martin Parr),
50 centre left (photo Bruce Davidson), 50 bottom
(photo Martin Parr), 74 top (photo Gilles Peress),
138 right (photo Martin Parr), 146 right (photo Misha
Erwitt); Panos Pictures: 2 right; Photostage: 49, 66 top;
Rex Features: 2 left, 10 left, 34 top left, 58 bottom,
66 centre left, 92 top left, 101 bottom left, 116,
130 left, 130 right, 132, 140 bottom; Science Photo
Library: 21 centre; Still Pictures: 15 top right, 101 top
right, 129; Tony Stone Images (Cosmo Condina,
Simeone Huber); Universal (courtesy Kobal): 44 top;
Werner Forman Archive: 15 top left; Zefa Picture
Library: 6 bottom, 15 bottom left, 15 centre, 15 bottom
right, 44 bottom, 58 top, 70, 76 centre right, 76 bottom
left, 90 bottom left, 92 top right, 92 centre left,
101 bottom right, 138 left

**The publisher would like to thank the following for
their help and assistance:**

George & Davis's Ice Cream, Oxford

ABOUT THE FIRST CERTICATE EXAM

Paper 1   Reading
(1 hour 15 minutes)

Paper 1 consists of four parts, which are always in the same order. Each part contains a text and comprehension task of some kind. The type of texts used include newspaper and magazine articles, advertisements, brochures, guides, letters, fiction, messages and reports.

Part 1 *Multiple matching*: text preceded by multiple matching questions.

Part 2 *Multiple choice*: text followed by multiple choice questions.

Part 3 *Gapped text*: text from which 6 or 7 sentences or paragraphs have been removed and put in jumbled order. The task is to fit the missing text into the gaps.

Part 4 *Multiple matching*: as in Part 1.

Paper 2   Writing
(1 hour 30 minutes)

Paper 2 consists of two parts.

Part 1 *Transactional letter* (this part is compulsory).

Part 2 Candidates can choose one of four questions. The writing tasks may include letters, articles, reports, applications, stories and compositions, and questions about the background reading texts.

Paper 3   Use of English
(1 hour 15 minutes)

This paper consists of five parts, which test the candidate's knowledge of grammar and vocabulary.

Part 1 *Multiple choice vocabulary cloze*: a text with 15 gaps followed by a choice of 4 answers for each gap.

Part 2 *Grammar cloze*: a text with 15 gaps; no answers are given.

Part 3 *Key word transformations*: a complete sentence followed by a gapped sentence, which must be completed using a given word.

Part 4 *Error correction*: a text where most lines contain an extra and unnecessary word. Candidates must identify the extra words.

Part 5 *Word formation*: a text containing 10 gaps each of which must be filled with a word formed from a given root word.

Paper 4   Listening
(about 40 minutes)

This paper contains four parts. Each part contains one or more recorded texts and accompanying comprehension questions.

Part 1 *Multiple choice*: short, unconnected extracts, each about 30 seconds long.

Part 2 *Note taking or blank filling*: a monologue or a text with more than one speaker, lasting about 3 minutes.

Part 3 *Multiple matching*: short connected extracts, each about 30 seconds long. Candidates match extracts with prompts.

Part 4 *Selection from 2 or 3 possible answers*: a text lasting about 3 minutes. Task types may include yes/no, true/false, 3 option multiple choice, which speaker said what.

Paper 5   Speaking
(about 15 minutes for 2 candidates)

This paper – the speaking test – contains four parts. Normally there are two examiners and two candidates. One examiner only assesses, the other gives instructions and talks to the candidates. Candidates should talk mainly to each other.

Part 1 Candidates are asked to give information about themselves.

Part 2 Each candidate is given two pictures to talk about in relation to themselves. They also comment on the other candidate's pictures.

Part 3 Candidates talk to each other in a communication task (for example making plans, solving a problem, making a decision, discussing an order of importance, speculating). Pictures or diagrams help candidates start the discussion.

Part 4 Candidates exchange opinions with each other. Discussion is related to the topic of Part 3.

ABOUT THE BOOK

New Success at First Certificate is an integrated course divided into 20 topic-based units. Every eight-page unit has five parts, each starting on a new page. Each of these five parts is called a 'Focus'.

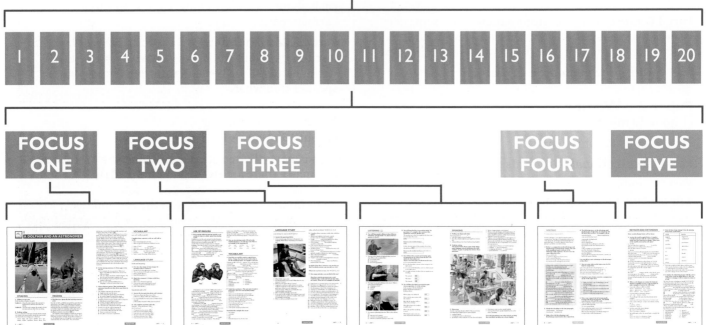

Each of *Focus 1–3* brings a fresh perspective to the unit topic together with integrated and varied language input and practice. The Focus input may be one or more of:

> USE OF ENGLISH
> READING
> LISTENING
> SPEAKING
> PASSAGES FOR COMMENT

Practice of vocabulary, structure and usage arises naturally from the input of the Focus. Practice activities and exercises may be one or more of:

> VOCABULARY
> LANGUAGE STUDY
> USE OF ENGLISH
> PROBLEM SOLVING
> WORD FORMATION
> WRITING

Focus 4 of each unit concentrates on the writing skill and the writing paper of the exam. It provides models, and practice of all the types of writing task (letter, narrative, speech, argument, description etc.) required in this part of the exam.

Focus 5 contains REVISION AND EXTENSION of key structures and vocabulary. Many of the exercises are in the form of the exam and there are cross-references where necessary to the Grammar Summary at the back of the book. This Summary provides clear grammatical explanations and examples.

The Syllabus pages show how each unit practises each of the five papers of the exam as well as listing the language study and vocabulary covered. ▷

SYLLABUS

1
A DOLPHIN AND AN ASTRONOMER

FOCUS	EXAM PRACTICE (P1 = Paper 1 etc.)	LANGUAGE STUDY/VOCABULARY
ONE	Speaking (P5) Reading (P1)	*say, tell, talk* or *speak*? Form and meaning Questions with *who*
TWO	Use of English (P3)	*stop doing* vs. *stop to do* *who, which* or *whose*? When do you have to use *the*?
THREE	Listening (P4) Speaking (P5)	Conversations
FOUR	Writing (argument 1) (P2)	Advantages and disadvantages; link words
FIVE	Revision and extension	Word building (verb to noun)

2
TRAVEL WISELY, TRAVEL WELL

ONE	Speaking (P5) Use of English (P3) Speaking (P5)	*travel, journey, voyage* or *trip*?
TWO	Reading (P1)	*may, should, must* and *will*
THREE	Listening (P4) Speaking (P5)	Verb and noun combinations: *give* and *take*
FOUR	Writing (transactional letter 1) (P2)	Informal letter 1
FIVE	Revision and extension (P3) Listening (P4)	Revision of Units 1 and 2

3
THE INTERVIEW

ONE	Speaking (P5) Reading (P1)	Phrasal verbs
TWO	Use of English (P3) Listening (P4)	Word building (noun to adjective/adverb)
THREE	Reading (P1)	Word building (*apply, applicant, application* etc.) Requests and intentions
FOUR	Writing (letter of application 1) (P2)	Formal letter
FIVE	Revision and extension	*do/does* or *am/is/are doing*? *will do* or *is/are doing*?

7 LETTERS TO AN ADVICE COLUMN

FOCUS	EXAM PRACTICE	LANGUAGE STUDY/VOCABULARY
ONE	Speaking (P5) Reading (P1)	Conditionals
TWO	Use of English (P3)	*fault, mistake, error, defect, blame* *Is it still going on?*
THREE	Listening (P4)	*suggest, recommend, advise* etc. *still, yet* or *already?* More about how we report what people say
FOUR	Writing (argument 2) (P2)	Expressing an opinion
FIVE	Revision and extension	Conditionals (1 and 2)

8 SPACE WARRIOR MADNESS

FOCUS	EXAM PRACTICE	LANGUAGE STUDY/VOCABULARY
ONE	Speaking (P5) Reading (P1)	Three types of past action
TWO	Reading (P1)	*so* or *such?* *ache* or *pain?*
THREE	Listening 1 (P4) Speaking (P5) Listening 2 (P4)	*used to do* or *be used to doing?*
FOUR	Writing (informal letter 1) (P2)	Adjective order
FIVE	Revision and extension (P3) Listening (P4)	Revision of Units 7 and 8

9 THE FACE BEHIND THE MASK

FOCUS	EXAM PRACTICE	LANGUAGE STUDY/VOCABULARY
ONE	Speaking (P5) Reading (P1)	*although* and *despite*
TWO	Listening (P4) Use of English (P3)	Phrasal verbs
THREE	Reading (P1)	*let* or *make?*
FOUR	Writing (article 1) (P2)	Adjectives describing character
FIVE	Revision and extension	Word building (noun ⇄ adjective)

10
WORDS AND FEELINGS

FOCUS	EXAM PRACTICE	LANGUAGE STUDY/VOCABULARY
ONE	Speaking (P5) Reading (P1)	Comparisons
TWO	Speaking (P5) Listening (P4)	Describing feelings
THREE	Use of English 1 (P3) Use of English 2 (P3)	Phrasal verbs Preferences
FOUR	Writing (transactional letter 3) (P2)	Informal letter 2
FIVE	Revision and extension (P3) Listening (P4)	Revision of Units 9 and 10

11
SCENES FROM A ROMANTIC NOVEL

FOCUS	EXAM PRACTICE	LANGUAGE STUDY/VOCABULARY
ONE	Speaking (P5) Reading (P1)	Prepositions Question structures
TWO	Reading (P1) Use of English (P3)	Gerund (*doing*) or infinitive (*to do*)? Infinitive with or without *to*?
THREE	Use of English (P3) Listening (P4)	*who*, *which* or *that*? More kinds of comparisons
FOUR	Writing (story 2) (P2)	Use of tenses to tell a story
FIVE	Revision and extension	Infinitive with or without *to*? Gerund (*going*) or infinitive (*to go*)? Changes in meaning

12
A STUDY IN CONTRASTS

FOCUS	EXAM PRACTICE	LANGUAGE STUDY/VOCABULARY
ONE	Reading (P1) Speaking (P5)	*Not only ... as well*
TWO	Speaking – problem solving (P5)	*have something done* *lie* or *lay*? *bring, take, fetch, carry* or *wear*?
THREE	Listening (P4)	What is the meaning of *they*? Verb and noun combinations: *make* and *do*
FOUR	Writing (letter of application 2) (P2)	Planning a letter of application
FIVE	Revision and extension (P3) Listening (P4)	Revision of Units 11 and 12

I
A DOLPHIN AND AN ASTRONOMER

SPEAKING

A Talking on your own
Work in pairs as Student A and B.

Student A: Describe and compare the animals in both pictures and say what they are doing.

Student B: Describe and compare the people in both pictures and say what they are doing.

B Problem solving
Here is a short list of animals. Decide which animal you think is the most useful, which the least useful and which the most dangerous to humans.

wolves dogs cats tigers spiders mice rats
whales sharks elephants horses sheep flies

READING

A Read the text. Ignore the four missing sentences (1–4).

One day in 1963, a dolphin named Elvar and a famous astronomer, Carl Sagan, were playing a little game. The astronomer was visiting an institute which was looking into the way dolphins communicate with each other. Sagan was standing on the edge of one of the tanks where several of these friendly, highly intelligent creatures were kept.

The dolphin wanted Sagan to scratch his stomach again, as the astronomer had done twice before. Elvar looked up at Sagan, waiting. Then, after a minute or so, the dolphin leapt up through the water and made a sound just like the word 'more'. The astonished

FOCUS ONE

astronomer went to the director of the institute and told him about the incident. [2]

Dolphins have bigger brains in proportion to their body size than humans have, and it has been known for a long time that they can make a number of sounds. What is more, these sounds seem to have different functions, such as warning each other of danger. Sound travels much faster and much further in water than it does in air. That is why the parts of the brain that deal with sound are much better developed in dolphins than in humans. [3] Scientists don't agree on this.

A language is not just a collection of sounds, or even words. A language has a structure and what we call a grammar. The structure and grammar of a language help to give it meaning. [4] If you stop to think about it, you will see that this difference doesn't come from the words in the question but from the difference in structure. That is why the question 'Can dolphins speak?' can't be answered until we find out if dolphins not only make sounds but also arrange them in a grammatical order which affects their meaning.

B Fit the missing sentences A–D into gaps 1–4 in the text.
   A For example, the two questions 'Who loves Mary?' and 'Who does Mary love?' mean very different things.
   B 'Oh, yes. That's one of the words he knows,' the director said, showing no surprise at all.
   C Elvar had just swum up alongside him and had turned on his back.
   D But can it be said that dolphins have a 'language', in the real sense of the word?

C Choose the best answer. Then read aloud the sentences from the text that show your choice is correct.
1 The dolphin leapt into the air because
   A Sagan was too near the water.
   B it was part of the game they were playing.
   C he wanted Sagan to scratch him again.
   D Sagan wanted to communicate with him.
2 Dolphins' brains are particularly well developed to
   A help them to travel fast in water.
   B arrange sounds in different structures.
   C respond to different kinds of sound.
   D communicate with humans through sound.
3 Sounds can only be called a language if
   A each sound has a different meaning.
   B each sound is different from the other.
   C there is a system of writing.
   D they have a structure or grammar.

VOCABULARY

say, *tell*, *talk* or *speak*?

Complete these sentences with *say*, *tell*, *talk* or *speak*.
1 How many languages can you _____?
2 What is the first word most children learn to _____?
3 Stop it! Don't _____ nonsense.
4 Can you _____ me that joke again?
5 When do children usually learn to _____?
6 Please _____ me when to get off the bus.
7 Actions _____ louder than words.
8 Sorry. I wasn't listening. What did you _____?

LANGUAGE STUDY

Form and meaning

A How does the change in form change the meaning of these sentences?
1 Sound travels through water very fast.
2 The sound travels through water very fast.
3 Stop to think about it.
4 Stop thinking about it.

B Match the sentences 1–4 above with these meanings.
a This is true of sound in general.
b This means a particular kind of sound.
c Stop for a moment and think about it.
d Don't think about it.

Questions with *who*

C Answer the two questions about each sentence.
1 Tom loves Mary but Mary loves Dick.
   a Who loves Mary? b Who does Mary love?
2 Lee Oswald killed Kennedy and Jack Ruby killed Oswald.
   a Who killed Oswald? b Who did Oswald kill?

D Ask complete questions with *who*.
Example: Someone phoned. Who?
➤ *Who phoned?*
1 Cleopatra loved someone. Who?
2 Someone loved Cleopatra. Who?
3 Someone saw you yesterday. Who?
4 You saw someone yesterday. Who?
5 You know someone here. Who?
6 Someone knows you here. Who?

USE OF ENGLISH

A First read the following passage quickly to get an idea of what it is about. Ignore the missing words.

Dolphins are not the only animals besides humans that use sounds in an apparently intelligent manner. Whales also use a complex system **(0)** _of_ sounds that is similar in many ways to a human language. One type of whale even sings, and its songs can go **(1)** _on_ for as long as three or four hours. What is more, they can be heard under water **(2)** _at_ distances of more than 300 kilometres. After analysing one of these songs, Carl Sagan said it contained at **(3)** _least_ a million 'bits' of information. This is approximately **(4)** _the_ same number of bits as in a long poem **(5)** _like_ the *Odyssey*.

'Ball'   'Listen'

Chimpanzees use a system of different sounds to communicate with **(6)** _each_ other. One type of cry seems to mean something like 'danger in the air' or 'big bird' and **(7)** _another_ apparently means 'danger on the ground' or 'snake'. The first cry causes **(8)** _them_ to hide in holes or under trees and look up at the sky. When they hear the second cry, they hide in the upper branches of trees **(9)** _and_ stare nervously at the grass.

Chimpanzees are **(10)** _also_ capable of learning sign language. One chimp called Washoe learned to make about 160 separate signs meaning **(11)** _such_ things as 'Give me a drink' and 'banana'. Washoe even learned to swear. She had a teacher called Jack **(12)** _who_ once refused to give her a drink. Washoe got angrier and angrier and used several signs **(13)** _which_ meant 'dirty Jack'.

A group of chimps at a research institute in Atlanta, Georgia, have recently **(14)** _been_ taught to type sentences using a computer. The chimps'

trainer was called Tim, and he kept correcting the mistakes made **(15)** _by_ one of the chimps. The chimp obviously wanted Tim to stop correcting him and typed out the following request: 'Tim, please leave room'.

B Here are the missing words. Fill each of the numbered spaces 1–15 with one word. There is an example at the beginning (0).

also	and	another ✓	at	been
by ✓	each ✓	least ✓	like	on
such ✓	the ✓	them ✓	who ✓	which ✓

VOCABULARY

A Read this text and the words in capital letters below. Change the form of each word so that it fits the numbered space. An example is given (0).

Chimps use **(0)** _different_ sounds. These sounds have various **(1)**_____ and chimps use these sounds as a means of **(2)**_____. This is one **(3)**_____ between chimps, whales and dolphins. There has been a great deal of **(4)**_____ research into this recently. However, this research has not produced **(5)**_____ that these animals really have a language. A **(6)**_____ of sounds is not the same thing as a language, which has some kind of **(7)**_____ structure. Most scientists are in **(8)**_____ about this.

0	DIFFERENCE	5	PROVE
1	MEAN	6	COLLECT
2	COMMUNICATE	7	GRAMMAR
3	SIMILAR	8	AGREE
4	SCIENCE		

B Study these sentences. The same pair of words is used twice. How does the meaning change?
► **GS 9.1**

1 Have you ever looked into a microscope?
2 Have you ever looked into the way animals communicate with each other?
3 Let's go to London. Let's go on the train.
4 Please don't go on talking about the problem.
5 Go up the stairs and turn left.
6 Prices often go up but rarely come down.
7 Come down here at once.
8 Look up at the sky.
9 Look up the meaning of that word.

Read aloud the example that means

1 investigate
2 continue
3 rise
4 fall
5 find information in a book or list

LANGUAGE STUDY

stop doing vs. *stop to do* ➤ GS 5.3

A Answer the questions below.

1 A few minutes ago, the man in the picture was working. What did he stop doing a few minutes ago?

2 What did he stop to do?
3 His lunch break is at 12 noon. What does he stop doing at 12 noon?
4 What does he stop to do at 12 noon?
5 Imagine he can hear a radio when he is eating. Suddenly someone on the radio says 'Ladies and gentlemen. Here is a very important announcement.' What do you think the man would probably stop doing?
6 What would he probably stop to do?
7 If you were in the middle of an English lesson and suddenly heard an explosion outside, what would you probably stop doing?
8 What would you probably stop to do?

who, which or *whose*? ➤ GS 11.1, 11.2

B Complete these sentences with *who, which* or *whose*.

1 Whales and dolphins both make sounds _which_ in some ways are similar to a language.
2 People _whose_ work with dolphins are often surprised at how intelligent they are.
3 One scientist _who_ has studied dolphins carefully is John Lilly.
4 Lilly was the director of an institute _which_ became famous for its research.
5 Another person _who_ work has become well known is Roger Fouts.
6 Fouts, _who_ has studied the behaviour of other animals, taught a chimpanzee sign language.
7 This is the kind of language _which_ is used by deaf and dumb people.
8 'Dumb' is the word used in English for someone _who_ is unable to speak.
9 The chimpanzee, _which_ name was Washoe, learned about 160 signs.

In which of the above sentences can you also use *that*? In which sentence can you only use *who*?

When do you have to use *the*? ➤ GS 3.2, 3.3

C How many mistakes can you find in this text?

Most lines contain an unnecessary word. Underline these words and tick any lines that are correct. There are two examples (0) and (00).

0	Roger Fouts is a scientist who is very interested in	✓
00	the behaviour of <u>the</u> animals. For years he has	
1	studied the animal behaviour. He has also studied	✓
2	the chimpanzees. One of <u>the</u> chimpanzees he	
3	studied was called Washoe. He taught Washoe to	✓
4	make the signs as <u>a</u> means of communication. All	
5	over the world, the deaf and dumb people use signs	✓
6	to communicate. The grammar of sign language is	
7	very different from the English grammar or the	
8	grammar of other languages of the world. Some	
9	people think the sign language is not a real	✓
10	language but they are completely wrong. The	✓
11	vocabulary and grammar of the sign language is	
12	very rich. Chimpanzees can learn the signs that	
13	are part of sign language but they cannot learn the	
14	grammar. That is why the communication is not	
15	very easy for them when they use sign language.	

LISTENING 😐

A **You will hear people talking in three different situations. For questions 1–3, choose the best answer, A, B or C.**

1 You are in the south of England when you hear this. What is the weather like?
   A It is much colder.
   B It may snow.
   C It is snowing heavily.

2 You hear two people talking in the street. What is one of them looking for?
   A a language school
   B a church
   C a hotel

3 A woman is phoning someone. Who is she talking to?
   A someone in Germany
   B a student at a language school
   C someone a student is going to stay with

B **You will hear the first conversation again. For questions 4–7, complete the sentences that summarize what the speaker says.**

The good news is that last night for the first time in seven days there was

   4 [   ].

However, this weather brings a

   5 [   ].

In fact, in some parts of the country there have already been **6** [   ].

However, the weather has been even worse in
   7 [   ].

C **You will hear the second conversation again. For questions 8–10, choose from the list A–D where the three places are.**
There is one letter that you do not need to use.

   A It is just around the corner.
   B It is the first place you see when you get to the right street.
   C It is next to the first place you see when you get to the right street.
   D It is right in front of where the two speakers are standing.

   The school   **8** [   ]
   The hotel   **9** [   ]
   The church   **10** [   ]

D **You will hear the third conversation again. Answer questions 11–16 by writing**
S (the speaker), **W** (Mrs Wellford),
H (Mrs Wellford's husband), or
K (Klaus Klein).

   Whose plane was delayed?   **11** [   ]

   Who is in the same room as the student?   **12** [   ]

   Who did the speaker talk to earlier this evening? **13** [   ]

   Who didn't know the student would be late?   **14** [   ]

   Who is the speaker speaking to now?   **15** [   ]

   Who forgot to give someone some important information? **16** [   ]

FOCUS THREE

SPEAKING

A Finding out about each other

Ask your partners:
- why they want to learn English.
- how they think English may help them in later life.
- what problems they have had learning English.

B Problem solving
The picture below shows some of the things many language schools in Britain offer their students. In pairs or groups first discuss these questions.

1 What is happening in each picture?
2 What are the advantages and disadvantages of learning English in Britain or another country where English is spoken, rather than learning English in your own country?
3 Suppose you are planning to study English at a school in Britain. Which of these facilities or features do you think are very important? Which do you think are not so important? Give reasons for your answers.

- small classes of between 6 and 9 students
- a library • use of computers
- a language laboratory • tennis courts
- sports facilities • a canteen

C Discussion
In pairs or groups discuss which of these activities you think have helped you to learn English.

- reading English
- looking up words in a dictionary
- speaking to other students in your class in English
- listening to your teacher speak English
- having a friend who speaks English as his or her native language

Now tell your partners one other activity or thing that you think can help you to learn English.

WRITING

Composition (argument) 1

In Part 2 of Paper 2, you may be asked to write a composition. One type of composition asks you to write about the advantages and disadvantages of a particular topic. You must organize what you are going to say before you start writing.

A **Below is a composition on the advantages and disadvantages of living in the country. Fill each of the numbered spaces with one of the following words or phrases. Try not to use the same expression twice.**

First of all/Firstly
In addition/ Moreover/Furthermore
So/As a result/Therefore
However/On the other hand/In contrast
In conclusion/To sum up/On the whole

> Living in the country is something that people from the city often dream about. **(1)**_____, in reality, it has both its advantages and disadvantages.
>
> There are certainly many advantages to living in the country. **(2)**_____, you can enjoy peace and quiet. **(3)**_____, people tend to be friendlier and more open. A further advantage is that there is less traffic, so it is safer for young children.
>
> **(4)**_____, there are certain drawbacks to life outside the city. **(5)**_____, because there are fewer people, you are likely to have fewer friends. **(6)**_____, entertainment is difficult to find, particularly in the evening. Furthermore, the fact that there are fewer shops and services means that it is harder to find work. **(7)**_____, you may have to travel a long way to work, which can be extremely expensive.
>
> **(8)**_____, it can be seen that the country is more suitable for some people than others. **(9)**_____, it is often the best place for those who are retired or who have young children. **(10)**_____, young, single people who have a career are better provided for in the city.

B **Match these headings to the four paragraphs.**

Disadvantages   Advantages
Conclusion   Introduction

C **Make a list of all the advantages and disadvantages mentioned in the composition.**

D **The following notes, on the advantages and disadvantages of television, are mixed up. Put the notes into two lists. An example is given.**

ADVANTAGES   DISADVANTAGES
stops people feeling lonely

stops people feeling lonely
bad for the eyes
can be educational
stops people from talking to each other
discourages people from taking exercise
cheap
makes reading seem less attractive
good for old people living alone
can create problems in the family
good for children
stops people from going to the theatre, cinema, etc.
bad for the sports industry

Can you add any more advantages or disadvantages to these lists?

E **Here are some other useful expressions for this kind of composition.**

One of the advantages/disadvantages of ... is ...
There are advantages and disadvantages to ...
The (main) advantage/disadvantage of ... is ...
The main drawback/problem with ... is ...
A further advantage (of)/problem (with) ... is

F **Read these notes before you write a composition on one of the topics in G.**

1 Make two lists – one of advantages, one of disadvantages.
2 Decide in what order you will mention the points.
3 Decide what to say in the introduction and the conclusion.
4 Use some of the words and phrases in A and E above to link your composition.

G **Write your composition in four paragraphs, leaving a line between each one. You should write between 120 and 180 words.**

1 Your teacher has asked you to write a composition with the following title:

   TV: is it a good thing?

2 Your teacher has asked you to write a composition answering the following question:

   What are the advantages and disadvantages of living at home with your parents?

FOCUS FOUR

REVISION AND EXTENSION

How words change from verb to noun

A Look at the word in capital letters. Complete each short passage with the correct form of the word. Does the word always change? What form of the word do you need in each space?

1 AGREE
The two sides have signed an _____ to end the fighting, and most independent observers _____ that the deal is fair to everyone.

2 MEAN
Have you ever been abroad and asked yourself 'What does that word _____?' Well, now you can find out with the help of the *Electronic Translator*, a small computer that lists the _____ of over 20,000 common words in six European languages.

3 ARRIVE
We went to the airport to collect Katie at 2.30. We checked the screens in the hall, but there was no news of the _____ of her flight. Then we went to the information desk, and were told that there would be a long delay and in the end she didn't _____ until 9.30.

4 COLLECT
My uncle _____ stamps, and the other day he went to see an expert. He took his _____ along, and he was told that it was worth thousands of pounds because he had a number of very rare and unusual stamps.

B When a verb changes to a noun, the form can change in a number of ways. Can you think of other examples of each of the following?

- A special ending (a suffix) is added:
  amuse – amusement   act – action
  appear – appearance   refer – reference
  refuse – refusal   tend – tendency

- A vowel and/or consonant changes:
  sell – sale   believe – belief

- The spelling is the same but the pronunciation changes:
  I don't use (/z/) soap. I have no use (/s/) for soap.

- Some verbs ending in -*se* have noun forms ending in -*ce*:
  to advise – advice
  to practise – practice

- In a few cases, the stress changes :
  We import (imPORT) cars.
  This is an import. (IMport)

- But with many verbs, the noun form is exactly the same:
  I love you. Love is a dangerous thing.
  I hate you. Hate is a strong feeling.

C How do these forms change? Give the missing form of the words below.

VERB	NOUN
suggest	*suggestion*
explain	explanation
satisfy	_____
_____	permission
interfere	_____
_____	appearance
encourage	_____
_____	delivery
see	_____
_____	breath
give	_____
_____	export
prove	_____
_____	practice
advise	_____

- From the completed table above and from any other words you know, make a list of endings like -*ion* which show you a word is a noun.
- Pronounce the words in the table. Do you notice any other changes from verb to noun?

D Complete the following passage with the correct form of the words in capital letters (1–10). You will have to change a verb to a noun or a noun to a verb.

The fear of crime is leading to the **(0)** *transformation* of housing estates into fortresses. In Rosemont, USA, the local council decided to fence off an entire neighbourhood of 2,000 people. It is only possible to **(1)**_____ the estate by two gateways, which are manned 24 hours a day by armed police. Anyone who wants to **(2)**_____ is asked to provide **(3)**_____ and has to give the police a reasonable **(4)**_____ of why they want to come in. A video camera films the **(5)**_____ plates of all the cars that come in and out. The people of Rosemont have had mixed **(6)**_____ to the scheme. Some residents **(7)**_____ it is a good idea, and point out that there have been no crimes since the **(8)**_____ of the scheme. However, others are not pleased. Linda Edwards, a **(9)**_____, said: 'These are public streets, there's no **(10)**_____ for the police to sit on our doorstep all the time. It's like living in a prison.'

0	TRANSFORM	6	REACT
1	ENTRANCE	7	THOUGHT
2	VISITOR	8	INTRODUCE
3	IDENTIFY	9	TEACH
4	EXPLAIN	10	NEED
5	LICENSE		

TRAVEL WISELY, TRAVEL WELL

SPEAKING

A Talking on your own
Work in pairs as Student A and B. Do not interrupt while your partner is speaking.

Student A: Describe and compare the forms of transport the people are using in both pictures. Say which form of transport you prefer.

Student B: Describe and compare the people and the places in both pictures. Say what reasons the people may have for travelling.

B Finding out about each other
Ask the other students in the class about the different means of transport (train, car, plane, bike, travelling on foot, etc.) they have used in the past month.

C Discussion
1 What advantages and disadvantages do people have when travelling by public transport and in their own cars?
2 What kind of problems can people have when travelling?

USE OF ENGLISH

A Read the text quickly, ignoring the missing words (1–8).

I have learned, often the hard **(0)** _way_ , that there are a few simple rules about how to make life easier both before and after the journey. First of all, you must always check and double-check departure times. This is absolutely essential. It is amazing how few people do this really carefully. Once I arrived at the airport a few minutes before ten. My secretary had got the ticket for me and I thought she had said that the plane left at 10.50. I walked calmly to the departure gate, thinking I **(1)**_____ had a little time to spare. I hadn't bothered to take a good look at the ticket. The clerk at the desk told me politely but firmly that the departure time was 10.15 and that, **(2)**_____ to international regulations, the flight was 'now closed'.

  Secondly, you should remember that even in this **(3)**_____ of credit cards, it is still important to have at least a little of the local currency with you when you arrive in a country. This can be absolutely essential if you are flying to a place few tourists normally visit. A few years ago I was sent to Tulsa, Oklahoma. I flew there from London via Dallas with very little time to **(4)**_____ planes in between. I arrived there at midnight and the bank at the airport was closed. The only **(5)**_____ to get to the hotel was by taxi and, since I had no American dollars, I offered to pay in British pounds instead.

  'Listen, buddy. I only take real money!' the driver said angrily. Luckily, I was able to **(6)**_____ a few dollars from a clerk at the hotel, but it was very embarrassing.

FOCUS ONE

The third and last rule is to find out as much as you can about the weather at your **(7)**_____ before you leave. It may be very different from the weather at home. I feel sorry for some of my colleagues who travel in heavy suits and raincoats in March or April, when it is still fairly cool in places like London, Berlin or New York, to places like Athens, Rome or Madrid, where it is already beginning to get quite warm during the day. Few people understand just how important it is to have the right sort of clothes with you in these days of rapid air **(8)**_____.

B **Decide which is the best word, A, B, C or D, to complete gaps 1–8. An example is given (0).**

0	**A** path	**C** way	
	B road	**D** street	
1	**A** still	**C** then	
	B yet	**D** already	
2	**A** regarding	**C** according	
	B relating	**D** referring	
3	**A** period	**C** term	
	B time	**D** age	
4	**A** exchange	**C** transfer	
	B change	**D** alter	
5	**A** way	**C** path	
	B manner	**D** route	
6	**A** borrow	**C** gain	
	B lend	**D** beg	
7	**A** goal	**C** objective	
	B aim	**D** destination	
8	**A** travel	**C** journeys	
	B trips	**D** voyages	

C **Discuss these questions. Compare your answers.**
1 Explain why the writer once arrived at the airport only a few minutes before the plane left.
2 Whose fault do you think it was, the writer's or his secretary's? Give reasons for your answer.
3 Explain why the writer thinks it is essential to have at least a little local currency when you arrive in a foreign country.
4 Describe some of the problems you could have if you ignore the advice in the last paragraph.

SPEAKING

Problem solving

In pairs or groups do the exercise below. Then compare your answers with others.

Imagine you are going to visit the United States in the winter for ten days. You are going to New York, where it is very cold and Los Angeles, where it is warm. You can take only one small suitcase and ten items each. Decide what you would take. Give reasons for taking each item.

VOCABULARY

travel, journey, voyage or *trip*?

A **Which word suggests the following?**
1 going somewhere by ship
2 going a long distance, perhaps by land
3 going somewhere for business/shopping or for a short period
4 the general idea of going from one place to another

B **Now complete these sentences.**
1 I'm going away tomorrow on a business _____.
2 How are you going to _____? By train or by plane?
3 The _____ over the mountains took two days.
4 Would you like to go on a long ocean _____?

flight, drive, ride or *tour*?

C **Use one of the words above to complete these sentences.**
1 Would you like a ____ on my motor-bike?
2 We went on a guided ____ of the city.
3 I took my grandparents on a nice, quiet ____ in my car.
4 Olympic Airways has a ____ from Athens to Tokyo early tomorrow morning.
5 The whole orchestra is going on a ____ of cities in Asia, Europe and the United States.
6 Thank you for flying with us. We hope you have had a good ____.
7 Can you ____ a car?
8 Can you ____ a bike, too?

READING

A You are going to read part of a leaflet about London's Heathrow Airport. After you have read it quickly, look at the questions in B on the next page.

A | Passport Control

If you are not transferring to another flight outside Britain or Northern Ireland, you must pass through Passport Control and Customs immediately after leaving your plane. If you are not British or a citizen of a country in the European Community, you must fill out a special form called a landing card before your passport is examined. This card should be given to you during the flight. However, you can also obtain one inside the terminal building.

When you enter the terminal building from your aircraft, follow the ARRIVALS signs. Make sure that you are in the right channel when you reach PASSPORT CONTROL. There is one channel for holders of European Community passports and a second channel marked 'Other Passports'.

B | Getting Your Luggage

If you have luggage which was carried in the aircraft hold, follow the BAGGAGE RECLAIM signs after your passport has been examined. If you have only hand luggage, pass through the baggage reclaim area and follow the CUSTOMS sign.

C | Customs

All passengers arriving from a country outside Britain and Northern Ireland are allowed to bring with them a certain quantity of duty free items. You can get information about how much you can bring by reading the signs marked Duty Free Allowances in the baggage reclaim area.

There are three Customs Channels; the Red Channel, the Green Channel and the Blue Channel. If you have something to declare, or if you are not sure about your Duty Free Allowance, you must go through the Red Channel. Passengers arriving from outside the European Community with nothing to declare must go through the Green Channel. Passengers arriving from countries in the European Community with nothing to declare must go through the Blue Channel.

Please note that Customs Officers may stop you at any time and examine your luggage as you go through the Green or Blue Channels.

D | Transit Passengers

If you are immediately transferring to another flight at Heathrow that is not bound for a destination in Britain or Northern Ireland, you are a transit passenger and do not have to go through the procedures above.

All transit passengers should follow the black and yellow TRANSFERS signs. Airport staff at the Transfer Desk and at other places in the terminal will direct you to your departure gate.

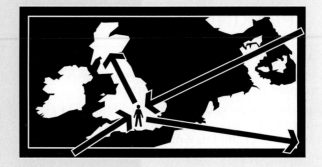

FOCUS TWO

B Which section refers to

people who may ask you questions
about what is in your luggage?

0	*C*

your suitcases and what is in
them?

1	
2	

people who are waiting for their
suitcases to come from the plane?

3	

something you must do if, for example,
you have a US or Japanese passport?

4	

people who are going to change planes
at Heathrow and go to another
foreign country?

5	

tobacco, alcohol and other things
with a special tax on them?

6	

people of all nationalities who have
just come from countries like Japan,
the USA, Argentina?

7	
8	

people of all nationalities who have
just come from countries like France,
Italy, Germany?

9	
10	

the first thing you do after you get
out of the plane at Heathrow?

11	

special signs for people who have
not yet completed their journey?

12	

C In pairs or groups, explain the following.

1 How passengers can get a landing card and what
they have to do with it.
2 The purpose of the three Customs Channels.
3 What exactly a duty free allowance is.

LANGUAGE STUDY

may, should, must, will ➤ GS 7

**A Study these examples. How does the meaning of
the underlined word change?**

a) Someone <u>may</u> stop you and ask you to open your
suitcase.
b) <u>May</u> I have a look in your suitcase, sir?
c) You're ill. You <u>should</u> see a doctor.
d) We <u>should</u> be arriving in Athens on time.
e) You <u>must</u> be tired after that long flight.
f) You <u>must</u> go through Passport Control.
g) <u>Will</u> this happen?
h) <u>Will</u> you show me your passport, please?

Repeat the sentence that is

1 a command or order
2 a request
3 someone asking for permission
4 advice

Now repeat the sentence that means

5 As long as there are no problems, this will happen.
6 This can happen – but perhaps it won't.
7 Give me your opinion about the future.
8 Surely the answer is 'Yes'. After all, it's logical, isn't
it?

**B Use *may*, *should*, *must* or *will* to complete these
sentences.**

1 You _____ be blind if you can't see that sign!
2 It's raining. You _____ take an umbrella.
3 Excuse me, but _____ I ask you something
personal?
4 Listen. I _____ be late this evening, so don't wait
for me.
5 If you see George, _____ you give him this
message?
6 Before the plane lands, the 'No Smoking' sign
_____ come on.
7 When the 'No Smoking' sign comes on, you
_____ stop smoking.
8 The train _____ be here in a few minutes, but
you never know.

You will hear people talking in six different situations. Choose the best answer for each question, A, B or C.

1 You overhear this conversation in the airport. Where exactly are you?
   A at Passport Control
   B in a Customs Channel
   C at Baggage Reclaim

2 A man and woman are talking. What is the man's problem?
   A His luggage is on the wrong plane.
   B He can't remember where he is staying in London.
   C He is looking for someone but doesn't know what the person looks like.

3 What is this announcement about?
   A which Customs Channel to use
   B who should get on the plane first
   C a delay of some kind

4 What question has this man just been asked at Passport Control?
   A What is your occupation?
   B Where have you just come from?
   C What is the purpose of your visit?

5 You live in Madrid and a friend has left this message on your answer phone. What is the message?
   A Your friend isn't coming to Madrid.
   B She will arrive later than expected.
   C She is already in Madrid and will contact you later this evening.

6 You and a friend are waiting to go on the next British Airways flight to Madrid. What should you say to your friend after hearing this announcement?
   A Don't worry. There's plenty of time yet.
   B Oh, no! Not another delay!
   C That must be our flight! Come on. Hurry!

LANGUAGE STUDY

Verb and noun combinations: *give* and *take*

A Which of the things below can we take? Which can we give? Say the complete phrases aloud with *give* or *take*.

• a party	• a talk about something
• an interest in something	• place in
• care of someone or something	• a long time to do something
• someone a call	• someone trouble
• birth to a baby	• a break from doing exercises like this
• someone a lift	
• part in something	

B Rewrite the second sentence in each pair. Use no more than five words including the word in bold. Do NOT change this word. An example is given (0).

0 Phone me tomorrow please.
   give Please _give me a call_ tomorrow.

1 What is the subject of your lecture tomorrow?
   talk What are _____ tomorrow?

2 There is a conference here today.
   taking A conference _____ today.

3 Do politics interest you?
   take Do you _____ politics?

4 My wife had twins last week.
   gave Last week _____ twins.

5 I spent an hour doing this exercise.
   took It _____ to do this exercise.

6 Get in my car. I'll take you to the station.
   give Let me _____ to the station.

7 When my mother was ill, I looked after her.
   took I _____ when she was ill.

8 Lately I've had problems with my back.
   trouble My back _____ lately.

9 There were three participants in the discussion.
   took Three people _____ the discussion.

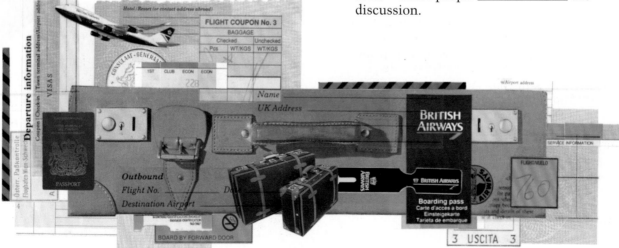

FOCUS THREE

SPEAKING

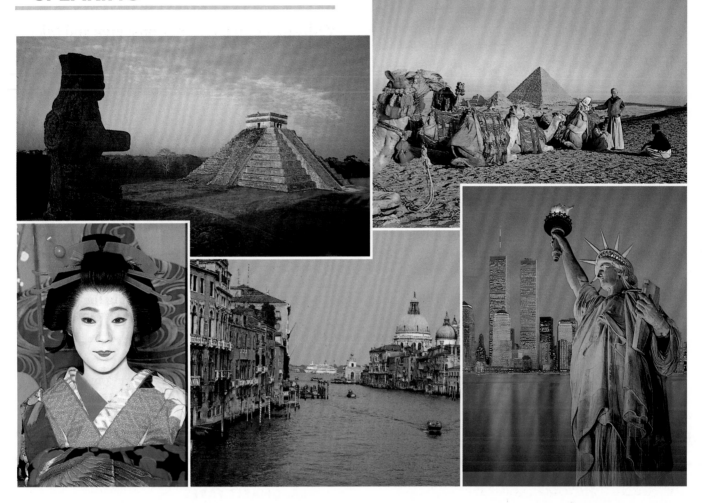

A In pairs, match the questions 1–5 with the answers a–e.

1 Have you ever been to Mexico?
2 Really? Why? What do you know about it?
3 Is there anything else you can tell me about it?
4 No, I'm afraid I haven't. Could you tell me about him?
5 So, just imagine you could spend a week there. What would you do? What would you want to see?

a) I'd like to see the places where the Aztecs and also the Mayas once lived. I'd also like to visit some museums.
b) He was an artist. He painted some wonderful pictures.
c) No, I haven't, but I'd like to go there.
d) It's a very big country. The climate is very warm. There were two great civilizations there before the Spaniards came, the Aztecs and the Mayas. Let's see… what else. The capital is Mexico City.
e) Yes, the food is supposed to be very good. The music is very interesting, too. And I'm also very interested in the work of Diego Rivera. Have you ever heard of him?

B Find out about each other's experiences. Ask questions like 1–5 about one of the places shown in the pictures. Also ask about the things below.

- What do they know about the money, the language, the customs, the food, etc.?
- Can they tell you anything about the weather and the kind of clothes you would need if you went there for a week?
- Is there anything else your partner hasn't mentioned which he or she can tell you?

C Now think of another place you think your partner would find interesting. It can be a place in your own country or somewhere else. Tell your partner a little about it and why you think he or she would find it interesting. You can use the language below.

- I'd like to tell you a little about…
- I think you'd find it interesting because…
- It's famous for its… and also its…
- If you go there, you should know a little about the climate there. The best time of the year to go there is… The worst time to visit it is… because…

WRITING

Transactional letter 1

In the first part of Paper 2 you will be asked to write a 'transactional' letter, based on some information that is provided. You should make sure that your letter covers all the points that are given.

A Sample task

Below is part of a letter you have received from a friend. Write a reply based on the notes you have made and the other information given.

> I don't know if you will be around when I come but if not, could you suggest somewhere to stay? I'll only be staying one night, but I thought there would probably be something on at the theatre. Could you find out for me and let me know? Hope to see you soon,
>
> Yours, Jerry

no - away in USA until 16th
Pickwick - £35 a night near theatre
R&J

WHAT'S ON
AT THE THEATRE

The Royal Shakespeare Company presents
Romeo and Juliet
by William Shakespeare
10 – 15 NOVEMBER TICKETS £20
RESERVATIONS: 01238-221143

B Read this reply. Choose the best options from the words in *italics*. Remember that this is an informal letter to a friend.

Many thanks for your letter – it was *great/a pleasure* to hear from you again.

I'm so sorry/I apologize, but I won't be here when you come, because I'll be away in the States, and I don't get back until the 16th. It's *such a shame/most unfortunate*.

Nevertheless/Anyway, I've asked around about places to stay in and a couple of people have suggested the Pickwick Hotel in Garfield Road. It costs about £35 a night and it's fairly close to the theatre, *and consequently/so* I think it would suit you quite well.

As far as the theatre is concerned, there's a performance of Romeo and Juliet on, which you would probably enjoy. It *starts/commences* at 7.30, and tickets are about £20.

Do *let me know/inform* me if there is anything you'd like me to do – I can book you a room and

get/obtain tickets for the play if you like. Hope to hear from you soon, and maybe we can meet up the next time you are here.
Yours/Yours faithfully, Billy

C Writing task

A friend is coming from Australia to do a two-week course in your country. Read the part of your friend's letter below, together with the other information. Then write a suitable reply in 120–180 words.

> The course finishes on Friday 18th, but I'm not flying back until the Sunday evening. Could I come and see you then? Do let me know if we can arrange something. There are a couple of other things. The flight in doesn't arrive until 11 in the evening. Are there any buses into the city centre that late? If so, could you find out how much they cost and how long they take?
> The other thing is that I need to know what the weather will be like, so I can bring the right sort of clothes. I don't want to arrive with all the wrong things! Anyway, I do hope we can meet up – it'd be great to see you again.
>
> Yours, Sandy

great! yes, we're all free

AIRLINK BUSES

Airport to City Centre

- **EVERY 20 MINUTES**
- **REASONABLE FARES**
- **24-HOUR SERVICE**

- weather
- clothes to bring
- plans - Saturday: sightseeing, restaurant in the evening; Sunday: lunch at home, will take to the airport

D Read these notes before you write your letter.

1 Use the following plan:
   Paragraph 1 introduction
   Paragraph 2 main details of airport buses
   Paragraph 3 details about the weather and what clothes to bring
   Paragraph 4 arrangements for the weekend (Use your imagination here.)
   Paragraph 5 ending

2 Make your paragraph divisions clear. Leave an empty line between paragraphs.

3 Remember to write in an informal style. Try to use phrases from the example in your letter.

4 Assume that you are writing to a friend who is the same age as you. You can use contractions like *I'll*, *we've*, *it's*, etc.

FOCUS FOUR

REVISION AND EXTENSION

Read this letter from someone who is doing a language course in France. Choose the best word, A, B, C or D, to fill spaces 1–15.

Dear Mum and Dad,

This is just a quick letter to let you know that I'm fine. We're all working quite hard because the exams are only a few weeks away, but our teacher (1)_____ he thinks we'll do well. (My landlady's not so sure – she keeps (2)_____ me I should stop (3)_____ so much TV and do a bit more reading!)

Anyway, we had a wonderful time at half-term. I went off to Paris for (4)_____ days with some of the others from the school, and we went on a guided (5)_____ of the city. We saw most of the famous (6)_____ like the Louvre, where they have an amazing (7)_____ of paintings, and the Eiffel Tower. Then we went down to the South of France (8)_____ train. It was so fast – the whole (9)_____ was only about four hours. We spent (10)_____ time in Nice and in Cannes as well, and we all really enjoyed it. On our last day we went to a small island (11)_____ the Ile des Pelerins, and we saw the castle where they used to keep the 'Man in the Iron Mask'. All in all, we had a great time and (12)_____ weather was really good as well. The only thing I felt (13)_____ about was that we didn't have enough time to (14)_____ to go swimming – maybe next time.

Anyway, I must go now as I've got to do a bit of homework for tomorrow. (15)_____ you write soon?

Love Janie

1. **A** says **C** speaks
   B tells **D** talks
2. **A** saying **C** speaking
   B telling **D** talking
3. **A** watch **C** to watch
   B watched **D** watching
4. **A** a little **C** a few
   B little **D** few
5. **A** trip **C** tour
   B visit **D** excursion
6. **A** shows **C** views
   B sights **D** looks
7. **A** set **C** gallery
   B group **D** collection
8. **A** in **C** with
   B by **D** on
9. **A** voyage **C** drive
   B travel **D** journey
10. **A** a little **C** few
    B little **D** a few
11. **A** spoken **C** called
    B said **D** told
12. **A** any **C** the
    B a **D** those
13. **A** sorry **C** displeased
    B apologetic **D** regretful
14. **A** spend **C** spare
    B waste **D** take
15. **A** Must **C** May
    B Should **D** Will

LISTENING 📇

You will hear a telephone conversation during which a man asks a tour company about the trips they organize. For questions 1–8 fill in the missing information in the man's notes.

TRAGICAL MYSTERY TOURS

Bus trip to (1)................. . Picked up at Temple (2)................ at (3)................. p.m. Evening meal at Greenwich. (4)................ commentary throughout. Runs every day except (5)................. . Ghost Bus to Chislehurst in Kent. Take a walk through the caves and (6)................. . Trips only on (7)................ and ....

Cost of trips: Adults (8) ....

　　　　　　　 Children   ....

SPEAKING

A Talking on your own

Work in pairs as Student A and B. Do not interrupt while your partner is speaking.

Student A: Describe and compare the places in both pictures. What do you think usually happens in these places?

Student B: Describe and compare the people in both pictures. What do you think they might be saying to each other?

B Discussion

1 Which of the two locations in the pictures is not a good place for an interview? Give reasons for your answer.

2 What are some of the questions that are asked in almost every interview?

3 Imagine you are going to be interviewed for a job with a large international organization next week. How could you prepare for the interview?

READING

The woman at the reception desk looked surprised when I told her why I had come.

'Take a seat over there,' she said, and pointed to some chairs where three young women were already sitting. They gave me a strange look. One of them giggled and whispered something to the other two. They seemed to find something amusing about me.

I sat down and spent a few minutes looking at the advertisement again.

Are you between 21 and 30? Are you fluent in Spanish, Portuguese or Greek? Are you good at communicating with people on the phone? Would you find it interesting to work as the assistant to the sales director of a small but growing software company? If your answer to at least two of these questions is 'Yes', write to us at the address below, giving details of your previous work experience.

SOFT LOGIC

⌐ **12 SOUTH STREET, BRIGHTON, SUSSEX BN1 3AQ**

I had come across the advertisement in the local newspaper and had immediately sent them a short letter about myself. A few days later I had got back a short note asking me to come for an interview. They hadn't sent me an application form to fill out or even asked for a photograph. Suddenly I remembered that I had signed my letter 'Chris Neale'. Had they assumed that 'Chris' meant 'Christine' and not 'Christopher'? Did 'assistant' in the advertisement mean 'Personal Assistant' – another word for 'Secretary'? Was this a job that only women could get? I hadn't personally come up against that difficulty before.

A man in his early thirties came out of one of the offices and asked the three young women if they had come about the advertisement. He didn't seem to notice me.

'Where's the other girl who applied?' he asked, looking at a list.

Discuss these questions.

1 Is the person who wrote the story a man or a woman? How old could he or she be?
2 Without looking at the advertisement again, describe the job that is advertised.
3 Now describe the things a person in such a job might do at work.
4 How do you think the writer felt after he spoke to the woman at the reception desk?
5 Explain what you think made him feel the way he did.
6 Do you think there was some kind of misunderstanding? If so, explain what the misunderstanding was and how it perhaps came about.
7 Give some examples of 'typical jobs for women' and 'typical jobs for men'.
8 What happened before the writer went to the interview?
9 How do you know this happened before the interview?

VOCABULARY

A In pairs or groups read the sentences below. Say which sentence in each pair contains a phrasal verb, explaining why you think it is a phrasal verb.

1 Where did you come across this information?
2 Come across the street with me.
3 Your name came up again in conversation.
4 The submarine came up slowly in the darkness.
5 This letter came about two days ago.
6 How did this misunderstanding come about?
7 The submarine came up against a dark sky, so nobody saw it.
8 Have you ever come up against this problem?

9 The boy went upstairs and then came down with a book in his hands.
10 The boy came down with a bad cold.
11 I almost passed out when I heard I had won first prize.
12 Oil comes into the engine through the blue tube and then passes out through the red tube.
13 The patient was given an anaesthetic and didn't come to for three hours.
14 The woman came to the door and looked at me.

B Match the meanings a–g with the phrasal verbs used in A.

a) meet or face a difficulty
b) happen
c) regain consciousness
d) find by accident or hear about
e) be talked about, mentioned or discussed
f) fall ill with
g) lose consciousness

LANGUAGE STUDY

Rewrite the second sentence in each pair. Use no more than five words including the word in bold. Do NOT change this word. An example is given (0).

0 All students face the problem of phrasal verbs.
come All students _come up against_ phrasal verbs.
1 Is it the first time you've heard of phrasal verbs?
come Have you ever _____ phrasal verbs before?
2 Are you as interested in them as I am?
find Do you _____ interesting as I do?
3 Do you use them well?
good Are you _____ them?
4 I have the impression you know something about them.
seem You _____ something about them.
5 What is another way of saying 'I fell ill with a cold'?
came How can I say 'I _____ a cold'?
6 What about 'We often discuss this subject in our lessons'?
comes What about 'This subject _____ our lessons'?
7 Some examples even amuse students.
find Students _____ amusing.
8 I think we've discussed phrasal verbs enough now.
stop Let's _____ now.
9 If you study any more, you may lose consciousness.
pass You may _____ if you go on studying.
10 Why don't you rest a little now?
break Why don't _____ now?

USE OF ENGLISH

Read the job advertisement quickly to get an idea of what it is about. Ignore the missing words.

MORGEN SUN

INTERNATIONAL

LEISURE PLANNER

We own hotels and holiday centres in England, France, Spain and Portugal. The leisure planner is responsible (1)_____ planning and organizing leisure activities for guests and other clients. The post requires someone (2)_____ the ages of 25 and 35 with an interest in encouraging people (3)_____ all ages to take part in (4)_____ wide range of leisure activities at our holiday centres. Fluency (5)_____ French and either Spanish or Portuguese is also desirable (6)_____ not essential. Although (7)_____ successful candidate for the post will be based in our London headquarters near Heathrow Airport, he or she will be required to travel frequently. Candidates must be capable of working (8)_____ their own but at the same time be able to cooperate (9)_____ other members of a busy team. In addition, the successful candidate must have (10)_____ international driving licence.

SENIOR PERSONAL ASSISTANT

We are also looking for someone (11)_____ has had at least five years' secretarial experience to assist the managing director. Good organizational and communication skills are essential, (12)_____ well as the ability to use computers, software and other information management systems.

Candidates for both positions must be ready to take (13)_____ their posts no later (14)_____ the end of the year and should apply in their own handwriting on standard forms, (15)_____ are available from the Personnel Department.

TELEPHONE 0171 497 3771

Fill spaces 1–15 with these words.

a   an   as   between   but   for   in   of
on   than   the   up   which   who   with

VOCABULARY

Read this text and the words in capital letters below it. Change the form of each word so that it fits the numbered space. An example is given (0).

The question 'What makes a manager (0) _successful_ ?' often comes up. First of all, a manager needs the right kind of (1)_____ support. In other words, a good manager requires the (2)_____ of a good secretary. A good secretary needs to have the right kind of (3)_____ skills. These include the (4)_____ to use modern technology, such as computers. There are (5)_____ skills that are just as important. More and more managers need secretaries who can speak several foreign languages (6)_____. Success or failure in international (7)_____ can depend on this. This (8)_____ is often stressed in job advertisements today. Many (9)_____ are rejected because the candidates lack such skills.

0	SUCCESS	5	ADDITION
1	PROFESSION	6	FLUENT
2	ASSIST	7	NEGOTIATE
3	SECRETARY	8	REQUIRE
4	ABLE	9	APPLY

SPEAKING

In pairs or groups, imagine the telephone conversation between speakers A and B. Discuss with each other exactly what you think they say to each other. Then, in pairs, take a role each.

A You have seen the advertisement on the left. Phone for an application form. Ask about the salary. Try to get more information.

B You work in the personnel department. Find out which job the caller is interested in and personal details (name, address, phone number, previous job experience). You are not allowed to give more information about either of the jobs.

LISTENING 📷

A You will hear part of two different job interviews. For questions 1–7, choose the best answer, A, B or C.

1 Has the first candidate any previous experience of the job he is applying for?
   A Yes.
   B No.
   C He isn't sure.

2 What does the job he is applying for not involve?
   A travelling
   B selling books
   C meeting people

3 Why did he leave his last job?
   A He doesn't want to say.
   B He wanted to travel and meet people.
   C He didn't like his boss.

4 Why is the second candidate interested in the job she is applying for?
   A It is similar to her previous job.
   B She can improve some skills she has already learned.
   C She wants to learn how to deal with different kinds of people.

5 Why did she argue with her previous boss?
   A She didn't do the things he asked her to do.
   B He wrongly thought he had asked her to do things.
   C He said she had done things that he had never asked her to do.

6 What else does she say about her previous job?
   A It taught her something important.
   B Her boss made her work too hard.
   C She liked the job itself very much.

7 Which of these things does she say she intends to do in her next job?
   A avoid arguing with the boss
   B listen only to what the boss tells her to do
   C talk to her boss and others about her job responsibilities

B You will now hear the two interviews again. Check your answers to 1–7.

C Explain to someone else the problem the second speaker had with her boss and what the cause of that problem was. Then suggest a way to solve it.

SPEAKING

A Talking about yourself

1 In pairs or small groups, describe a job you would not like to do, giving reasons why you would not want to do it.

2 Talk about a job you wanted to do when you were younger. Say why you wanted to do it then. If you no longer want to do it, explain why not.

B Discussion

1 Are the jobs below usually done by men or women? Why do you think this is?

   astronaut   coal miner   dancer   lorry driver   nurse   pilot   police officer   shop assistant   surgeon

2 There are many jobs in which a knowledge of English is essential or desirable. Name some of these jobs and say why English is important for them.

READING

You are going to read part of a leaflet prepared by a large employment agency. It gives advice on what to do and what not to do at interviews. Choose the most suitable heading from the list A–F for each part (1–4). There is an example at the beginning (0). Notice that there is one heading which you do NOT need to use.

A 'Why did you leave your last job?'
B What else should you do during the interview?
C 'What did you do in your last job?'
D How should you prepare for the interview?
E 'Why do you want to work for us?'
F What questions should I ask my interviewers?

0 D

- Find out as much as you can about your prospective employers and the business they are in. Think about the questions you are most likely to be asked, and at least three questions you would like to ask them. Then make sure you arrive for the interview at least fifteen minutes early. Here, by the way, are four of the most frequent questions interviewers ask. Think calmly about them while you are waiting.

1

- Don't just give the name of the job. Describe the main duties and responsibilities the job involved. Then pause and see if your interviewer has any further questions.

- Be as positive as possible. Emphasize all the things you learned that you think will be useful in the new job. Be sure to mention any promotion or advancement you had.

2

- Never say 'It was boring'. Instead, say that you didn't think you could make use of your full abilities. Don't criticize your previous employer. If you lost your job through no fault of your own, briefly describe the problems the company had. Never give your prospective employers the impression that you are bitter.

3

- Don't talk only about what you hope to get from the firm. Emphasize what you think you can do for them and all the things in your previous experience and training that you think will be useful in the new job. Be sure also to mention something you have learned about your prospective employers that interests you.

4

- Relax. Be yourself.

- Look at your interviewer when he or she asks you questions.

- If you don't understand a question, politely say 'I'm not sure if I understand. Do you mean...'

- Remember the questions you would like to ask. Be sure to ask at least one or two before the interview is over.

- At the end, thank your interviewers for seeing you.

VOCABULARY

A Work in pairs. Take it in turns to read out a question (1–6). Your partner should then read aloud the answer, choosing from a–f.

1 Where are the new applicants?
2 Where are the new applications?
3 Do you need any assistance?
4 Do you need an assistant?
5 Who's your new employer?
6 Who's your new employee?

a) Yes, I'd like some information, please.
b) They're waiting to be interviewed.
c) On your desk.
d) Do you mean my new secretary?
e) An American company.
f) Yes, someone with secretarial skills.

B Complete the table. The first two examples have been done for you.

	ACTION	PERSON	THING
1	apply	*applicant*	*application*
2	_____	assistant	_____
3	_____	_____	translation
4	_____	adviser	_____
5	_____	_____	invention
6	_____	interviewer/ interviewee	_____
7	_____	lover	_____
8	criticize	_____	_____
9	use	_____	_____
10	_____	employer	_____
11	_____	_____	speech
12	discover	_____	_____

C Explain how the choice of words changes the meaning in 1–4 below.

1 Are you the new trainer/trainee?
2 Look at the interviewee/interviewer when you speak.
3 Don't throw the critic/criticism in the waste basket.
4 Do you want to kill the competitor/competition?

LANGUAGE STUDY

Requests and intentions ➤ GS 7.1, 7.3, 13.3

A What's the difference?
a) Will you do a favour for me?
b) Would you do a favour for me?
c) Are you going to do this favour for me?

1 Which sentence means *Do you intend to ...?*
2 Which sentences often have *please* at the end?

B Use *Are you going to . . .* or *Will you . . .* to rephrase these sentences.

1 Do you intend to help me?
2 Please help me.
3 Do you plan to get married soon?
4 Please marry me.
5 Do you intend to answer these questions?
6 Please answer these questions.
7 Please take this to the post office.
8 Do you intend to take this to the post office?
9 Do you intend to explain the difference between *will* and *going to . . .*?
10 Please explain it again.

C In each of the following sentences, fill one space with a form of *going to* and the other space with *will*.

Example:
(Janet) *Janet is going to* catch the 8.30 train tomorrow, so (you) *will you* take her to the station?

1 (You) _____ give me a hand moving the furniture as (I) _____ clean the floor later?
2 (We) _____ go out for dinner at 8.00, so (you) _____ make sure you're back in time?
3 If (you) _____ play tennis with Richard, (you) _____ let Emily come and watch?
4 (You) _____ look after the children for an hour, as (I) _____ get a few things from the supermarket?

D Find out what your partner intends to do. Ask questions with *going to*, using 1–7 below and your own ideas. If the answer is *No*, ask why not.

1 take the Cambridge exam this year
2 study this weekend
3 do anything interesting next weekend
4 spend most of their free time studying
5 have a party if they pass
6 come to your party if you pass
7 do anything else interesting this year

WRITING

Letter of application 1

In Part 2 of Paper 2, you may be asked to write a letter applying for a job. If you are replying to an advertisement, you must be careful to cover all the points. You should write in a suitably formal style.

A Read this advertisement.

SOCIAL EVENTS *ORGANIZER*

We are looking for someone to arrange weekend and evening events for a group of students from Europe, who will be studying at a London language school in July and August. Could it be you? Are you

- a good organizer?
- sociable and outgoing?
- good at languages?
- familiar with the local area?

If you are, please write to us, saying why you would be suitable for this job.

B Read this letter of application for the job that is advertised above. Choose the words or phrases in *italics* that you think are more formal.

> Dear Sir or Madam,
>
>   I am writing to apply for the *post / job* of Social Events Organizer which was advertised in last week's edition of Summer Jobs.
>
>   I am *now / currently* studying French and Italian at London University, so I speak both languages well.
>
>   I feel I would be *suitable / right* for this position because I have good organizational skills, and I greatly enjoy going out and meeting new people. I have lived in London all my life so I know many of the places that young students would enjoy.
>
>   I have experience of this kind of work. Last summer I *was employed by / worked for* Imperial Hotels as a Tour Organizer, and I arranged excursions to places of interest in and around London. I also worked for London Life last Christmas, which involved taking *groups of / some* American tourists around the capital.
>
>   My course finishes in the middle of June, so I *would be available for work / can start working* at any time during July and August.
>
>   Please do not hesitate to contact me if you *need / require* any *more / further* information. I look forward to hearing from you.
>
> Yours faithfully,

C Read the advice (notes 1–7) on how to write a good letter of application. Then find the part of the letter in B that relates to each piece of advice. Finally, re-arrange the advice so that it is in the same order as the letter.

1 Make it clear which post you are interested in and how you heard or learned about the job.
2 Describe your present position or situation briefly and clearly.
3 Begin the letter with 'Dear Mr …', 'Dear Ms …' or 'Dear Mrs …'. However, if you don't know the name of the person, remember that there is another phrase you can use.
4 Sign off correctly. Use a suitable formal phrase.
5 Make it clear when you can begin the job if it is offered to you.
6 The final paragraph of your letter is just as important as the first paragraph. It must be polite but it must also give them the impression you are really interested in the job.
7 Explain why you think you would be particularly good for the job. You can make up any details you like here.

D Writing task

You see this advertisement and decide to apply:

WANTED!

We are looking for Summer Camp Hosts to help teach and entertain children aged 10–12 at our Summer Camp in August.
If you are good with children, keen on sports and other outdoor activities, and have a lively and outgoing personality, then we'd like to hear from you. We offer good rates of pay and free accommodation.

REPLY TO SUMMER CAMP TRAVEL, BOX 100

E Follow these notes when you write your letter of application.

1 Remember it is not necessary to write any addresses.
2 Write in a formal style. Avoid informal language.
3 Cover the three qualities they ask for (good with children, sports, personality), explaining clearly why you think you have these qualities. Use your imagination here. Don't be afraid to exaggerate a little.
4 Use some of the phrases from the letter in B.
5 Be sure to tell them something about your present situation and when you could begin working.
6 Arrange your letter in clear paragraphs.
7 Don't write more than 180 words.

REVISION AND EXTENSION

do/does or *am/is/are doing*? ➤ GS 13.1

A The writer of the following letter works in a travel agency. Which form of the verbs in brackets do you need to complete her letter, the present simple (*do/does*) or the present progressive (*am/is/are doing*)? For example, is the first answer *write* or *am writing*? Notice that sometimes the verb in brackets does not need to be changed at all.

Dear Sally,

I (write) just to let you know that I've arrived and that everything's fine.

At the moment I (stay) at a hotel in Athens and I (do) quite a lot of sightseeing. Next week, I (move) to the island of Crete, which is where most of the people in the company (live). I (rent) a villa there for the summer, which should be nice.

The weather's not particularly good – as a matter of fact, it (rain) at the moment. Still, it (get) better slowly, and I'm sure it'll be fine when you (come) in the summer. I (look) forward to it already.

The job (not seem) to be too demanding. Most of the time I (deal) with bookings and (answer) inquiries. But I (suppose) it'll be different when the tourist season (start) next month. Even now the restaurants (begin) to get busier.

See you soon.
Love,

Jenny

B Again, change the verb in brackets if necessary.
1 He (not like) his job, so he (think) about moving.
2 I (want) to see the new film by Neil Jordan, as I (hear) it's very good.
3 I (love) the roses you sent me, and they (smell) wonderful.
4 She (prefer) tea because it (not taste) so bitter.
5 I (doubt) if they (understand) what you (talk) about.
6 It (appear) that the house now (belong) to Mrs Johnson.
7 I (see) from the report that you (meet) the Manager tomorrow.
8 He (work) very hard at the moment and (deserve) to succeed.
9 I (imagine) that she (feel) a bit better now.
10 I (measure) the room to see what size carpet we (need).

will do or *is/are doing*? ➤ GS 13.3

C Complete the following conversation. Use only the *will do* form or the *is/are doing* form; for example, is the first answer *Will you do* or *Are you doing*?
A (You do) anything this weekend?
B No, not really.
A Well, I (go) to Wales on Friday. Would you like to come?
B Yes, I'd love to. Wait a minute . . . did you say Friday? Let me look at my diary. Oh dear, I'm afraid I (not be able) to come. I (meet) James at six, and we (go) to a film.
A Tell him to come too. He (want) to come, (not) he?
B Yes, I should think so. All right, I (give) him a ring and I (tell) you what he says.
A OK, if you decide to come, I (pick) you up here on Friday. I (be) here at three. I must go now, I (see) Jill for lunch and she (not be) pleased if I am late.

D Look at statements a–h below. How certain are you that these things will happen in your lifetime? Circle one of the following numbers (1–5) to show how you feel about each statement.
1 It definitely will happen.
2 It probably will happen.
3 It may happen.
4 It probably won't happen.
5 It definitely won't happen.

a) You will become a grandparent.		1 2 3 4 5
b) You will earn a lot of money.		1 2 3 4 5
c) Many people will live for more than 150 years.		1 2 3 4 5
d) There will be a war in your country.		1 2 3 4 5
e The world will become over-populated.		1 2 3 4 5
f) Computers will be able to understand languages.		1 2 3 4 5
g) You will live abroad for more than ten years.		1 2 3 4 5
h) You will appear on television.		1 2 3 4 5

Now write a few sentences about each statement giving reasons for the way you feel.

Example: *I'm bound to become a grandparent, because...*

... (be) bound to..., because...
I'm quite convinced that... will..., because...
... probably will..., because...
... may well..., because...

There's a chance that... will..., because...
... might..., because...

I doubt if... will, because...
I shouldn't think... will..., because...

I'm quite sure... won't..., because...
I'm convinced... won't..., because...

SECRET MESSAGES TO OURSELVES

READING

Late one night more than a hundred years ago, an American inventor ran into a problem that seemed impossible to solve. He was trying to design a sewing machine, but he couldn't think of a way to get the thread to run smoothly around the needle.

He was exhausted and finally went to bed. However he was so worried that he slept very badly. He had a nightmare in which he dreamt that he had been captured by a tribe of terrible savages. Their king threatened to kill and eat him unless he could build a perfect sewing machine. When he tried to do so, he ran into the same problem as before. The king was so angry that he ordered his soldiers to kill him immediately. Suddenly, the inventor noticed something. The soldiers were all carrying spears, and in the tip of each one of them, there was a hole that looked just like an eye.

The inventor woke up and realized that he had just found the solution to the problem. Instead of trying to make the thread run around the needle, he should make it run through a small 'eye' or hole in the tip.

The inventor's name was Elias Howe, and this simple idea enabled him to design and build the first really successful sewing machine. He was not the only famous person to find solutions to difficult problems in this way. Thomas Edison, who invented the electric light bulb, said that his best ideas came to him in his dreams. So did Albert Einstein, the great mathematician and physicist. The novelist Charlotte Brontë also got inspiration from her dreams when writing *Jane Eyre*. Igor Stravinsky, the great composer, said that he 'slept' on his problems, and when he woke up they were solved.

Few people understand the meaning of dreams. In order to do so, you have to understand what happens when you sleep. When you are awake, you notice all sorts of things and get lots of ideas without realizing it. When you are asleep, the unconscious part of your brain is active and it begins to 'digest' this information mentally. Sometimes it is that part of the brain that notices something important that the conscious part of your brain didn't. The unconscious part of your mind, however, has its own logic and language. This is why the strange images in our dreams are sometimes called 'secret messages to ourselves'.

SPEAKING

A Finding out about each other

Ask your partners:

* how often they dream.
* if they dream in colour or in black and white.
* if they can describe a dream they had recently.
* if they know the difference between the words below.

  dream   daydream   fantasy   nightmare
  illusion   hallucination

B Discussion

1 A successful doctor dreams that he or she suddenly falls down some stairs. What could this dream mean?
2 Some scientists study dreams. Why? What do you think they are trying to find out?
3 Why do we dream? Is there any reason?

FOCUS ONE

A Choose the best answer.

1 What was the inventor's problem?
 A He was so tired he couldn't think.
 B He wasn't using the right kind of thread.
 C He hadn't designed the needle correctly.
 D The needle was in the wrong place.

2 The idea for the solution came from something
 A the king said in the dream.
 B the inventor noticed about the soldiers' weapons.
 C the inventor saw after he woke up.
 D he saw in the eyes of one of the soldiers.

3 Albert Einstein is mentioned because he
 A was a great physicist and mathematician.
 B got inspiration from Howe and Edison.
 C also had strange dreams.
 D got many good ideas from his dreams.

4 Dreams are sometimes called 'secret messages to ourselves' because
 A it is better if other people don't understand them.
 B they often tell us important things through strange images.
 C we have them when we are asleep and never understand their real meaning.
 D our brains notice things other people don't want us to notice.

5 What do you think is the general 'message' of the whole story?
 A Only inventors, artists and scientists can understand what their dreams are trying to say.
 B If you work too hard and too late, you may have terrible nightmares.
 C Elias Howe wasn't the only person who solved problems when he was asleep.
 D Howe was the first person we know who solved a problem while he was asleep.

B Discuss the difference in meaning in these pairs of sentences.

1 Very few people understand the value of dreams.
2 A few people understand the value of dreams.
3 The inventor got very little sleep that night.
4 The inventor got a little sleep that night.

Which sentences sound more positive, and could mean 'at least some people' or 'at least a little sleep'?

LANGUAGE STUDY

Rewrite the second sentence in each pair. Use no more than five words including the word in bold. Do NOT change this word. An example is given (0).

0 I don't know many people here at all.
 few I *know very few* people here.

1 I don't know many people but at least I know some.
 few I _____ people here.

2 I haven't got much money at all.
 little I _____ money.

3 At least I've got some money – not much.
 little I _____ money.

4 I don't understand many of these words at all.
 few I _____ these words.

5 I didn't understand very much of that story.
 little I _____ that story.

6 The inventor couldn't sleep because he was worried.
 so The inventor _____ couldn't sleep.

7 I fell asleep because the story was boring.
 so The story _____ fell asleep.

8 'I'll kill you if you don't do it,' the king said.
 unless The king said '_____ I'll kill you.'

9 'Kill him!' the king shouted at his soldiers.
 ordered The king _____ him.

10 'Please sit down,' the teacher said to the student.
 asked The teacher _____ down.

11 Please open your suitcase.
 mind Would _____ your suitcase?

12 Don't ask so many questions.
 stop Please _____ questions.

13 I have the impression that something is wrong.
 seems Something _____ wrong.

14 Do you find it easy to make friends?
 good Are you _____ friends?

15 I didn't go to the party. I studied.
 instead I _____ to the party.

LISTENING

A You will hear a radio talk about dreams. Listen to the first part. Then answer questions 1–4.

1 Why did the speaker talk to psychiatrists and psychologists?
   A She wanted them to explain her dreams.
   B She was writing a book about dreams.
   C She wanted advice about which books to read.

2 What was probably the cause of the successful businessman's dreams?
   A He was afraid he would be poor again.
   B He had lost a lot of money before he had the dream.
   C He thought he had seen a wolf somewhere.

3 What was strange about the other people in the second businessman's dream?
   A They sat in a circle, looking down at him.
   B They were laughing at him because he was naked.
   C They were wearing strange clothes.

4 What was the cause of the second businessman's dream?
   A He was afraid of losing a lot of money he had put in a foreign bank.
   B He was afraid that tax officials already knew too much about him.
   C He didn't want the officials to learn more about him.

B Now listen to the second part. Then complete sentences 1–7. Compare your completed sentences with a partner's sentences.

Before an important performance, the singer usually had a dream about [1   ].

The baby she gave birth to was
[2   ].

The cause of the dream was
[3   ].

If you want to understand dreams, you have to understand that a dream never
[4   ].

The fact that the singer dreamt of having a baby did not [5   ].

You have to know a lot about people before you can
[6   ].

People's dreams also tell you something about
[7   ].

FOCUS TWO

VOCABULARY

Read through this text. Then use the words in capital letters below it to form a word that fits each space. An example is given (0).

Like all (0) *inventors*, Elias Howe had sudden 'flashes of (1)_____'. His strange dream is just one example of (2)_____ processes that are still beyond our (3)_____. This is why there is so much (4)_____ about dreams and what they really are. Dreams have no (5)_____ at the time we have them. Our (6)_____ of dreams happens after they are over. Some (7)_____ think that our dreams are partly the (8)_____ of our unconscious minds. Our memory of the dream may be (9)_____ different from the dream we (10)_____ had.

0	INVENT	6	INTERPRET
1	INSPIRE	7	SCIENCE
2	PSYCHOLOGY	8	PRODUCE
3	UNDERSTAND	9	COMPLETE
4	AGREE	10	ACTUAL
5	MEAN		

LANGUAGE STUDY

Reporting what people say ➤ GS 12.1 & 12.2

A Match sentences 1–8 with the actual words the speaker probably used when he or she said it (a–h).

1 He admitted doing it.
2 She denied doing it.
3 He asked her to do it.
4 She promised to do it.
5 He agreed to do it.
6 She refused to do it.
7 He advised her to do it.
8 She told him to do it.

a 'I'll do it. You have my word.'
b 'I didn't do it. I didn't!'
c 'If I were you, I'd do it.'
d 'Do it! Now! Don't argue!'
e 'Would you mind doing it?'
f 'No, I won't!'
g 'Yes, I did it. I'm sorry but I had to.'
h 'All right, if that's what you want, I'll do it.'

B Look at the sentences below. Then say what you think the speaker actually said.

Example: The singer said she often had the same dream before an important performance.

➤ *'I often have the same dream before an important performance.'*

1 One day Joe, a tax official, phoned Tom, a businessman, and asked if he could see him.
2 Tom said he was too busy to see anybody.
3 Tom's partner advised Tom to talk to the tax official immediately.
4 Tom phoned Joe and asked him to come to his office.
5 Joe thanked Tom for agreeing to see him.
6 Joe asked Tom if he had any money in Switzerland.
7 Tom denied having any money there.
8 He refused to discuss the matter any further.
9 Then he admitted he had 'forgotten' something.

C Rewrite the second sentence in each pair. Use no more than five words including the word in bold. Do NOT change this word. An example is given (0).

0 'Can I see you?' Joe said to Tom.
asked Joe *asked Tom if he could* see him.

1 'I'm very busy,' Tom said to Joe.
told Tom _____ busy.

2 'Would you mind coming to my office?' Tom said to his partner.
asked Tom _____ his office.

3 'If I were you, Tom, I'd talk to a good lawyer,' the partner said.
advised Tom's partner _____ a good lawyer.

4 'No, I won't talk to a lawyer,' Tom said.
refused Tom _____ a lawyer.

5 'All right. I'll see you,' Tom said to Joe.
agreed Tom _____ Joe.

6 'I haven't done anything wrong,' Tom said.
denied Tom _____ wrong.

7 'I'll tell you the truth,' he said to Joe.
promised Tom _____ Joe the truth.

8 'Yes, I have a little money in Switzerland,' he said.
admitted Tom _____ in Switzerland.

USE OF ENGLISH

Read this text about a dream a young man called Martin Ellward once had. Most lines of the text contain an unnecessary word. Underline these words and tick any lines that are correct. There are two examples (0 and 00).

 0   I still remember this dream very well, even   ✓
00   though I had it <u>since</u> four years ago. I was
 1   trying to persuade to my girlfriend to get into
 2   a small aeroplane with me. She didn't want to,
 3   but finally she agreed me. I started the engine
 4   and we took off. I wanted to impress on her, so
 5   I started doing some dives and other things.
 6   Then I noticed that the weather had turned into
 7   bad. Suddenly the engine stopped. I wondered me
 8   what was wrong. 'What is it happening?' my
 9   girlfriend asked me. I tried to make her to believe
10   that everything was all right. While that I was
11   trying to start the engine again, I realized that
12   we had run out of the fuel. Then I looked down
13   and suddenly saw that we were very much near
14   a mountain. 'This is all your fault,' my girlfriend
15   said. Then we were crashed.

Read aloud each corrected complete sentence.

Example: *I still remember this dream very well, even though I had it four years ago.*

SPEAKING

A Read what Martin Ellward says.

'At the time I had this dream, I was engaged to a woman who had a much better job. She was earning much more money than I was and liked eating in expensive restaurants. I didn't want to tell her but sometimes I was afraid I couldn't afford to pay my share. Not long after this, we broke off our engagement.'

In pairs or groups discuss what the following things in Martin's dream could symbolize.

1   the plane
2   running out of fuel
3   his desire to impress his girlfriend by doing some dives and rolls
4   the mountain
5   the crash

B First discuss with each other what A and B might say to each other. Say the actual words they would say. A and B could be Martin and his girlfriend, or just two friends of the same sex.

Example: A suggests having a meal together this evening.

➤ *Let's have a meal together this evening.*
    OR
    Why don't we have a meal together this evening?

1   A suggests going to a new restaurant called 'Harry's'.
2   B tries to get some information from A about the food and the price of a typical meal there.
3   A recommends 'Harry's' but admits that it is 'a bit pricey'.
4   B is short of money but doesn't want to admit it and tries to think of an excuse why he or she can't go there.

C What do you think happens after that? What do A and B say to each other?

D Now in pairs take the roles of A and B. Decide whether you are 'boy friend and girl friend' or just friends of the same sex.

VOCABULARY

Phrasal verbs with *take*, *look* and *run*

A Work in pairs. One of you reads aloud an example (1–9). Your partner repeats only the phrasal verb in the example and then says what it means, choosing one of the meanings a–i below.

Example: The plane ran out of fuel.

➤ *run out – to have no more of something*

1 The inventor ran into a serious problem.
2 The driver ran over a cat and killed it.
3 Let's run through the instructions once more.
4 BMW took over the English car manufacturer Rover several years ago.
5 This table takes up a lot of room.
6 I just can't take in all these phrasal verbs!
7 Look the word up in your dictionary.
8 The police are looking into the matter.
9 Are you looking forward to doing another exercise on phrasal verbs?

a to expect to enjoy something
b to hit something or someone with a car
c to occupy
d understand, mentally 'digest'
e to investigate
f to find information about something in a book or list
g to discuss, repeat, or read something quickly
h to get control over something, by buying it or in some other way
i to meet something unexpectedly

B Now complete each sentence, using one of the phrasal verbs.

1 Can you really _____ all this information?
2 We _____ hearing from you again.
3 What is the meaning of dreams? Scientists who have _____ the question do not agree.
4 These books _____ ten shelves. Can't you get rid of a few of them?
5 I _____ your number _____ in the telephone book.
6 The lorry went out of control and _____ two people.
7 An American organization may _____ this company.
8 They _____ difficulties on board and had to return to the port.
9 Let's _____ the plan for tomorrow again, just to make sure everybody knows exactly what to do.

LANGUAGE STUDY

Review of verb forms ➤ GS 5.2.3

A Explain the difference in meaning in these pairs of sentences.

1 In my dream, a man ate a bird. I saw him do it.
2 In my dream a man was eating a bird. I saw him doing it.
3 I saw him cut the bird into pieces.
4 I saw him cutting the bird into pieces.
5 He shot at another bird. I saw him do that, too.
6 He was shooting at another bird. I saw him doing it.

• Which sentences suggest most clearly that you saw a *complete* action from beginning to end?
• Which sentences could mean that you perhaps saw only part of an action and not the action from beginning to end?
• Which sentence could mean that the man did the same thing more than once?

B Complete the sentences below with the correct form of the verbs in brackets.

Example: Last night I (sleep) very badly.

➤ *Last night I slept very badly.*

Last night I (**1** have) a very strange dream. In this dream, I was in a restaurant. I (**2** sit) alone and (**3** read) a book. Suddenly I (**4** look) up and (**5** see) a man (**6** stare) at me. I (**7** look) around and (**8** see) a lot of other people (**9** sit) at tables near him. They (**10** laugh) and (**11** smile) about something. The waiter (**12** come) over to me. He (**13** begin) to smile. I (**14** ask) him why he (**15** smile). The other people (**16** begin) to laugh even louder. The waiter (**17** point) to my legs. Then I (**18** understand) why everybody (**19** laugh). I (**20** not wear) any trousers.

One person in each pair or group should now read aloud his or her completed exercise. Can your partner or partners find any mistakes in your version?

WRITING

Story 1

In Part 2 of Paper 2 you may be asked to write a story. Often, you are given the first sentence and asked to continue the story. You may want to use direct and reported speech, but be careful not to use dialogue throughout.

A Sample task

You have been asked to write a short story for a class competition. Begin your story with these words:

It was nearly midnight when the doorbell rang.

Write your **story** in 120–180 words.

B Read the following story and answer these questions.

1 What do you notice about the punctuation and layout of direct speech? Find three things to say.
2 What do you notice about the tenses in reported speech?
3 How many words can you find in the story that refer to ways of talking (for example, *say*)?

It was nearly midnight when the doorbell rang. I opened the door and saw a girl with a motorbike helmet. She was covered in blood.

'Oh, no,' I said. 'What has happened?'

'Please help me,' the girl said weakly. 'There's been an accident. My boyfriend is outside.'

I helped her to a chair. She was bleeding a lot.

'I'll call an ambulance,' I said.

I ran to the sitting room and phoned for an ambulance. Then I ran back to the girl. But she had disappeared. I went outside, but there was no sign of her or the motorbike in the silent street.

When the ambulance arrived, I explained what had happened. The driver went pale. He said that <u>exactly ten years ago, his daughter and her boyfriend had had a motorbike crash</u>. He went on to say that <u>the boy had been killed instantly. His daughter had gone to ask for help in the house I was now living in, but she had died a few minutes later</u>.

The ambulance left. As I stood in the hall, I noticed there was no longer any blood on the chair where the girl had been sitting.

C Change the underlined parts of the story into direct speech.

Example: *The driver said 'Exactly ten years ago, ...*

D Writing task

You have been asked to write a short story for a school competition. Your story must begin with these words:

I was woken in the night by a noise downstairs.

Write your **story** in 120–180 words.

E Plan what you are going to say in the story. Think about the following questions:

Was anyone else in the house at the time? What time was it? What sort of noise was it? What or who did you think it might be? Did you think about going downstairs yourself? Did you phone for help? Where was the phone?
Who decided to go downstairs to have a look? Who/What did they find? What were they doing? How had they got in? What (if anything) did they say? What happened in the end?

F When you have decided what the story will be about, add a few details to the following plan.

1 Setting the scene
   Woke up, heard a noise... crept to Mum and Dad's room.
2 Deciding what to do
3 What happened next
4 What they said
5 Ending

G Try and use some direct and reported speech in your story. For example, you could relate your first conversation with the other people in the house (your mother or father) in direct speech, and the conversation with the intruder or police in reported speech.

H Remember the following points about the punctuation and layout of direct speech.

1 Start a new paragraph every time the speaker changes.
2 Use opening and closing inverted commas for direct speech.
3 If the speech is broken by *he said/he replied* etc., then a comma is put before the closing inverted commas, for example 'Come in,' he said.

REVISION AND EXTENSION

Read this text. Then choose the best word, A, B, C or D, to fill spaces 1–15.

Operation Stargate

Operation Stargate was the name of a secret spying operation that was run by the Pentagon in the United States for over 20 years. The aim of the operation was to **(1)**_____ the possibility of using mind readers, clairvoyants and astrologers to help with spying operations.

The Pentagon **(2)**_____ six of these psychic people, and the experiments were held at a secret military base in Maryland. Put in special rooms, the psychics were asked to concentrate on particular spying operations. By using a technique called 'remote viewing', they were asked to **(3)**_____ solutions to specific problems.

The team had a limited number of successes. They were able to give **(4)**_____ of the layout of the building where American diplomats were held hostage in 1979, and on another occasion they **(5)**_____ Customs officials by describing exactly where a drug dealer could be found. When a US diplomat was kidnapped in Italy, they described the town he was in and in **(6)**_____ said exactly what the building looked like.

(7)_____, they had many more failures than successes. In the end, the government ordered the CIA to **(8)**_____ the mission. The team was then examined by a group of experts, who were not **(9)**_____ by the results. They decided that **(10)**_____ the psychics had been right a **(11)**_____ times, this had probably just happened by **(12)**_____. At other times, they were probably repeating information that they had **(13)**_____ in newspapers. The military authorities now have the **(14)**_____ task of explaining to **(15)**_____ that they wasted $20 million on the project.

1 **A** look through   **C** look up
   B look down on   **D** look into

2 **A** employee   **C** employed
   B employer   **D** employment

3 **A** come up against   **C** come across
   B come up with   **D** come into

4 **A** description   **C** plan
   B definition   **D** details

5 **A** assisted   **C** supervised
   B employed   **D** conducted

6 **A** also   **C** addition
   B more   **D** else

7 **A** But   **C** Although
   B Yet   **D** However

8 **A** take over   **C** take after
   B take up   **D** take in

9 **A** impressive   **C** impressed
   B impressing   **D** impression

10 **A** despite   **C** in spite of
   B although   **D** besides

11 **A** little   **C** few
   B some   **D** number

12 **A** chance   **C** occasion
   B possibility   **D** opportunity

13 **A** come into   **C** come across
   B come round   **D** come up against

14 **A** embarrassed   **C** embarrassment
   B embarrassing   **D** embarrass

15 **A** critical   **C** criticism
   B criticize   **D** critics

LISTENING

Listen to the interview with a psychologist who studies dreams. Then choose the best answer, A, B or C.

1 Directed dreamers are people who
   A wake up in the middle of a dream.
   B remember what they have dreamt.
   C can control what they are dreaming.

2 Dr Border is trying to find out if people can
   A dream the same dream regularly.
   B meet each other in their dreams.
   C talk in their sleep.

3 The experiment required the three people to
   A dream about a particular situation.
   B go to a river.
   C sleep in the same room.

4 The interviewer found it interesting that
   A the woman had only dreamt about one of the men.
   B neither of the men dreamt that they met the woman.
   C all the dreamers had the same dream.

SPEAKING

A Talking on your own

Work in pairs as Student A and B. Try to speak for about one minute.

Student A: Describe and compare the places in both pictures. Say what time of day it is and what you could hear if you were there.

Student B: Describe and compare the buildings in both pictures. Say what kind of people you think live in them and which place you would prefer to live in.

B Talking about yourself

Do these tasks in pairs or groups.

• Describe your own home. How many rooms are there? Who else lives there with you?

• Describe your 'ideal home'.

READING

Alison closed the door of her small flat and put down her briefcase. It had been another exhausting day at the travel agency where she worked, and she was looking forward to being alone. There was an interesting programme she wanted to watch on television later in the evening. She had just started preparing her dinner when there was a knock at her door.

'Oh, no! Who on earth could that be?' she muttered. She went to the door and looked through the 'spy hole'. A man of about sixty was standing there. It took her a few seconds to realize who he was. He lived in the flat below. They had passed on the stairs once or twice and had exchanged the usual greetings. He had a long, thin face with two large front teeth that made him look like a rabbit.

'Sorry to bother you, but …uh… there's something I'd like to …er… talk to you about,' he mumbled when she opened the door. Alison hesitated but then asked him to come in. Then she noticed the dog. Alison detested dogs, particularly big ones. This one was a very old and very fat bulldog.

The man went into her small living room and sat down on the sofa. The dog followed him and climbed

FOCUS ONE

up on the sofa next to him. Its mouth was open and it was breathing heavily. Alison saw several drops of the dog's saliva fall on the light green material that covered the sofa.

'Do you mind if I smoke?' the man asked. Without waiting for an answer, he lit a cigarette.

'You must be wondering why I've come. Well, I hope you won't be offended, but …' He stopped suddenly and coughed. His face went very red. Another cough exploded from somewhere very deep inside him. He pulled a dirty, grey handkerchief out of his pocket and spat into it. Some ashes from his cigarette fell on the floor. He looked around the room. Alison glanced at her watch. The man seemed to have forgotten what he wanted to say.

'Nice place you've got here,' he said at last.

A Choose the best answer.

1 How do you think Alison felt when she heard the knock at her door?
   A afraid
   B irritated
   C pleased
   D curious

2 Who was the man at the door?
   A Someone she worked with.
   B A friend who needed advice.
   C A complete stranger.
   D A neighbour she hardly knew.

3 What do you think Alison said to herself when she saw the dog?
   A 'I wish he hadn't brought that dog in here.'
   B 'Oh, what a nice dog.'
   C 'I wonder what's wrong with the poor thing.'
   D 'I like some dogs but not this one.'

4 Why did the man want to talk to Alison?
   A He had forgotten to tell her something.
   B He wanted to tell her how nice her flat was.
   C The text doesn't tell us.
   D He wanted to apologize for offending her.

5 What do you think was Alison's general impression of the man after he came in?
   A She had no feelings about him at all.
   B She thought he was very interesting.
   C She liked him but not his dog.
   D He had some very annoying habits.

B Discuss these questions.

1 What do you think is probably a typical day in Alison's life?
2 Now try to describe a typical day in the man's life, too.
3 What are some possible reasons for the man wanting to talk to her?
4 Why do people sometimes get annoyed with their neighbours? Describe two or three typical reasons.

LANGUAGE STUDY

Ways of asking for permission

A The following examples are all ways of asking for permission. What are the differences between them?
a) Do you mind if I smoke?
b) May I smoke here?
c) You don't mind if I smoke, do you?
d) Is smoking permitted here?
e) Is it okay to smoke here?

Which example seems to be

1 something you can say about official regulations?
2 what people say when they think it is all right to smoke?
3 very polite – the kind of thing you say when you don't know the other person very well?
4 not very formal but still polite?
5 very informal?

B Rewrite the second sentence in each pair. Use no more than five words including the word in bold. Do NOT change this word.

1 I'm sure it's all right if I open the window.
   mind You don't _____ the window, do you?

2 Do regulations allow people to park here?
   permitted Is _____ here?

3 May I close the window?
   mind Do you _____ the window?

4 Don't worry. You can park here.
   okay I'm sure _____ here.

5 Will you permit me to use your dictionary?
   mind I hope you _____ your dictionary?

6 Selling drugs is against the law here.
   permitted The sale _____ here.

7 Are you sure singing is permitted in this place?
   okay Do you know if _____ here?

8 I hope it's all right to do this.
   mind You don't _____, do you?

9 Is it all right if I turn on the radio?
   may Excuse me, but _____ the radio?

10 Can I ask you something?
   mind Do you _____ something?

LISTENING

A You will hear the conversation between Alison and the man. Answer the six questions below by writing
W (for Alison, the woman)
M (for the man)
D (for the dog)

The answer to the first question (0) is given as an example.

0 Who apologizes for not knowing the other's name? **0** | W

1 Who stops doing something the other speaker doesn't like? **I** |

2 Who complains about something the other speaker often does? **2** |

3 Who promises to do something about a problem? **3** |

4 Who apologizes for saying something? **4** |

5 Who dislikes a particular kind of music? **5** |

6 Who seems to enjoy a particular kind of popular music? **6** |

B Listen a second time. Then answer these questions, too.

1 Look at question 2 again. What exactly is it that the speaker is complaining about?
2 Look at question 3 again. What exactly does the speaker say when making the promise?
3 Look at question 4 again. What are the words the speaker uses that tell you the speaker is apologizing?
4 Look at question 5 again. What is the particular kind of music in the question?
5 Look at question 6 again. What kind of popular music does one of the characters enjoy?

VOCABULARY

Which is the word in each group that does not belong? Explain why it does not belong with the other three words.

1 offend   embarrass   amuse   upset
2 offended   bored   annoyed   insulted
3 embarrassed   self-conscious   ashamed   confident
4 apologize   complain   protest   object
5 disturb   bother   dislike   annoy

SPEAKING

In pairs or groups suggest first what you would do and then what you would actually say in the following situations.

Example: One of your neighbours plays very loud music late at night.

➤ *I think I would probably complain. I would say 'Please stop playing that music so loud. It disturbs me.'*

1 Your neighbour's dog often barks all night long.
2 You are having a party tomorrow evening in your new flat. You want to develop good relations with your neighbours.
3 You have quickly parked your car outside a friend's house in order to give the friend some important news. You have just begun telling your friend the news when you hear someone shouting outside. 'Whose car is this? It's blocking my driveway and I can't get my car out!'

USE OF ENGLISH

The man who visited Alison wrote this letter to her two weeks later. Look at each line carefully. Most lines contain an unnecessary word. Underline these words and tick any lines that are correct. There are two examples (0 and 00).

0 I hope you remember <u>of</u> my conversation with
00 you two weeks ago when I told you about the ✓
1 disturbance that which your music has caused.
2 When we had spoke, you agreed to turn your
3 music down so as that it would not disturb my
4 dog, Bruno. Unfortunately, this has not been
5 happened. Several evenings later, I could heard
6 music again coming from your flat. Although
7 Bruno was very disturbed by it, I decided I
8 would not complain, hoping that it would not
9 still happen again. However, since then there
10 have been two more times there that this has
11 happened. Both times Bruno was very disturbed.
12 I hope you will agree that not only we humans
13 but also the dogs have certain rights. Please
14 remember that if you will do this again, I will
15 inform to the police about this disturbance.

In groups, discuss each mistake. Then correct the sentence in which each mistake occurs. Afterwards your teacher will ask some of you to read aloud your corrected version.

LANGUAGE STUDY

Asking and telling people not to do things

A Repeat these examples. Then answer the questions about them.

a) Put that cigarette out!
b) Excuse me but would you mind not smoking here?
c) No smoking!
d) Smoking is strictly forbidden.
e) I'm sorry but you can't smoke here.
f) Don't smoke here.
g) Thank you for not smoking.

1 Which three are often seen in written notices or signs?
2 Which of these three written notices do you think is the most polite?
3 Which of the other examples do you think are polite ways of asking someone not to smoke?
4 Which example or examples sound more like orders or commands?

Reporting questions, polite requests and other things people say ➤ GS 12

B The examples below show two different ways of reporting what people said. In pairs or groups, read each example aloud. Then discuss what you think the speaker actually said.

Example: A woman in a restaurant asked the man she was with not to shout because the other people in the restaurant were looking at them.

➤ *I think she probably said, 'Would you mind not shouting?' or 'Please don't shout. The other people here are looking at us.'*

1 He told her he wasn't shouting.
2 She asked him why everyone was looking at them if he wasn't shouting.
3 He told her not to worry about the other people.
4 She asked him again not to shout and not to shake his fist at her.
5 He told her to stop giving him orders.
6 She asked him if he knew the difference between an order and a polite request.
7 The manager of the restaurant came and asked the man not to disturb the other people in the restaurant.
8 The man told the manager not to interrupt his conversation with his girlfriend.
9 The manager threatened to call the police but the woman politely asked him not to.
10 Afterwards, the man begged the woman to forgive him.

C Report the conversation between the man and the woman in the restaurant by completing the second sentence in each pair.

1 'Please lower your voice,' she said to him.
   asked She ＿＿＿＿＿＿＿＿＿＿ to lower his voice.
2 'Listen to what I'm saying,' he shouted at her.
   told He ＿＿＿＿＿＿＿＿＿＿ to what he was saying.
3 'I'll leave unless you lower your voice,' she said.
   threatened She ＿＿＿＿＿＿＿＿＿＿ if he didn't lower his voice.
4 'Please don't leave. Please don't,' he said to her.
   begged He ＿＿＿＿＿＿＿＿＿＿ to leave.
5 'I'll speak calmly, I really will!' he said.
   promised He ＿＿＿＿＿＿＿＿＿＿ calmly.
6 'Am I still speaking too loud?' he asked.
   asked He ＿＿＿＿＿＿＿＿＿＿ he was still speaking too loud.
7 'I'm afraid I can't hear you very well,' she answered.
   told She ＿＿＿＿＿＿＿＿＿＿ hear him very well.
8 'Why are you speaking so quietly?' she asked.
   asked She ＿＿＿＿＿＿＿＿＿＿ speaking so quietly.

D Suppose you lived in the same building as Alison and the man with the dog. Yesterday you heard them talking in the hall. In pairs, discuss how you could report their conversation today. Report what the man said to Alison (1–5) and then what she said to him (6–10).

1 Can I talk to you for a few minutes?
2 Do you know how thin the ceiling is?
3 I can still hear the music you play in the evenings and it's very loud.
4 Don't disturb my dog any more.
5 If you disturb my dog and me again, I'll call the police.
6 Now what do you want to talk to me about?
7 Can't we talk about this later?
8 All right. I'll turn it down even lower.
9 Are you crazy? I don't disturb your dog. He disturbs me !
10 Would you mind not raising your voice?

USE OF ENGLISH

A The article below appeared recently in a local newspaper. Read it quickly to get an idea of what it is about, ignoring the missing words.

DOGS' MISERY IN SMALL HOUSE

A seventy-two-year-old widow, Mrs Francis Lovell, pleaded guilty yesterday to causing unnecessary suffering to the dogs she (0) _kept_ in her small three-roomed house in the village of Wheatley near Oxford.

The court was told that Mrs Lovell's neighbours repeatedly complained to her for more than six months about the (1)_____ in which the dogs were kept. The dogs often (2)_____ all night long. Despite these complaints, she (3)_____ to do anything about the problem. Finally, one of the neighbours who was unable to (4)_____ up with the noise any longer, called the police.

The police (5)_____ in touch with the RSPCA★, who sent one of their inspectors to call on Mrs Lovell. The widow claimed that she had 'only a few pets', and that she (6)_____ after them very well. At first she tried to (7)_____ the inspector from entering her house. However, he (8)_____ on seeing the dogs for himself. It (9)_____ out that she had forty-four dogs, most of them poodles, and that she never let them out of the house.

According to the inspector, John Carey, the dogs were all suffering from neglect, malnutrition and the (10)_____ of being kept all day in a very small house. Seventeen of them were in such a (11)_____ state that they had to be destroyed.

The lawyer defending Mrs Lovell said that she had never intended any (12)_____ to the animals.

'My (13)_____ is a lonely old woman whose only companions were her dogs. She was afraid that if she let them out of the house, something bad would (14)_____ to them. Her only (15)_____ of income is a very small pension, most of which she used in order to purchase food for them,' he said.

★ Royal Society for the Prevention of Cruelty to Animals

B Decide which is the best word, A, B, C or D, to complete the sentences with missing words in them. An example is given (0).

0   A   maintained   C   kept
        B   held   D   stopped
1   A   states   C   situations
        B   conditions   D   positions
2   A   cried   C   sounded
        B   barked   D   called
3   A   denied   C   disagreed
        B   resisted   D   refused
4   A   put   C   pass
        B   stand   D   let
5   A   came   C   became
        B   went   D   got
6   A   saw   C   cared
        B   watched   D   looked
7   A   avoid   C   escape
        B   prevent   D   refuse
8   A   insisted   C   emphasized
        B   commanded   D   impressed
9   A   showed   C   turned
        B   proved   D   found
10   A   results   C   effects
        B   returns   D   affects
11   A   wrong   C   poor
        B   ill   D   ruined
12   A   harm   C   hurt
        B   damage   D   injury
13   A   client   C   patient
        B   customer   D   passenger
14   A   occur   C   happen
        B   succeed   D   come
15   A   origin   C   stock
        B   supply   D   source

SPEAKING

In pairs or groups, discuss the following possible punishments for Mrs Lovell. Give reasons why you think each punishment is bad or good in her case.

1 Send her to prison for several months.
2 Order her to pay a very heavy fine.
3 Permit her to keep only one dog, but order her to allow an RSPCA inspector to visit her regularly to see how she is treating the dog.

Here is some useful language.

'I don't think the court should... because...'
'In my opinion, the best thing would be to... My reasons for saying this are as follows. First,... Second,...'
'I disagree with you because...'
'Yes, I agree with you. However, I think the court should also...'
'I'd like to make another suggestion. I think the best thing would be to...'

VOCABULARY

Phrasal verbs

A **In pairs or groups, underline the phrasal verbs in each question (a–h). Then match the phrasal verb with its meaning (1–8). Finally, answer each of the questions. If your answer is 'Yes' or 'No', give a reason for your answer.**

a) Do you think you could put up with Mrs Lovell if she were your neighbour?

b) What do you think the RSPCA inspector said to her when he called on her?

c) What did she do when he said he wanted to look into the complaints that her neighbours had made?

d) What do you think he said when it turned out that she had forty-four dogs in the house?

e) Do you think people should be allowed to keep pets if they can't look after them properly?

f) In your opinion, does Mrs Lovell's case call for understanding or punishment?

g) Do you think she should give up all her dogs except one?

h) Can you explain how she got through her money so quickly?

1 require or demand something that is best in a particular situation

2 visit

3 take care of

4 what you can say when you mean 'the result of our investigation showed that ... '

5 live with, in the sense of 'tolerate' or 'accept'

6 no longer have something or no longer do something

7 spend completely

8 find the cause of, investigate

B **Complete the following sentences with a phrasal verb from A above.**

Yesterday I decided to **(1)**_____ a woman who lives next door. Her father is very old, so she has to **(2)**_____ him. She finds it very difficult to **(3)**_____ some of his habits. He **(4)**_____ a large amount of money every week. She couldn't understand what he was spending it on, so she decided to **(5)**_____ the matter. It **(6)**_____ that he was buying a large amount of cat food. There are a lot of hungry cats in the neighbourhood and he is convinced that their condition **(7)**_____ him to feed them all. My neighbour wants her father to **(8)**_____ this habit, but she can't persuade him to do so.

WORD FORMATION

Read through this text. Then use the words in capital letters below to form a word that fits each space. An example is given (0).

It is very difficult to decide on the correct **(0)** _punishment_ in cases like these. This was why it took the judge so long to reach a **(1)**_____ in Mrs Lovell's case. Her lawyer said in her **(2)**_____ that she was lonely and confused and that this was why she had ignored the **(3)**_____ of her neighbours for so long. He also argued that this was not a case of deliberate **(4)**_____. In other words, Mrs Lovell had no **(5)**_____ of causing suffering. He also argued that a case like this called for **(6)**_____.

The judge finally found her **(7)**_____, but gave her **(8)**_____ to keep one dog for a period of a year, subject to good **(9)**_____. In other words, if she repeats her **(10)**_____, the dog will be taken away from her.

0	PUNISH	6	UNDERSTAND
1	DECIDE	7	GUILT
2	DEFEND	8	PERMIT
3	COMPLAIN	9	BEHAVE
4	CRUEL	10	OFFEND
5	INTEND		

LANGUAGE STUDY

Verbs and prepositions

Complete the text by filling the spaces with the correct prepositions.

Mrs Lovell was accused **(1)**_____ treating the dogs badly. They all belonged **(2)**_____ her and they all suffered **(3)**_____ neglect. This was one reason her neighbours complained **(4)**_____ them and why they wanted to prevent her **(5)**_____ getting any more dogs. They blame her **(6)**_____ the poor condition **(7)**_____ the animals. The judge has said that he does not believe **(8)**_____ punishment for cases like this and that sending her **(9)**_____ prison would be 'completely wrong'.

WRITING

Report 1

In Part 2, you may be asked to write a report for a company or other organization. This will contain factual information and may include a recommendation. You will have to supply the necessary details for the report.

A Sample task

Mr Klimt is a Swiss executive who is moving to your country with his family and will be working for your company for a year. You have been asked to look at possible housing for him by the Personnel Officer in your company.

Write a **report** on your findings, recommending a suitable home for Mr Klimt and his family.

B Read this answer.

To: J Harman,
Personnel Department

From: H Hunter

Re: Housing for Mr Klimt and family

FINDINGS

Here is the information on the three places I visited last week:

1 Apartment 41, Victoria Tower (£1800 per month) This is a two-bedroom flat, and although it is luxurious, it would be rather small for a family of four.

2 Meadow Farmhouse (£2050 per month) This is a five-bedroom farmhouse in the country with good rail links into the city centre. However, it is expensive and there are no suitable schools nearby.

3 Holly House, Ashton Street (£1550 per month) This is a three-bedroom house with a small garden. Although the house is in need of redecoration, the garden is pleasant and the rent is reasonable. The house is on a bus route and close to the Ashton International School.

RECOMMENDATIONS

I recommend that we rent Holly House and arrange for it to be redecorated before the Klimt family arrive. I look forward to discussing the matter with you at our next meeting.

C Answer these questions about the report.

1 Would you describe the language as informal or formal? Which words and expressions make you think so?
2 What do you notice about the layout of the report?
3 How much of the detail in the report has been supplied by the writer?
4 Which words and expressions would you be able to use in a similar type of report?

D Writing task

An American College is going to hold a five-day conference in your country. You have been asked by the College Principal to suggest three possible hotels where the conference could be held.

Write a **report** on what you have found out and recommend a suitable hotel.

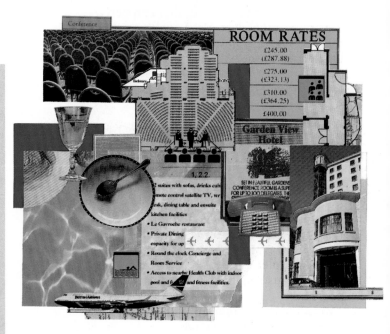

E Divide your report into three parts.

1 Opening
2 Findings
   Include factors you think are relevant, such as the following:
   Price and standard of the hotel (eg 4/5 star)
   Location (city centre or out of town? near the airport or near town facilities?)
   Facilities (conference rooms? number of bedrooms available? restaurants?)
3 Recommendations
   Say which of the hotels you thought was the most suitable, and include an appropriate ending.

REVISION AND EXTENSION

Review of verb forms ➤ GS 13

A **Complete the table below. The first one has been done for you as an example.**

Infinitive present	Past simple	Participle after *have/had*
go	*went*	*gone*
_____	swam	_____
rise	_____	_____
_____	_____	drunk
lay	_____	_____
forgive	_____	_____
_____	lay	_____
blow	_____	_____
_____	_____	lit
_____	stuck	_____

Present perfect or past simple?
➤ GS 13.1.3, 13.2.1

B **Complete the following conversation with the correct form of the verb in brackets. Use only the present perfect or the past simple, for example, is the first answer *have left* or *left*?**

A Since you (leave) school, you (travel) a lot, (not you)?

B Yes, so far I (live) in eight countries, but of course I (visit) more than that.

A What is the most interesting place you (be) to?

B It's hard to say. I (be) in Paris a few years ago and I really (enjoy) it.

A (you do) a lot of sightseeing while you (be) there?

B Yes, I (do).

A Where (you go)?

B I (go) up the Eiffel Tower, and I (see) a play at the Comédie Française. I must say, the play (be) really good.

A (you ever be) to South America?

B No, I (not have) the chance to go there yet, but I (hear) a lot about it and I hope to go there next year.

C **Match the sentences 1–10 with suitable contexts a–j.**

1 My parents have lived in London for three years.
2 My parents lived in London for three years.
3 Have you eaten breakfast?
4 Did you eat breakfast?
5 I hope you have enjoyed the party.
6 I hope you enjoyed the party.
7 The teacher hasn't come.
8 The teacher didn't come.
9 Have you seen that film?
10 Did you see that film?

a) There's a good film on this week.
b) The students are still waiting for the teacher.
c) It is eight o'clock in the morning.
d) It is eight o'clock at night.
e) The party has just finished or is just about to finish.
f) There was a good film on last night.
g) They live in London now.
h) The party was last week.
i) The students waited for the teacher and the lesson is now over.
j) They lived there from 1980 to 1983.

D **Use the correct form of the verb in brackets and choose one of the words *for*, *since* or *ago* for the following sentences.**

1 I (not speak) to her (for, since, ago) she (go) to London.
2 He (leave) school three years (for, since, ago), then he (work) in France (for, since, ago) a few months before coming back to England.
3 She (have) a headache (for, since, ago) she (get) up this morning.
4 How long (you know) him?
5 I (be) here (for, since, ago) an hour! Where (you be)?
6 He (just get) a new job, and he's going to work in the States (for, since, ago) six years.
7 It's two weeks (for, since, ago) I (see) him.

E **Rewrite the second sentence in each pair. Use no more than five words including the word in bold. Do NOT change this word.**

1 Is smoking permitted in British cinemas?
allowed Are _____ in British cinemas?

2 Please don't play your music so loudly.
playing Would _____ your music so loudly?

3 I'm going to take the car – that's okay by you, isn't it?
take You don't _____ the car, do you?

4 Alcohol is bad for you and so are cigarettes.
good Neither _____ for you.

5 I said to the waiter 'Could I have another coffee?'
bring I asked _____ another coffee.

6 The doctor asked 'Why didn't you make an appointment?'
made The doctor asked her _____ an appointment.

7 We haven't got enough room for this huge sofa.
takes This huge sofa _____ space.

8 Howe finally solved the problem in a dream.
final The _____ came to Howe in a dream.

SPEAKING

Talking on your own

Work in pairs as Student A and B. Try to speak for about one minute.

Student A: Describe and compare the situations in both pictures. Say what you think each person might be going to say.

Student B: Describe and compare the gestures the people are making in both pictures. Say how the people might be feeling and why they might be making these gestures.

READING

A **Read this article quickly, ignoring the missing paragraphs. Then read paragraphs A–E and choose the one that fits each gap in the text (1–3). There is one extra paragraph which you do not need. An example is given (0).**

All American schoolchildren learn that George Washington, the first President of the United States, once said, 'I cannot tell a lie.' But what is a lie? Is it anything we say which we know is untrue?

0	*E*

Professor Jerald Jellison, of the University of California, has made a scientific study of lying. According to his research, women are better liars than men. They are especially good at telling 'white lies', such as when a woman at a party tells another woman that she likes her dress, even though she really thinks it is awful.

1	

Some psychologists believe that certain gestures give liars away. For example, they may make sudden, unconscious movements if they are sitting down when they tell a lie. This suggests that they are thinking , 'I wish I weren't here.'

2	

In Miami, Florida, a man was recently found guilty of murdering his wife. He had accused her of having an affair with another man. When denying this, she had rubbed her nose several times. He believed this was proof that she was lying.

3	

This is just one small example of how gestures can deceive people, often with tragic consequences.

FOCUS ONE

A Her doctor later testified that he had seen her the day before she was killed. She had come to him because she was suffering from a rare skin condition. This caused a strange, itching sensation, especially in her nose.

B When he was very young, he chopped down his father's favourite cherry tree. When his father asked him if he had done it, he confessed immediately.

C However, this is only one side of the story. Other researchers say that men are more likely to tell more serious lies, such as making a promise which they do not intend to keep. This is the kind of lie politicians and some businessmen are supposed to be good at; the kind of lie they can profit from in some way.

D They may also touch their lips or rub their noses, as if to say 'If only I could stop myself from lying.' Perhaps these gestures are caused by the mental stress involved in telling a lie. However, we should remember that they can tragically mislead us in other ways.

E For example, suppose a friend asks you to lend him some money. You refuse because he often forgets to re-pay his debts. However, rather than hurt his feelings, you say, 'Sorry, I'm short of money myself.' Is this really a lie?

B Discuss these questions

1 Explain the meaning of the term 'a white lie'.
2 Describe the kind of lie men are probably better at than women.
3 What are some of the things liars do which may show that they are lying?
4 Explain why it can be dangerous to believe these gestures are always proof that someone is lying.
5 What does the case of the man who killed his wife in Miami have to do with the rest of the text?
6 There is a connection between the rest of the text and the paragraph you do not need. What is this connection?

SPEAKING

In pairs or groups, discuss what you would do and say in the following situation.

A friend tries to borrow money from you. You are not short of money. However, you lent this friend a large sum last year. Your friend has not repaid the debt and seems to have forgotten all about it. You have never mentioned this to your friend because you don't want to hurt your friend's feelings.

LANGUAGE STUDY

I wish and *If only* ➤ GS 14.1

A Which of these sentences (a or b) expresses most clearly that the speaker is sorry about something or regrets it?

1 a I don't want to be here.
   b I wish I weren't here.
2 a I want to have more money.
   b If only I had more money.
3 a I hope I can come to your party.
   b I wish I could come to your party.
4 a I want to be in London now.
   b If only I were in London now.

B Rewrite the second sentence in each pair. Use no more than five words including the word in bold. Do NOT change this word.

1 I'm sorry I can't speak English perfectly.
   wish I _____ English perfectly.
2 I'm sorry I can't do this exercise.
   only If _____ this exercise.
3 I'm sorry I'm not rich.
   only If _____ rich.
4 Are you ever sorry that you aren't rich?
   wish Do you ever _____ rich?
5 I'm sorry I can't answer that question.
   wish I _____ that question.
6 It's a pity the weather isn't better today.
   only If _____ better today.
7 I'm sorry you don't love me.
   only If _____ me.
8 It's a pity you can't understand how I feel about you.
   wish I _____ how I feel about you.

VOCABULARY

In groups or pairs, discuss which word you need to complete each of these sentences.

borrow   lend   pay   earn   gain   win   lose

1 I wonder if you could _____ me a few dollars?
2 You mean you want to _____ more money from me?
3 If I give it to you, you'll _____ it in a card game.
4 I never play cards any more. I know I can't _____.
5 I want a job so that I can _____ some money.
6 Then I promise I'll _____ you all the money I owe you.
7 What do you hope to _____ by telling such lies?

READING

A **You and a friend want to choose a film to watch on TV this evening. Read the two reviews and decide together which film you would prefer and why.**

The Sting   (9–10.30 PM, C4)

Brilliant! A classic – recently voted one of the ten best films in the last fifty years. The story takes place in Chicago in the 1930s. Two small-time crooks (Paul Newman and Robert Redford) get together in order to cheat a powerful New York gangster (Robert Shaw) out of a huge sum of money. They want revenge on him for the murder of one of Redford's friends. It is sometimes difficult to work out who is cheating who. However, in the end Newman and Redford bring their plan off. Watch it and you'll never be bored.

Ring of Deception   (10.15 TO MIDNIGHT, C 3)

A depressing story about Steve, an insurance salesman (played by Kevin Hart) who falls for Jenny (Amanda Crown). At first she is not at all interested in him, but he takes her in with a story he makes up about being a rich playboy. He asks her to marry him and she almost says 'yes'. However, she finally turns him down when she finds out the diamond ring he gives her, like everything else he has told her, is a fake. The plot soon runs out of what little interest there is in the beginning. If you can't sleep at night, go on watching this for a few minutes and you'll soon drop off.

B **In pairs or groups, read aloud all the phrasal verbs you can find in the texts. Then match these phrasal verbs with the meanings below.**

1 do something successfully even though it is difficult
2 use up, no longer have something
3 be deeply attracted to
4 get something from people dishonestly
5 meet
6 discover, learn
7 continue
8 make someone believe something that is not true
9 calculate or understand
10 invent
11 refuse, say no to an offer or request
12 fall asleep

C **Work in pairs. One of you completes the questions below and asks them. The other answers each completed question.**

1 Where … 'The Sting' take …?
2 Why … Redford and Newman … together?
3 Why … they want revenge … the New York gangster?
4 … they … their plan off?
5 What … the second film about?
6 Why … Steve make … a story about being a rich playboy?
7 … he manage to … her in?
8 What … happen if you … on watching this for very long?

SPEAKING

Finding out about each other

Ask your partners:

- how often they go to the cinema.
- when they last saw a good film.
- where they saw it.
- where the story took place.
- why they enjoyed it.
- who they were with when they saw the film.
- what kinds of film they don't like.

WRITING

Write 120 words about a film you have seen. Use the sentences below and go on to briefly describe what happens in the film. Then give your opinion of it. Was it brilliant? Boring? Exciting? Frightening? Depressing?

The film is called…
It stars…
It takes place in…
The film is about…

VOCABULARY

Which word or phrase in each group doesn't belong with the other three? Explain why.

Example: film game music programme

➤ *Music – because you can't watch it.*

1 salesman crook criminal thief
2 borrow steal rob cheat
3 fake false genuine imitation
4 brilliant depressing wonderful entertaining
5 event plot story plan
6 betray deceive take in take over
7 fill up run out of get through finish
8 bring off succeed achieve fail

LANGUAGE STUDY ➤ GS 1.2

A Explain the difference in meaning in these pairs of sentences.

1 I don't think you're very interested.
  I don't think you are very interesting.
2 The problem with you is that you're bored.
  The problem with you is that you're boring.
3 You aren't very amusing.
  You aren't very amused.

Repeat the sentences that people do not like to hear about themselves. Then describe a situation or situations in which you might say the other sentences.

Example: I don't think you're very interested.

➤ *Perhaps I would say this if I told someone a story and I could see that he or she wasn't listening.*

B Read this text and the words in capital letters below it. Change the form of the word so that it fits the numbered space. An example is given (0).

I saw a film last week that was not very **(0)** *interesting*. It was a comedy but it was not very **(1)**_____. But perhaps the real problem was not that the film was bad but that I was **(2)**_____. The weather was very **(3)**_____ that day too. To add to my problems, I was **(4)**_____ because I had just had some very **(5)**_____ news. I had been hoping to get a very **(6)**_____ job that someone else got instead. In fact, I was very **(7)**_____ I didn't get it because I was **(8)**_____ that I had all the right qualifications. However, **(9)**_____ things like this happen all the time, don't they? So why was I **(10)**_____?

0	INTEREST	6	INTEREST
1	AMUSE	7	SHOCK
2	DEPRESS	8	CONVINCE
3	DEPRESS	9	DISAPPOINT
4	DISAPPOINT	10	SURPRISE
5	SURPRISE		

C In groups or pairs, say one or two sentences about each of the following things.

1 Some news that you would find surprising.
2 What you do when you are bored.
3 Something which you have found boring.

USE OF ENGLISH

A Read the text below. Think of the best word to fill each space. Use only one word each time. An example is given (0).

THE LIEBUSTER
THE MODERN ELECTRONIC MIRACLE!

At last, thanks to modern technology, (0) _there_ is a way to find out if people (1)_____ telling the truth: The Liebuster. Don't be taken in (2)_____ the fact that it looks like an ordinary watch. It's far more (3)_____ that. In addition (4)_____ telling the time, it buzzes when it detects a lie.

This miracle of modern technology is one of the smallest and (5)_____ accurate lie-detectors ever made. By means of high-tech microchips, it measures the stress (6)_____ people's voices. Nobody will ever get (7)_____ with lying if you use it (8)_____ important business negotiations.

Take it with you (9)_____ all those special 'romantic' occasions, and it will warn you if your wife, husband, girlfriend or boyfriend is lying when you ask questions (10)_____ as 'Do you really love me?' or 'What did you (11)_____ when I was away on business?' The bigger the lie, (12)_____ louder the buzz. Nobody can do (13)_____ one . So hurry now, (14)_____ stocks last, and buy your personal LIEBUSTER (15)_____ an amazingly low price.

Here are ten of the words. Did you include them?

at   away   by   during   in
on   than   to   while   without

B In pairs or groups, think of the exact questions the following people with Liebusters would ask other people to find out if they were lying.

Example: Customs Officers at airports

➤ *Have you anything to declare? Is this all your luggage?*

1 detectives or police officers
2 jealous husbands or wives
3 interviewers
4 interviewees
5 shoppers in open-air markets

LISTENING

A A man and a woman are talking. Listen and decide which of the statements below are true and which are false.

1 The man has never been late before.
2 He phoned the woman earlier to tell her he would be late.
3 Dinner is ready when he arrives.
4 The woman often has to go away on business at the weekend.
5 The man says he saw some friends last weekend.
6 The woman believes him.
7 The woman has a special way of finding out if the man is telling the truth.
8 The only person who tells a lie in this conversation is the man.

B In pairs or groups, discuss these questions. Then compare your answers with other pairs or groups.

1 What do you think is the relationship between the man and the woman? Are they married? Business colleagues? Or something else?
2 Who do you think Carla is?
3 What is the disadvantage of the technology the woman uses in order to find out if the man is lying?

C Now listen to five different people talking (1–5). Choose from the list A–F which speaker is talking. There is one extra letter which you do not need. The first answer has been given for you.

SPEAKER ONE	D

SPEAKER TWO	

SPEAKER THREE	

SPEAKER FOUR	

SPEAKER FIVE	

A Someone who has decided not to sell Liebusters.
B Someone who has a Liebuster and is very satisfied.
C Someone who would never buy one.
D Someone who may buy one or who may not.
E Someone who had a Liebuster but no longer has it.
F Someone who thinks it might make an excellent gift for someone else.

SPEAKING

A **Read the description of one of the objects shown below. Then say which object you think is being described.**

The purpose of this is to tell you the time. It also makes a very loud noise in the morning when you want to wake up. Its main advantage is that it is very cheap and very simple to operate. All you have to do is wind it up. You don't need batteries or any other form of electricity. However, it doesn't always tell the time very accurately.

B **Now work in pairs. One of you describes one of the objects above. Do NOT say which object you are describing. See if your partners can guess which object you are talking about. Be sure to do these things:**

- Describe the purpose of the object.
- Explain what else you need in order to use it.
- Give at least one advantage of using the object.
- If you can, describe a possible disadvantage.

C **Decide together which are the two most useful objects, giving your reasons why.**

LANGUAGE STUDY

I wish you would/wouldn't do it
I wish you had/hadn't done it ➤ GS 14.1

A **Which two examples below could mean 'Please do or don't do this in the future'? Explain what the other two examples mean.**

1 I wish you would phone me.
2 I wish you had phoned me.
3 I wish you wouldn't lie to me.
4 I wish you hadn't lied to me.

B **Complete the second sentence in each pair. Always begin the second sentence with *I wish*.**

Example: I'm sorry I said that.

➤ *I wish I hadn't said that.*

1 Please don't say things like that.
2 Please don't do that.
3 I'm angry because you said that.
4 I'm angry because you did that.
5 Don't ask me so many questions.
6 Don't smoke here!
7 I'm sorry I asked you that question.
8 It was wrong of you to ask me that question.

VOCABULARY

Word combinations (compound nouns)

A **Study the definitions (1–3). Then match them with the things they define (a–c).**

1 A machine that is used to detect lies.
2 A medicine or something else you can use to make your hair grow again.
3 A person who steals things from people's pockets.

a) a pickpocket b) a lie-detector c) a hair restorer

B **Now define the words below in the same way.**

Example: a cassette player

➤ *Something you can use to play cassettes.*

1   a stain remover
2   a company director
3   an air traffic controller
4   a hair-dryer
5   a weedkiller
6   a water softener
7   an office cleaner
8   a textbook writer
9   a photocopier
10 a toilet cleaner

WRITING

Transactional letter 2

The transactional letter in Part 1 of Paper 2 is either informal (see Unit 2) or formal. Decide which style is more appropriate by thinking about the purpose of the letter and who you are writing to.

A Sample task

Read the following information and write a letter of complaint to the Manager of the Multiplex Cinema Centre, explaining why you are not satisfied and saying what you think they should do.

B Read this sample answer. Choose the best option from the words in *italics*.

Dear *Sir/Manager*

I am writing to complain about/This is about your advertisement for the Multiplex Cinema, which is misleading in a number of ways.

Firstly, you state in *the advertisement/your advert* that seats cost £3.00. *But you know/However*, when I went to the cinema, the only seats that were available cost £10 each. I *feel/reckon* that it should have been made clear that only a limited number of seats cost £3, and that the others are *far/loads* more expensive.

Secondly/And then you say that there is free car parking. However, when I asked about this at the box office, I was told that the free car park was twenty minutes' walk away. There is a £10 charge for using the car park next to the cinema, but your advertisement does not make this clear at all.

So all in all/Under the circumstances, I feel justified in asking for a refund. I would therefore be grateful if you could refund the extra £14 I had to spend on the tickets and the £10 charge for parking. *I am enclosing/Here are* the receipts for these.

I look forward to hearing/Hope to hear from you.

Yours *faithfully/sincerely*

D D Jones

C Look again at the task and the sample letter. Answer these questions with yes or no.

Has the writer of the letter …
1 written to the Manager?
2 chosen a formal style?
3 covered all the points mentioned in the writer's notes?
4 mentioned the five films in the advertisement?
5 explained clearly what the complaint is about?
6 suggested a course of action the manager should take?
7 been offensive?

Where you have answered no, think about why the writer has chosen not to do this.

D Writing task

You have recently been on a short holiday organized by a local company, but you were not happy with some of the things that happened. Read the information from Comfy Cottages and your notes. Then write **a letter of complaint** to the manager of the company.

> Holiday dates: Fri Feb 13 – Sun Feb 15
> Accommodation: Holly Tree Cottage
>
> ## Comfy Cottages
>
> We have been specializing in short break holidays in countryside cottages for over 10 years. We have an excellent range of first class cottages to choose from. Our cottages combine traditional charm with every modern facility.
>
> *No dishwasher*
> *TV broken*
>
> Your cottage will be cleaned prior to your arrival. You will receive a Welcome Pack with a few essential groceries and a bottle of wine, along with an Information Pack telling you all about the local area.
>
> *Terrible mess.*
> *Not until*
> *Saturday!*
> *Had no coffee or*
> *milk on day 1 –*
> *all shops shut!*
>
> We pride ourselves on our level of service. If there is anything you are unhappy about, let us know. If you are delighted, please tell your friends.
>
> *Yes! Refund*
> *£100?*
> *Free weekend*
> *somewhere else?*

E Read through these notes before you write your answer.

1 Opening: remember you are writing to the manager.
2 Paragraph 1: explain why you are writing and give details of where you stayed and when.
3 Paragraph 2: describe the problems you had with the facilities.
4 Paragraph 3: describe what other problems you had.
5 Paragraph 4: suggest a course of action.
6 Ending: finish the letter in a suitable way.

REVISION AND EXTENSION

Read the following theatre review. Choose the best word, A, B, C or D, to fill spaces 1–15.

The Misanthropist

The latest production at the Playhouse is a modern version of Molière's great play of 1666, *Le Misanthrope*. As in many of his other comedies, Molière takes an aspect of human nature and **(1)**_____ it, so creating a rich variety of comic scenes and situations. In the past, many directors have **(2)**_____ to stress the serious **(3)**_____ of the play, but here, **(4)**_____ Jack Long has kept the tone light and **(5)**_____.

Peter Fowler plays the central character, Alceste. He is a man who has no **(6)**_____ of people's emotions. He refuses to **(7)**_____ any of the small **(8)**_____ lies that are necessary in normal society; he doesn't mind **(9)**_____ people and ends up hurting the **(10)**_____ of almost everyone he meets. It would be easy to feel some sympathy for Alceste – after all, his only fault is that he is too **(11)**_____ – but Peter Fowler **(12)**_____ to make him look a rather ridiculous figure.

There are some excellent performances from other **(13)**_____. The long-suffering Philinte (Sam Kirby) comes across as a very sympathetic character. The romantic interest is provided by Celimene (Amanda Carter), although in the end she **(14)**_____ to persuade him to change his ways.

The Misanthropist is on every night for the next three weeks **(15)**_____ Sundays.

1. A increases   C expands
   B grows   D exaggerates
2. A used   C tended
   B selected   D leaned
3. A side   C view
   B angle   D edge
4. A direct   C direction
   B directive   D director
5. A fun   C comic
   B pleasant   D amused
6. A knowledge   C conscience
   B understanding D thought
7. A speak   C tell
   B say   D talk
8. A green   C grey
   B red   D white
9. A upsetting   C wounding
   B injuring   D damaging
10. A sensations C spirits
    B emotions   D feelings
11. A honest   C right
    B true   D accurate
12. A succeeds   C achieves
    B can   D manages
13. A casts   C players
    B actors   D roles
14. A fails   C mistakes
    B misses   D drops
15. A apart   C unless
    B without   D except

LISTENING 📷

Listen to the speech made at a prize-giving ceremony, and decide which of the following statements are true (T) and which are false (F).

1. There are four categories in the 'Product of the Year' competition. ☐
2. The music plug is designed to be used with computers. ☐
3. The telephone imager sends a picture of the person who is using the telephone. ☐
4. The powered parachute has been entered in the transport category. ☐
5. The concrete mixer can be carried around easily. ☐
6. Inventors depend on scientists to put their ideas into production. ☐
7. Many inventors get their ideas suddenly. ☐
8. Inventors need to know how to make use of computers. ☐
9. Successful inventors are usually good businessmen. ☐
10. The competition has been won by an engineer. ☐

LETTERS TO AN ADVICE COLUMN

SPEAKING

Talking on your own

Work in pairs as Student A and B. Try to speak for about one minute.

Student A: Describe and compare the people in both pictures. Say what you think they might have just said to each other.

Student B: Describe and compare the relationships in both pictures. Say which of the relationships you think is closer.

READING

A You are going to read three letters to an advice column in a magazine. Before you read them, study the statements (0–11) about the three letters. Then say which letter (A, B or C) contains the answer. An example is given (0).

0 She earns more than her partner. ___ B

1 Someone predicted something that came true. ☐

2 There were problems to do with money. ☐

3 Someone she loved wants to see her again. ☐

4 She predicts money problems if she does something. ☐

5 Her problems with her love life caused another problem in her family life. ☐

6 He wants her to make a choice that is very difficult. ☐

7 She is afraid to tell him the truth about her feelings. ☐

8 Her boyfriend wants to be a father. ☐

9 She trusted someone who deceived her in more than one way. ☐

10 She does not want to admit she made a mistake. ☐

11 He left her for another woman. ☐

Letter A

I have been going out for several months with a man called Peter. In many ways he is everything I have ever wanted. He has asked me to marry him. I would say yes if it weren't for Roger, my ex-boyfriend.

Although we had lots of fights, my relationship with him was very exciting and deeply satisfying in many ways. We broke up because Roger fell in love with another woman. I didn't hear from him for a long time but last week he phoned me again. He has been thinking about me all the time and wants to make a fresh start. I have told him I will think about it.

I know that Peter loves me very deeply and it would hurt him very much if he knew that I still love Roger. What would you do if you were me?

FOCUS ONE

Letter B

I find my career extremely interesting but I am in love with a man who wants me to give my job up so that we can get married and start a family. I know that if I stopped working I would be very unhappy. His salary is much lower than mine and we wouldn't have enough to live on. However he keeps saying, 'Money isn't the most important thing in life,' and 'If you really loved me, you'd do what I want.'

I don't want to give him up – but I don't want to give up my job, either. What should I do?

Letter C

A year ago, my mother told me that I should not trust the man I was going out with. She was convinced he would let me down. I told her not to interfere in my personal life, and we have not spoken to each other since then. However, she was right. Later, he often borrowed large sums from me but never kept his promises to pay them back. I finally left him when I found out that he was having an affair with another woman.

My mother always used to say that I was a poor judge of character, especially when it comes to men. Now I am afraid that if I contact her and tell her what has happened, she will only say 'See! I told you so.' Nevertheless, I'd like to have a friendly relationship with her again. What would you do if you were me?

B Now look again at the statements 1–11. Read aloud the sentence or sentences in each letter that give you the answers.

Example: She earns more than her partner.
➤ *His salary is much lower than mine. (B)*

C In pairs or groups, discuss these questions.

1 Look at letter A again. What did the writer's ex-boyfriend actually say to her when he phoned again? What did she say to him?
2 The writer of letter B is talking to her boyfriend about their problem. What do you think they actually say to each other?
3 The writer of letter C decides to phone her mother. How does the conversation begin? What do they say after that?

LANGUAGE STUDY

Conditionals ➤ GS 4.1, 4.2

A Match the first part of each sentence (a–d) with the second part of that sentence (1–4).

a) I'd come and see you …
b) I'll come and see you, …
c) If you understand English, …
d) If you understood English, …

1 you won't find this difficult.
2 if I have time.
3 if I had time.
4 you wouldn't find this difficult.

• Repeat only the sentences that give a reason why something is impossible.
• Now repeat the sentences that suggest something is or may be possible.

B Rephrase the following sentences using *if*.

Example: You don't understand this because you don't speak English.
➤ *You would understand this if you spoke English.*

1 You don't want to marry me because you don't love me.
2 I don't eat that kind of food because I don't like it.
3 I won't come to see you because I have no time.
4 Jack has no chance of passing the exam because he never studies.
5 Perhaps I'll have time. If so, I'll come and see you.
6 Perhaps I'll get a better job. I'll earn more then.
7 Perhaps it'll rain. If so, we'll cancel the picnic.

C Complete the second sentence in each pair. Use no more than five words including the word in bold. Do NOT change this word.

1 It's impossible to do this because we have no time.
   would   If we _____ be able to do this.
2 Perhaps it will be possible to do this if we have time.
   will   If we _____ be able to do this.
3 Her boyfriend does such things because he doesn't really love her.
   would   If her boyfriend really _____ do such things.
4 You steal because you aren't honest.
   wouldn't   If you _____ steal.
5 Will you tell the truth? If so, people will trust you.
   will   If you _____ trust you.
6 People don't trust him because he tells lies.
   would   If he did _____ trust him.

USE OF ENGLISH

Read the letter below, which answers letter A on page 50. Think of the best word for each space. Use only one word each time. An example is given (0). Here are five of the words.

if   let   still   unless   yourself

If I had more information about your relationship, it **(0)** _would_ be easier for me to give you advice. So rather than suggest what you should do, **(1)**_____ me ask you a few questions which you should ask yourself. How long **(2)**_____ your relationship with Roger last? You say your relationship with Peter **(3)**_____ lasted for several months. Are you getting rather bored with him only because you have been with him longer than you **(4)**_____ with Roger? And what about the woman Roger fell in love **(5)**_____? Does he **(6)**_____ love her? And if he **(7)**_____, can you really believe that he loves you as well?

    You must remember that if you **(8)**_____ up your relationship with Peter, it will be your fault, not Roger's. What will happen **(9)**_____ Roger is not satisfied in his new relationship with you? Will you blame Roger or **(10)**_____ because you left Peter for him?

Last of all, **(11)**_____ haven't you told Peter about your feelings for Roger? Are you really afraid **(12)**_____ hurting him? Won't he **(13)**_____ far more hurt if you don't give him a chance to talk about your feelings? How would you feel if Peter **(14)**_____ the same thing to you? You will never make the right decision **(15)**_____ you answer these questions honestly.

WRITING

A Write to a friend. Briefly describe a problem you have or have had recently and ask for advice about it. Use about 120 words. Then give the letter to someone in your class.

B If you get a letter from someone else asking for advice, write a short reply saying what you would do if you were the person who wrote the letter. Again, use no more than 120 words.

VOCABULARY

fault   mistake   error   defect   blame

A Study the following definitions from the OXFORD Wordpower DICTIONARY.

fault *noun* **1** something wrong or not perfect in a person's character: *One of my faults is that I am always late.* **2** responsibility for a mistake: *It will be your own fault if you don't pass your exams.*

mistake *noun* something that you do or think that is wrong: *Waiter! I think you've made a mistake over the bill.* (IDIOM) as a result of a mistake or carelessness: *The terrorists shot the wrong man by mistake.*

error *noun* **1** more formal than **mistake**: *The telephone bill was far too high due to a computer error.* (IDIOM) There are some expressions, for example *an error of judgement, human error* where only **error** can be used.

defect *noun* something that is wrong with or missing from someone or something: *There are defects in our educational system.*

blame *verb* to think or say that someone or something is responsible for something bad that has happened: *The teacher blamed me for the accident.*

B Complete the sentences below, using one of the words in A.

1 The accident was the result of pilot _____.
2 Even native-speakers sometimes make _____ in English.
3 Who do you _____ for your problems? Me? Or yourself?
4 There's a _____ in this computer.
5 Whose _____ do you think the accident was? Yours? Or the other driver's?
6 Oh, I'm sorry. I took your jacket by _____. It looks just like mine.
7 My father was not perfect. He had several _____, but he was still a good man.
8 Don't _____ me if this happens again. I warned you!
9 As a result of an accounting _____, you were overcharged in your previous bill.

C In pairs or groups, decide whether the following things are examples of mistakes, faults, errors, or defects. Then explain why.

Example: You have a new car. When you turn on the engine, nothing happens.

➤ *A defect, because something is wrong with the car.*

1 The word 'business' is spelled 'busyness'.
2 Some people always blame other people for their own mistakes.
3 You receive a bill for something you did not buy.
4 A part of a new machine regularly breaks down.
5 Someone says, 'If you will listen, you would understand.'
6 A company director who usually makes the right choices in employing people makes one very bad choice.
7 Some people always judge other people only by their appearance.
8 You buy a cassette recorder. The 'pause' button doesn't work.

D In pairs, answer these questions. Then ask other pairs to tell you their answers, too.

1 Describe a defect in something you have bought recently.
2 What are two mistakes you often make in English?
3 Give an example of an error that the post office or some other service in your country has been responsible for.
4 Describe a fault that you think can be found in your own character or in the character of someone you know.
5 A man got drunk in a pub. The owner of the pub knew the man was drunk but still sold him alcohol. The man got into his car and had a terrible accident. Who do you blame for the accident? Why?

LANGUAGE STUDY

Is it still going on? ➤ GS 13.1, 13.2

A Explain the difference in meaning

1 How long did your relationship with Roger last?
2 How long has your relationship with Peter lasted?
3 How long did you go out with him?
4 How long have you been going out with him?

• Repeat the sentences that suggest the relationship is still going on.
• What do the other two sentences suggest about time?

B Complete each sentence using the correct form of the verb.

Example: I (learn) English for the last five years.

➤ *I have been learning English for the last five years.*

1 I (go out) with my present boyfriend for nine months.
2 Before that, I (go out) with another man for two years.
3 Before I got this job, I (work) for a bank for three years.
4 I like my present job. I (do) it for more than a year now.
5 There is a strange man outside. He (stand) there for two hours.
6 I (see) him there yesterday, too.
7 He (stand) there yesterday for almost nine hours.
8 Do you mind if I ask you how long you (live) at your present address?
9 Can you also tell me where you (live) before that?

C In pairs or groups, ask your partners questions, in order to find out if they

1 do something now that they did not do ten years ago.
2 have any habits now which they did not have when they were younger.

Now find out how long they have been doing those things. Afterwards, tell someone else what you have found out about your partners.

Example:

My partner (name) has been going to dancing lessons for six months. He/She has also been studying English for several years.

D Most lines contain an unnecessary word. Underline these words and tick any lines that are correct. There are two examples (0) and (00).

0 Five years ago, I <u>have</u> lived in a very big city
00 far away from the small town where I was   ✓
1 born. I had a job in a bank there. I have left
2 last year because of the pay and working
3 conditions, which they were not very good. The
4 cost of the living there was very high. It was
5 very difficult for me to make the ends meet. I
6 am glad I came back home. I have been working
7 in a small office here. My salary here is about
8 the same but living here is more cheaper than
9 in the big city. Life is more simpler and better
10 in many ways. I have been going out with a
11 woman. I like her a lot and I would like to ask
12 her to marry with me. I hope very much that if I
13 will do this she will say 'Yes'. I wanted to ask her
14 yesterday but I felt myself very nervous. We are
15 going to meet us tomorrow and I will try again.

LISTENING 😐

A **You are going to hear a conversation between two people, Dan and Mary. After you have listened for the first time, answer questions 1–6.**

1 How old do you think Dan and Mary are?
2 Where do you think they are when they speak?
3 What time of day do you think it is?
4 What do you think is the relationship between Dan and Mary? Friends? Colleagues at work? Or something else? If so, what?
5 What does one of them do at the very end?
6 Why does he or she do this?

B **Now listen again. Then answer questions 7–13 by writing D (for Dan) or M (for Mary) in the boxes. An example is given (0). If you aren't sure what some of the words in the questions mean, look at the vocabulary exercise below first.**

Who wants to talk about something important?	**0**	M
Who is looking for something?	**7**	
Who apologizes for something?	**8**	
Who tries to change the subject?	**9**	
Who suggests doing something?	**10**	
Who has noticed a big change in the other person's behaviour?	**11**	
Who threatens to do something?	**12**	
Who promises to do something after it is too late?	**13**	

VOCABULARY

suggest   recommend   advise   threaten apologize   promise   offer   object

A **Which word describes what you do when you say**

1 you are sorry that you did something?
2 you are ready to help or do something for someone?
3 someone or something would be good or suitable for a job or purpose?
4 someone can be sure you will do something?
5 you will do something a person will not like unless he or she does what you want them to do?
6 what you think someone else should do?
7 you do not like or are against something?
8 something that is an idea or plan for other people to think about or consider?

B **Now complete these sentences, choosing one of the words in A.**

1 I _____ to pay this money back in a week.
2 Can you _____ a good hotel in Paris?
3 What would you _____ me to do in this situation?
4 I'd like to _____ for getting so angry yesterday.
5 When our car broke down yesterday, another car stopped and the driver _____ to help us.
6 I think this plan is very unfair. I _____ to it!
7 Yesterday Mary _____ to leave her husband.
8 I'd like to _____ that we do something else now.

C **Read this text and the words in capital letters below it. Change the form of each word if necessary, so that it fits the numbered space. An example is given (0).**

We all welcomed the teacher's (0) *suggestion* that we should do something else after the last exercise. Usually the teacher gives us very good (1)_____ and we have faith in all her (2)_____. So we were rather (3)_____ when she asked us to make small (4)_____ in the form of words like 'suggest', 'advise', and so on. In fact, one of the students seemed to have a very strong (5)_____ to the idea because there was such a clear (6)_____ between these words and the words we had just studied. 'I'll jump out of the window if we go on doing this,' he said. The teacher smiled because she knew the student was only (7)_____ and then asked 'Are you making a promise or is that a (8)_____?' There was a great deal of (9)_____ as we listened to the student's (10)_____.

0	SUGGEST	6	CONNECT
1	ADVISE	7	JOKE
2	RECOMMEND	8	THREATEN
3	SURPRISE	9	LAUGH
4	CHANGE	10	APOLOGIZE
5	OBJECT		

FOCUS THREE

LANGUAGE STUDY

still, yet or *already*?

A Complete the following sentences with *still, yet* or *already*.

1 Has that film you want to watch started ____?
2 No, it hasn't. Do you ____ want to watch it, too?
3 I'm not sure. I think I've ____ seen it.
4 I think the news is ____ on. Let's watch it.
5 What, you mean it hasn't finished ____?
6 No, and it's ____ nine thirty.
7 Do you want to watch it? Have you decided ____?
8 I've ____ told you. I'm not sure.
9 In other words, you're ____ thinking about it.

More about how we report what people say
➤ GS 12.2 –12.5

B Look at the sentences below. Then say what you think the speaker or speakers actually said.

Example: Mary threatened to leave Dan if he didn't do something about the problem.

➤ *'I'll leave you if you don't do something about this problem.'*

1 Mary asked a friend if she could recommend a good restaurant.
2 Her friend recommended one called 'Da Mario'.
3 When Dan came home that evening, he asked what they were having for dinner.
4 Mary suggested going to a restaurant rather than eating at home.
5 Dan objected to the idea because he thought eating in restaurants was too expensive.
6 Mary asked him why he was afraid to spend money.
7 She offered to pay for the meal in a restaurant and even for a taxi there and back.
8 Dan claimed to be very tired.
9 Mary advised him to see a doctor.
10 Dan accused her of wanting to waste money.
11 Mary apologized for troubling him.
12 Then she told him to cook his own meal because she was going out without him.

C Look again at sentences 1, 3 and 6 above. What is the difference between the actual words of the question and the way the question is reported? (See GS 12.4)

D Rewrite the second sentence in each pair. Use no more than five words including the word in bold. Do NOT change this word.

1 'Please sit down,' the teacher said to me.
   asked   The teacher _____ down.

2 'Have you any questions?' the teacher said to me.
   asked   The teacher _____ any questions.
3 'Why are you learning English?' was her next question.
   asked   Then the teacher _____ learning English.
4 'Let's go for a walk,' Mary said.
   suggested   Mary _____ for a walk.
5 'If I were you, I wouldn't watch so much TV,' Dan's doctor said to him.
   advised   Dan's doctor _____ so much TV.
6 'Let me help you carry that suitcase,' I said to the old lady.
   offered   I _____ the old lady's suitcase.
7 'Thank you for helping me,' the old lady said to me.
   thanked   The old lady _____ her.
8 'I'm innocent,' the criminal said.
   claimed   The criminal _____ innocent.
9 'You're lying,' the detective said to him.
   accused   The detective _____ lying.
10 'I hope you'll forgive me for coming so late,' the student said to the teacher.
   apologized   The student _____ so late.

SPEAKING

A In pairs or groups, discuss what you would say if you were visiting a friend in hospital who had had an accident. What questions would be asked? What would be said? What advice would be given?

B Imagine you are with another friend the day after your visit. Report the conversation you had with the friend in hospital.

WRITING

Composition 2 Expressing an opinion

In Part 2 of Paper 2, you may be asked to write a composition giving your opinion on a subject. This type of question is similar to the advantages and disadvantages composition (see Unit 1), except that in this case you talk about the subject from one point of view only.

A Sample task

You have been doing a project on crime and punishment. Your English teacher has asked you to write a composition commenting on this statement:

The death penalty cannot be defended. Do you agree?

Write your composition.

B Read this answer, ignoring spaces 1–10. Describe the writer's opinion briefly.

1 — Some countries still have the death penalty, **(1)**_____ it no longer exists in Britain. **(2)**_____, after a particularly violent murder, British people sometimes call for it to be brought back. **(3)**_____ my opinion, the death penalty cannot be defended for a number of reasons.

2 — **(4)**_____ and most important reason is that one can never be entirely certain that the accused person is guilty. In the **(5)**_____, people have been sentenced to death and later it is discovered that they were completely innocent.

3 — It is often **(6)**_____ that the death penalty prevents crime and that the risk of death acts as a deterrent. **(7)**_____, many serious crimes are caused by a sudden and very powerful emotion. In these cases, the individual is not thinking sensibly and does not stop to consider the risks.

4 — One final **(8)**_____ against the death penalty is that it sets a bad example. The laws of society should reflect its values. If it is wrong for one individual to murder another, **(9)**_____ it is also wrong for the state to execute an individual.

5 — **(10)**_____, I believe the death penalty cannot be defended. There are other ways of punishing criminals and these ways should always be tried.

C Complete the composition by choosing the best answer, A, B, C or D.

1	**A** and	**C**	although
	B despite	**D**	moreover
2	**A** In addition	**C**	Nevertheless
	B Also	**D**	In contrast
3	**A** In	**C**	About
	B For	**D**	With
4	**A** Firstly	**C**	The one
	B The first	**D**	Initially
5	**A** future	**C**	beginning
	B present	**D**	past
6	**A** told	**C**	spoken
	B heard	**D**	suggested
7	**A** Therefore	**C**	Moreover
	B However	**D**	Despite
8	**A** reason	**C**	argument
	B view	**D**	opinion
9	**A** then	**C**	and
	B as	**D**	too
10	**A** In contrast	**C**	At last
	B To sum up	**D**	Fourthly

D Read these notes before you write a composition on one of the subjects in E below.

- Plan before you write. Think of three or four points to support your view. Make each of these points a paragraph, and give more details and examples where possible.

- Don't get emotional. Comments like 'people who think this are stupid...' won't get you marks!

- Although you are expressing your opinion, use 'I' as little as possible. This is because you want to suggest that your ideas are facts. For example, rather than say: I think courts of law sometimes make mistakes... , it is better to use an impersonal style: Courts of law sometimes make mistakes.

- You may want to take an argument against your opinion and say why that argument is wrong. There is an example of this in paragraph 3 above: It is often suggested that...

E Now write a composition in 120–180 words on one of these subjects.

1 'Wars are always wrong.' Do you agree?
2 'Exams are not useful.' What is your opinion?
3 Perhaps you believe that the death penalty can be defended? Explain why.

FOCUS FOUR

REVISION AND EXTENSION

Conditional 1 ➤ GS 4.1

A Complete the following conversation with the correct form of the verb in brackets.

A Jack's coming this evening.

B When?

A Well, I'm not sure, it depends on the buses. He said he might catch the 7.30. If he (do), he (be) here at about 8.30, but if he (miss) it, he (have to) get the one at 8.15.

B What time he (get) here if he (take) the later one?

A I should think he (be) here at about 9.30, unless the traffic (be) bad, in which case he (may) not arrive until about 10.

B What do you want me to do about supper?

A Mmm. If he (get) here early, we (can) eat together, but if he (be) late, just (put) something in the oven to keep warm. But don't make too much, because if he (already eat) he (not be) very hungry.

B There's only one problem. What he (do) if I (be) out shopping when he (get) here?

A I wouldn't worry about that if I were you. If you (not be) here when he (arrive), he (have to) wait.

B No, I know what – if I (go) out, I (leave) a key and a note so that he (can) let himself in.

Conditional 2 ➤ GS 4.2

B Explain what you would do if these things happened.

Example: You found a wallet in the street.

➤ *If I found a wallet in the street, I would take it to the police.*

1 You heard a stranger shouting for help.
2 Someone insulted you.
3 You were offered a job in China for three years.
4 Someone you had never seen before said, 'I love you'.
5 You saw a strange light in the sky, which looked like a flying saucer.

C On what conditions would you do the following things?

Example: When would you be rude to a stranger?

➤ *I wouldn't be rude to a stranger unless the stranger were rude to me.*

1 When would you shout 'Help!'?
2 When would you steal food from a shop?
3 When would you ring up the fire-brigade?
4 When would you borrow money from a stranger?
5 When would you knock on your neighbour's door after midnight?

Conditional 1 or 2?

D Complete the following sentences with the correct form of the verb in brackets.

1 If I (be) you, I (apply) for a job as soon as possible.
2 If I (speak) perfect English, I (not need) to take the exam.
3 If he (be) taller, he (be able) to join the police.
4 You (be) rich if you (win) the pools.
5 You (not be able) to travel next week unless you (get) a visa.
6 If the weather (be) nice next weekend, they (go) to the country.
7 Unless you (hear) otherwise, I (come) at 8.15.
8 If I (be) the Prime Minister, I (change) a lot of things.
9 If the bus (leave) by the time I arrive, I (get) a taxi.
10 If my headache (not go away) soon, I (take) an aspirin.

E Rewrite the second sentence in each pair. Use no more than five words including the word in bold. Do NOT change this word.

1 She is so busy that she can't come to the party.
   could   If she was _____ come to the party.

2 John asked Mary 'Can I borrow some money?'
   would   John asked Mary _____ _____ some money.

3 He said 'I'm sorry I didn't reply to the letter.'
   apologized   He _____ to the letter.

4 Oh, don't complain all the time!
   wish   I _____ all the time!

5 He bought his car five years ago.
   had   He _____ five years.

6 It's three months since she started learning English.
   for   She _____ three months.

7 I'm upset because I have so much work to do.
   wish   I _____ so much work to do.

8 I haven't got the money, so I'm not going on holiday.
   would   If I _____ go on holiday.

9 She said 'I'll call the police if you don't leave immediately!'
   threatened   She _____ if he didn't leave immediately.

10 There were a lot of errors in his composition.
    mistakes   He _____ in his composition.

8

SPACE WARRIOR MADNESS

SPEAKING

A Talking on your own

Work in pairs as Student A and B. Try to speak for about one minute.

Student A: Describe and compare the places in both pictures. Say whether you have ever been to such places and why.

Student B: Describe and compare what the people are doing and how they might be feeling in both pictures. Say whether you would enjoy activities like these.

B Discussion

1 What attracts people to places like these?
2 What problems do people have if they go to such places too often?

READING

A This letter recently appeared in an English magazine. Read it quickly, to get a general idea of what it is about. Ignore the five missing sentences.

I have recently become very worried about my 16-year-old son, Nick. Although he was never brilliant at school, he always used to get reasonably good marks. **0** | *F* |

He used to be such a good swimmer that he won several prizes. But now he has given up training. And instead of the neat clothes he used to wear, all he ever puts on is the same pair of shabby old jeans and a dirty sweatshirt.

1 | | Nick was in the kitchen. The radio was on so loud that he didn't hear me come in behind him. My handbag was on the table. **2** | |

We had a terrible row. Finally, he broke down and confessed everything. He has been going every day to a big amusement arcade near his school and playing electronic games with names like Space Warrior and Alien Invaders. I had always thought they were harmless. **3** | |

He has promised he won't go there again, but I think he's too addicted to stop. **4** | | What can I do to help him?

FOCUS ONE

B Match the gaps in the text (1–4) with the sentences (A–F) below. There is one extra sentence which you do not need. An example is given (0).

A But now I realize that he's so hooked on them, he'll even steal from his own mother in order to pay for the habit.

B Even if he wanted to, he couldn't – and he doesn't.

C I often leave it there so that I won't forget it when I go out.

D He had taken some money out of it and was just about to put it in his pocket.

E But that isn't all – last Sunday, I got up earlier than usual.

F But now his work has become so bad that his teachers say he is just wasting his time there.

C In pairs or groups, discuss these questions.

1 How do you think Nick's mother felt after she saw Nick in the kitchen last Sunday?

2 What connection do you think there is between the changes she noticed before last Sunday and what happened on Sunday morning?

3 What are some of the things she probably said to Nick last Sunday? Try to imagine her exact words.

4 What do you think Nick said to her?

D Explain the full meaning of the words in *italics* below.

1 Even if he *wanted to*, he *couldn't* – and he *doesn't*.

2 He had taken some money out of *it*, and was about to put *it* in his pocket.

3 I had always thought *they* were harmless.

4 He has promised he won't go *there* again.

LANGUAGE STUDY

Three types of past action ➤ GS 13.2, 13.3

A Match the examples (a–c) with the meanings (1–3).

a) When I saw him, he was taking the money.

b) When I saw him, he was about to take the money.

c) When I saw him, he had taken the money.

1 He took the money before I saw him.

2 I saw him a moment before he took it.

3 I saw him at the same time that he took it.

B In groups or pairs, say what you think was about to happen, was happening or had happened.

Example: Nick looked inside his mother's handbag. He saw some money there. He put his hand into the handbag.

➤ *He was just about to steal the money.*

1 His mother was upstairs. The newspaper was open in front of her.

2 Outside, a raindrop fell. Then another fell. Then another.

3 A man was at the bus stop. He looked at his watch.

4 Nick took his hand out of the handbag. The money wasn't there any longer. It was in his pocket.

5 Nick looked out of the window and saw the front of the Number 12 bus not far from the bus stop.

6 The bus stopped. The man waited for the door to open.

7 A minute later, his mother came downstairs. Nick wasn't in the house.

8 She looked out of the window. Nobody was at the bus stop. She saw the back of the number 12 bus.

9 She put on her coat and went towards the door. Then she stopped suddenly.

10 She heard a sound. It was the telephone. She heard it again. And again.

11 A few minutes later, after saying, 'Good bye, Edna,' she put the phone down. Edna was a friend who phoned almost every day.

12 Nick was on the bus. He thought of the money in his pocket and the shop with all the electronic games.

READING

A Read the article below. It is in five parts. Choose the sentence (A–G) that summarizes what each part is about. You do not need one of these sentences. An example is given (0).

> A There is a link between computer games and crime.
> B The brain can be affected, too.
> C Weight problems are another result.
> D Girl's father is also blamed.
> E Playing computer games can actually hurt you.
> F Why are younger people getting weaker?
> G The health of teenagers causes concern in two countries.

0 | G |

Newspapers in Japan recently reported that standard tests show that the average Japanese teenager is 'significantly weaker than the average teenager forty years ago'. Almost exactly at the same time newspapers in England carried similar stories about the identical age-group in Britain.

1 | |

In both countries, the same four things were identified as the causes. The first was too much television. The second was too much convenience food and the third was not enough exercise. However, the fourth cause – computer games – was the focus of more comment in Britain than Japan.

2 | |

One London newspaper reported that a boy of 12 had become so obsessed with various computer games that he stole from his parents and his schoolmates in order to buy more. This is not the only such case. The head of a primary school recently claimed that many of the children at his school steal each other's lunch money for the same reason.

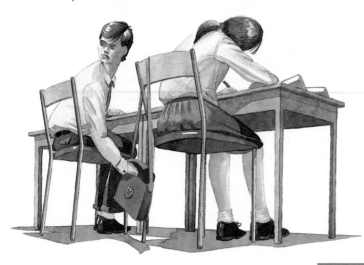

3 | |

Dr Leonora Keller, a health expert, said that many children play these games with such enthusiasm that they suffer from 'Space Warrior's Wrist'. The muscles of the lower arm become inflamed as a result of repeated movements of the wrist and constant pressure on the computer control stick. This also causes other aches and pains in their elbows and shoulders as well as strange sores on their hands.

4 | |

Dr Keller has also found that children who spend a lot of time playing electronic games have a tendency to be fatter than those who do not. She said that 'for some reason these children tend to eat more sugar and fat' and that 'many of them get too little exercise to burn up these things.'

5 | |

Another alarming problem was recently reported in the *British Medical Journal*. A 17-year-old girl spent hours playing computer games every day. Her father repaired computers and she took games from his workshop. One day she suddenly fell to the floor and began to jerk about wildly. The doctors who treated her found that she was suffering from an unusual form of epilepsy. The attack was caused by the signals on the computer screen blinking at a particular frequency.

B Now answer these questions.

1 Why, according to this article, are young people in Japan and Britain weaker than young people forty years ago?
2 Which crimes are blamed on computer games?
3 Describe three different kinds of health problems that can be caused by electronic games.

C In pairs or groups, discuss these questions.

1 Find out how much time your partners spend every day sitting down.
2 Now find out what they do while sitting down.
3 Find out what forms of exercise they get.

LANGUAGE STUDY

so or *such* ➤ GS 6.1

A Complete the following sentences with *so* or *such*.

1 He is _____ obsessed with these games that he has no time for anything else.
2 He plays these games with _____ enthusiasm that he is completely exhausted afterwards.

3 Nick was _____ a good swimmer that he won prizes.
4 Nick swam _____ well that he won prizes.

B Rewrite these sentences using *too*.

Example: Nick can't stop playing these games because he's addicted.

➤ *Nick is too addicted to stop playing these games.*

1 Some children don't get any exercise because they're lazy.
Some children are _____ any exercise.

2 My son is so young that he can't understand this.
My son is _____ this.

3 I'm so tired that I can't concentrate.
I'm _____.

4 He's so obsessed with football that he can't think about anything else.
He's _____ about anything else.

C Rewrite the second sentence in each pair. Use no more than five words including the word in bold. Do NOT change this word.

1 The film was very amusing. I couldn't stop laughing.
such It was _____ I couldn't stop laughing.

2 I couldn't stop laughing. I was very amused.
so I was _____ stop laughing.

3 I didn't go to the party because I was very busy.
too I was _____ the party.

4 I couldn't keep my eyes open because I was very tired.
so I was _____ keep my eyes open.

5 It was a very cold day. I didn't want to go out.
such It was _____ didn't want to go out.

6 Nick can't give these games up because he's obsessed.
too Nick's _____ up these games.

7 He does nothing else because of his interest in them.
so He's _____ he doesn't do anything else.

8 It's a very interesting game. I can't stop playing it.
such It's _____ I can't stop playing it.

9 Don't waste your time like this. Life is very short.
too Life _____ for you to waste your time like this.

VOCABULARY

A Match the six words below with the definitions 1–6.

ache   constant   continuous
convenient   pain   suitable

1 going on and on; not stopping
2 happening again and again, or always there
3 a bad feeling that can suddenly come and then stop
4 a bad feeling which doesn't start or stop suddenly
5 easy to do or prepare, or practical in some way
6 acceptable or good for a particular purpose

B Complete the sentences using the six words in A.

1 Is three o'clock a _____ time for us to meet?
2 Is red a _____ colour to wear to a very formal party?
3 A _____ line of policemen blocked the street.
4 The patient was in _____ pain.
5 I had a terrible head _____ yesterday.
6 Suddenly I felt a terrible _____ in my shoulder.

C Use the words given in capital letters below the text to form a word that fits the numbered space.

'Space Warrior's Wrist' is only one of the **(0)** _painful_ conditions that can be caused by **(1)**_____ playing computer games. Children also suffer from a strange **(2)**_____ feeling in their upper arms or shoulders. Another problem that doctors have reported is a **(3)**_____ of appetite in some children. The **(4)**_____ for this seems to be that they don't get enough exercise. This may also explain the **(5)**_____ of some children to put on weight. The high sugar **(6)**_____ of the convenience foods the same children eat is **(7)**_____ also a cause. Some people believe that it is the **(8)**_____ of the government to do something about this problem. However, it is difficult for even the most **(9)**_____ government to stop people doing what they want to do. One official recently said 'All we can do is put a **(10)**_____ on the games, saying that they can harm your health.'

0	PAIN	6	CONTAIN
1	CONSTANT	7	PROBABLE
2	ACHE	8	RESPONSIBLE
3	LOSE	9	POWER
4	EXPLAIN	10	WARN
5	TEND		

LISTENING 😐

You will hear two people, Michael and Fiona, discussing a birthday present. Listen to the tape and answer the questions about what they say. For each question write one of the following letters:

M (for what Michael says)
F (for what Fiona says)
N (for what neither of them say)

Who says it's their birthday soon?	**0**	*N*
Who suggests giving two different presents?	**1**	
Who suggests a computer game?	**2**	
Who points out the disadvantages of buying a computer game?	**3**	
Who is against the idea of an encyclopaedia?	**4**	
Who suggests a present that costs a lot?	**5**	
Who agrees that a light for a bicycle would be a good present?	**6**	

VOCABULARY

In groups or pairs, read aloud the examples 1–14 below. Each time, decide which of these categories the example belongs to (a–d).

a) making a suggestion
b) asking for someone else's opinion
c) agreeing
d) disagreeing and/or expressing doubt

1 What do you think we should do?
2 The best thing to do would be to …
3 Does that sound like a good idea to you?
4 I think we should …
5 It would be better to …
6 Do you agree?
7 I'm not sure about that.
8 Why don't we … ?
9 That sounds like a good idea.
10 What about …ing …… ?
11 I really don't think that would work.
12 We could …
13 Mmm… maybe, but …
14 I don't think we should …

SPEAKING

Problem solving
Carry out the following task in pairs or groups.

You are a member of a local committee that has been given a large sum of money. You have been asked to choose the best way of converting an old building in your area so that it can be used by young people.

Look at the four proposals in the picture and decide which one you would choose. Don't forget to give reasons for your choice.

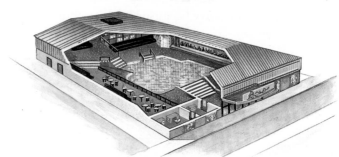

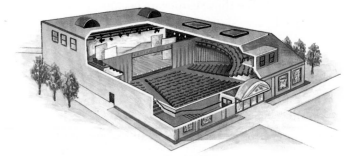

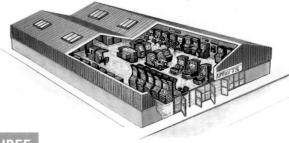

FOCUS THREE

LISTENING 🔈

You will hear a young man talking about his work and how he likes to spend his free time. Listen and choose the best answer.

1 What kind of business does he work in?
   A a delivery service
   B a bakery
   C a cake shop
2 What did the speaker's mother do in the last years before her husband's death?
   A She was a nurse.
   B She helped to run the business.
   C She worked for an accountant.
3 The speaker prefers to relax by
   A making furniture.
   B playing football.
   C walking or fishing.
4 The speaker lives in
   A the country.
   B a small village.
   C a small town.
5 The speaker doesn't watch television very much in the evenings because
   A he is too tired.
   B he prefers to make furniture.
   C he is too busy.

LANGUAGE STUDY

used to do or *be used to doing*? ➤ GS 13.2.2

A What's the difference?
a) My mother used to run the business.
b) My mother is used to running the business.
c) I never used to watch football.
d) I used to watch football.

B Match each of the sentences above with one of the following sentences.
1 I watch football now.
2 Running the business isn't difficult for my mother because she has done it for some time.
3 My mother ran the business before but doesn't any more.
4 I don't watch football any more.

C Work in pairs. One of you reads out the first part of a sentence (1–4). The other reads out the second part of the sentence, choosing from a–e. There is one extra which you don't need.
1 I never used to
2 I used to
3 I'm not used to
4 I'm used to

a) doing this kind of work so it may be difficult for me.
b) do this kind of work but I don't any more.
c) and I still am.
d) do this kind of work but I do now.
e) doing this kind of work so it won't be difficult for me.

D Rewrite these sentences using *used to do* or *be used to doing*.

Example: It isn't difficult for me to get up early because I have done it for some time.
➤ *I'm used to getting up early.*
1 I'm shocked when I hear bad language. I'm just not used to it.
2 I smoked a lot when I was younger but I don't any more.
3 It isn't difficult for me to travel long distances to work because I have done it for some time.
4 Not so long ago, Julia saw Ronald almost every day but she doesn't any more.
5 I don't work in that shop any more but I did once.
6 Because English people drive on the left, it's difficult for them to drive in other countries.

Your own opinion	Size/weight	Age	Shape	Colour	Country of origin	Material	NOUN
	small			blue	German		hair-dryer
beautiful		old		green		glass	bottle
	enormous		round	red	Dutch		cheese
mysterious	large			brown		paper	parcel

WRITING

Informal letter 1

A Look at the following types of adjective. Think of at least five more adjectives for each type except Age.

Age	young, old, ...
Colour	blue, light green, ...
Country of origin	Japanese, Greek, ...
Shape	oval, rectangular, ...
Material	cast-iron, wooden, ...
Size/weight	large, heavy, ...

B Use the table above to put the adjectives into the correct order.

Example: a hair-dryer German blue small

➤ *a small blue German hair-dryer*

1 a leather flat black small wallet
2 a Japanese fountain-pen beautiful red
3 an Pakistani writing-desk mahogany old
4 a china white round table-lamp

C What do you think it is?

Example: It's small and round, made of china and you drink out of it.

➤ *a cup*

In pairs, without naming the item, describe as fully as you can

1 an article of clothing someone is wearing
2 an object in the room

See if your partner can guess what it is.

D Which adjectives would you use to describe these things? Use at least three and no more than four.

E Complete the following letter by filling in the spaces with adjectives. Describe EITHER a very enjoyable holiday OR a terrible holiday.

This is just a quick note to tell you how the holiday is going. We're staying in a _____ _____ hotel in a _____ _____ part of town, so you can imagine how we feel. As you know, this is a _____ _____ city, and the people are very _____ and _____. We have had some _____ weather since we got here, so we are feeling very _____. We have seen some of the _____ sights and a few _____ museums, and we thought they were very _____. Yesterday we decided to go for a swim, and we went to a _____ _____ beach where the water was _____ and _____.

Last night we had a _____ meal in a _____ _____ restaurant. It was quite an experience. We were served by a _____ _____ _____ waiter, and the food and the service were _____. When the bill came, we could hardly believe it, as it was so _____.

Anyway, I'd better stop and catch the post, but I'll write again soon.

Lots of love, Marianne

F Writing task

You are about to return home after three months abroad at a language school. Write a letter to an English-speaking friend describing some of the presents you have bought for your friends and family.

G Use the following notes to help you.

1 Introduction – say why you are writing and say that you have been shopping.
2 Give details of what you have bought, eg clothes, food, souvenirs, books, etc.
3 Finish the letter in a suitable way, saying you hope to see your friend before you leave.

Include some adjectives describing the things you have bought. Do not use more than three adjectives in front of any noun.

This is an informal letter, so use contractions like *I've*, *it's*, etc. You can also use some of the more conversational adjectives like *nice*, *great*, etc.

Write your letter in 120–180 words.

FOCUS FOUR

REVISION AND EXTENSION

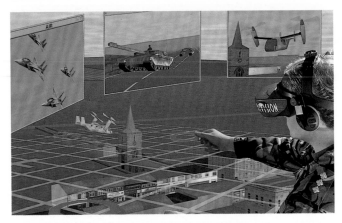

Choose the best answer, A, B, C or D.

A new VR (virtual reality) headset for the home user will be in the shops soon. The makers **(1)**_____ that it will change the way that computer games are played. Unlike the heavy VR headsets that people have been using in arcades **(2)**_____ the last few years, the new sets look more like a pair of sunglasses than a fireman's **(3)**_____. A spokesman for the company said 'A lot of people had **(4)**_____ with the old headsets. They were **(5)**_____ heavy that if you wore them **(6)**_____ for more than an hour or so, they could cause quite a lot of **(7)**_____. Our new headsets are very comfortable, and will be perfect for games, as well as in education.'

Some scientists, however, are **(8)**_____ about the effects of VR. Child psychologist Brenda Smith explained 'There have **(9)**_____ been several cases of violence among young children where computer games were to **(10)**_____. With VR, we will soon have children who are not **(11)**_____ to playing with other people. **(12)**_____ your life in a constant battle with aliens and monsters is not really a **(13)**_____ environment for someone young. We **(14)**_____ that a child should experience actual reality, not virtual reality, and it would be a great **(15)**_____ for parents to bring this sort of technology into the home.'

1 A claim   C offer
   B threaten   D recommend
2 A since   C among
   B ago   D for
3 A hat   C helmet
   B cap   D hood
4 A mistakes   C problems
   B faults   D errors
5 A very   C so
   B too   D such
6 A continuously   C always
   B throughout   D regularly
7 A hurt   C pain
   B ache   D suffering

8 A afraid   C scared
   B worried   D threatened
9 A yet   C still
   B ever   D already
10 A fault   C defect
   B error   D blame
11 A used   C allowed
   B made   D interested
12 A Spending   C Making
   B Doing   D Passing
13 A convenient   C real
   B suitable   D right
14 A recommend   C offer
   B tell   D speak
15 A defect   C mistake
   B fault   D blame

LISTENING

Listen to the news report about a robbery, and then complete the notes from the detective's notebook.

Time of robbery: 9(1) _____
Place: Halifax Building Society,
(2) _____ Street.
Amount stolen: (3) £

MAN
Height: (4) _____ Age: (5) _____
Eye colour: (6) _____
Hair: (7) _____
Clothes: (8) _____, green sweater,
(9) _____ Name: (10)_____
Accent: (11) _____

WOMAN
Height: (12) _____ Age: (13) _____
Eye colour: (14) _____
Hair: (15) _____
Clothes: (16) _____

CAR
(17) _____, Ford Escort.
(18) _____ number G595 ER1
Headlight (19) _____

THE FACE BEHIND THE MASK

SPEAKING

Talking on your own

Work in pairs as Student A and B. Try to speak for about one minute.

Student A: Describe and compare what the people are wearing in both pictures. Say why you think they are dressed like this.

Student B: Describe and compare what the people are doing and say how you think they might be feeling in both pictures.

READING

A Read the following story, which appeared in a British newspaper.

For almost two months Dominic York, a 23-year-old hairdresser, wandered about hospitals at night, wearing a white coat and pretending he was a doctor. Yesterday he proudly claimed in court that despite his complete lack of medical experience or qualifications, he had saved several people's lives. He had even been allowed to assist a surgeon during an emergency operation on a patient who was choking to death on something she had swallowed.

'I watched one of those TV dramas about a hospital and suddenly I felt like playing one of the roles myself. So I put on a white jacket and a stethoscope and walked around one of the biggest hospitals in London. At first I just watched. Once you learn how doctors talk to patients, nurses and other doctors, it's easy to take people in,' he said.

One of the patients he treated was Laura Kennan. She had almost been run over by a car and passed out. When she came to in hospital, York was standing over her.

'He looked very professional. He told me his name was Doctor Simon. Then he gave me some sort of injection,' she said. Although he left a very nasty bruise on her arm, and then suddenly cleared off when a nurse asked who he was, she didn't think there was anything wrong. 'I would never have realized he was a fake if a policewoman hadn't showed me his photograph a week later. When the policewoman told me who he really was, I could hardly believe my ears.'

Judge Raymond Adams told York that he was 'shocked and horrified' that he got away with his deception for so long, and then sentenced him to eighteen months in a special prison for criminals with mental disorders.

'I can only hope that this will not lead to further problems. After all, you will have considerable opportunity to study the behaviour of the psychiatrists who will look after you while you are there. If you try to persuade people that you yourself are a psychiatrist after your release, I shall make sure that you are given a much longer sentence,' Judge Adams warned York.

B **Choose the best answer.**

1 York was proud of the fact that
  A people thought he was a real doctor.
  B a surgeon let him watch an operation.
  C he had performed a doctor's duties successfully.
  D he had pretended for so long to be a doctor.

2 York learned how to behave like a doctor by
  A getting some training and experience.
  B watching doctors while he pretended to be one.
  C observing doctors while he was a patient.
  D acting the part of a doctor in a television drama.

3 Why was Laura Kennan in hospital?
  A She had swallowed something and almost died.
  B She had to have an emergency operation.
  C She had been involved in a road accident.
  D She had lost consciousness while driving.

4 When York gave Laura Kennan an injection, she
  A had no idea he was not a proper doctor.
  B realized he was not her usual doctor.
  C told a policewoman about him.
  D asked a nurse who he was.

5 The judge at his trial was shocked because York
  A felt he had done nothing wrong.
  B had had no proper medical training.
  C seemed so proud of what he had done.
  D had not been detected earlier.

6 The judge was worried that York would
  A be in prison for only eighteen months.
  B not get the treatment he needed.
  C learn to act just like a psychiatrist.
  D persuade himself that he was a psychiatrist.

7 What general impression does the article give us of Dominic York?
  A He wanted to train to be a doctor.
  B He was good at pretending to be a doctor.
  C He wanted to cause other people suffering.
  D He actually believed he was a doctor.

C **Find the phrasal verbs in 1–3 below and answer the questions.**

1 What will Dominic York have to give up doing if he doesn't want to spend more time in prison?
2 Do people look up to doctors in your country?
3 If you don't understand a word here, where can you look it up?

LANGUAGE STUDY

although and *despite* ➤ GS 6.4

A **Which sentences suggest something unusual?**

a) He was able to do such things because of his medical qualifications.
b) He was able to do such things despite his lack of medical qualifications.
c) He saved the patient's life although he had no medical qualifications.
d) He saved the patient's life because he had medical qualifications.

B **In which of the above sentences can you take one word out and use these words instead?**

1 in spite of   2 even though

C **Rewrite the second sentence in each pair. Use no more than five words including the word in bold. Do NOT change this word.**

1 The weather was good but we stayed indoors.
  despite We stayed indoors _____ _____ weather.

2 Cars cause pollution but people still want them.
  although People still want cars _____ _____ pollution.

3 He has a pleasant manner but he's a bad doctor.
  despite He isn't a good doctor _____ _____ manner.

4 In spite of her illness, my mother never complained.
  although My mother never complained _____ ill.

5 The weather is terrible but tourists come here.
  despite Tourists come here _____ _____ weather.

6 Dan never talks to Mary but she still loves him.
  although Mary still loves Dan _____ _____ her.

7 I don't like this job although the salary is good.
  despite I don't like this job _____ _____ salary.

8 This exercise is very long but I hope it isn't boring.
  although I hope this exercise isn't _____ _____ very long.

LISTENING

You are going to hear a short news report from a local radio station in England. Listen at least once and then choose the best answer, A, B or C.

1 This is a story about a man who
   A was attacked by a gorilla.
   B pretended to be a gorilla.
   C saw a gorilla attack someone in a park.

2 When the man's mother was alive, she
   A didn't want him to meet other people.
   B introduced him to other people.
   C used to disturb him at night.

3 After his mother died, he
   A began having more contact with women.
   B attacked a gorilla in a zoo.
   C got a strange idea from watching television.

4 One evening he frightened some people in a park by
   A pretending to be a wild animal.
   B hiding in a tree and making loud noises.
   C shouting that there was a gorilla in the trees.

5 Three months later, the man
   A took away an old woman's dog.
   B was caught after running away from a woman.
   C helped a policeman to arrest a man.

6 The woman didn't think he was dangerous because
   A his movements were so strange.
   B his skin was so white under his hair.
   C his feet did not look like a gorilla's.

VOCABULARY

A In pairs or groups, find the phrasal verb in each question (a–i). Then match the phrasal verb with its meaning (1–9).

a) What did Rodney Bunting (the man in the park) start doing after his mother passed away?
b) What did he put on before he went into the park?
c) What happened after he tried to get away from the old woman and her dog?
d) What gave him away?
e) How long did Dominic York (the man who pretended to be a doctor) get away with his deception?
f) Was Laura Kennan taken in by him?
g) What had happened to her just before she passed out?
h) Does the article say who almost ran her over?
i) Why did York suddenly clear off after he gave her an injection?

1 do something bad and not be caught
2 lose consciousness
3 show the truth about
4 die
5 leave suddenly
6 get dressed in
7 escape from
8 hit with a car
9 be deceived

B Now answer questions a–i in A.

FOCUS TWO

USE OF ENGLISH

Most lines contain an unnecessary word. Underline these words and tick any lines that are correct. There are two examples (0) and (00).

00	I have <u>been</u> read the article about Dominic	
0	York several times. However, I feel that it	✓
1	raises up many questions which I cannot	
2	find answers to them. How could he deceive	
3	people despite of his lack of medical	
4	qualifications? It seems as very strange that	
5	nobody questioned him and asked for proof	
6	that he was a real doctor. It seems like	
7	impossible that nobody asked him what he	
8	was doing even though there were many of	
9	people in the hospital. Also, how could he	
10	keep coming back day after a day without	
11	someone stopping him and making him to	
12	show proof that he was really a doctor? I also	
13	wonder me how he could have been allowed	
14	to help to a surgeon. I must say that I can't	
15	help it thinking that this is not a true story.	

After you have corrected the lines with words that should not be there, read aloud to each other complete and correct sentences from the text. However, pause just before the last word of each sentence. Can your partner remember the word without looking at the text?

LANGUAGE STUDY

A In pairs or groups, study the pairs of sentences below for a few minutes. In which pairs do the sentences have a similar meaning? Where there is a difference in meaning, change the phrasal verb in the first sentence.

1 The thief cleared up before the police came.
The thief left before the police came.
2 The manager told the waiter to clear off.
The manager told the waiter to clean the tables.
3 The restaurant manager has taken in three new waitresses.
The restaurant manager has given jobs to three new waitresses.
4 What gave him away was the fact that he was wearing tennis shoes.
The fact that he was wearing tennis shoes showed that he was not really a gorilla.
5 She passed away yesterday.
She fainted yesterday.
6 I ran over an old friend yesterday.
I happened to meet an old friend yesterday.

B Rewrite the second sentence in each pair. Use no more than five words including the word in bold. Do NOT change this word.

1 His mother died last year.
passed His mother _____ year.
2 When I heard the news, I fainted.
passed I _____ the news.
3 The driver skidded and hit a dog.
ran The driver skidded and _____ _____ a dog.
4 Please help me to make this room tidy.
clear Will you _____ this room?
5 The thief left with all the money.
cleared The thief _____ with all the money.
6 When you lie, some gestures can show you are lying.
give Some gestures can _____ when you lie.
7 Is it true that you haven't found a job yet?
looking Are you still _____ job?
8 Did that man deceive you too?
take Did he _____ as well?

READING

A You are going to read an article written by Linda Rossner, a young comedian who performs in small clubs in London and on the South Coast of England. First look at the eight headings below (A–H). Then read the article. It is in seven parts. Choose the heading that you think best summarizes each part. There is one heading you don't need.

A   The secret I had to keep

B   Learning through observation

C   How I suddenly became a star performer

D   A painful but important lesson

E   Then it happened again

F   The most important skill of all

G   How I first realized I could be a comedian

H   Losing my first job

0 | H |

I left school when I was seventeen. Even though I didn't have the right qualifications, I managed to find a job as a secretary in a private bus company. Then the company was taken over by a bigger company that cut back on running costs and laid thirty people off, including me.

1 | |

My older sister was sharing a small flat with two other girls in London. She agreed to put me up until I found a job and a place of my own there. At first, things didn't seem too bad. I soon got a part-time job in a video shop, but I didn't get on with my boss. After I'd been there for a week, we had a terrible row and I walked out.

2 | |

I didn't say a word about this to my sister. I pretended to go to work every day. I got up every morning, just as usual, and then walked the streets. I even stopped people and asked them for money. I wasn't too proud to do that, even though I was too proud to tell my sister what had really happened. I knew that if I told her, she'd tell my parents back home and they'd insist that I come back to live with them. I just couldn't let them know.

3 | |

Then I found another part-time job selling drinks at the bar of a comedy club in South London. One evening, one of the acts was a man imitating famous people. The manager of the club happened to be standing next to me and asked me what I thought of the act. I said 'It's terrible. I could do better myself!' I meant it, too. I'd always been good at doing things like that and making people laugh at school, but it had never occurred to me until then that perhaps I could actually make a living that way.

4 | |

I wish I could say that all my troubles ended there, and that the manager immediately gave me a chance and I was huge success. What really happened was that I spent a year working every evening at the bar. I learned as much as I could by watching the performers.

5 | |

Then I got a chance to do my own act at another club in Brighton. To be honest, at first I was awful. I quickly learned it isn't enough to imitate famous people. You have to make the audience laugh at the same time and that's a thousand times more difficult.

6 | |

Since then, I've learned a lot about the art of timing. You have to get your timing as sharp as a razor. Just before the 'punch line' – the words the audience is supposed to laugh at – a good comedian slows down just a little, and pauses so slightly that you're hardly aware of it. You don't notice it at all if a performer is really good. Comedy is sometimes very hard work, I can tell you!

FOCUS THREE

B In pairs or groups, decide which of the statements below about Linda Rossner are true and which are false. Always read aloud the part of the text that you think gives you the answer.

Example: She got a university education.

➤ *False. 'I left school when I was seventeen.'*

1 She was lucky to get her first job.
2 She lost her first job after an argument with the management.
3 She lived with her sister in London for a while.
4 She had serious problems in her second job.
5 She didn't want her family to know what she was really doing after suddenly leaving her second job.
6 Something very important happened in her next job.
7 As soon as she became a comedian, she was a great success.
8 She finds it very difficult to understand how comedians make people laugh.
9 Good comedians do something that most of us never really notice.

SPEAKING

A In pairs or groups, first read aloud to your partners the short text below. It was also written by Linda Rossner.

One of the people I most admire is a great comedian you have probably never heard of. His name was Frankie Howerd. He died while I was still at school. When I first saw him on TV, I didn't think he was funny at all and just couldn't understand why everyone was laughing. Now I realise it was his wonderful art of timing.

B Continue working in pairs or groups. Ask and answer these questions.

1 Who is someone you admire?
2 Why do you admire him or her?
3 Can you remember the first time you heard, saw or read about this person? How old were you? What was your first impression of this person from what you heard, saw or read?

LANGUAGE STUDY ➤ GS 5.2.3

A Explain the difference in meaning.

a) You can't let me do this.
b) You can't make me do this.
c) It's your fault. You let me do it.
d) It's your fault. You made me do it.
e) Frankie Howerd had a great talent for making people laugh.
f) This new petrol will make your car go faster.

• Repeat only the sentences that mean 'allow me to'.
• Now repeat the sentences that mean 'force me to'.
• Repeat the sentences in which *make* has the meaning 'cause someone or something to do something'.

B Complete the following sentences.

1 You can't come in here. I won't _____ you!
2 You don't understand. Please _____ me explain.
3 Please, I beg you. _____ me speak!
4 There is no way to _____ people learn if they don't want to.
5 Do you really expect me to believe that? Don't _____ me laugh.
6 My boss tried to _____ me work for nothing.
7 You will tell me your secrets. I have ways of _____ you tell them to me!
8 Would you _____ me use your dictionary for a moment?

C Rewrite the second sentence in each pair. Use no more than five words including the word in bold. Do NOT change this word.

1 If you put this in your car, it will go faster.
   make   This will _____ faster.
2 I tried to explain the problem to you but you refused to listen.
   let   You wouldn't _____ the problem to you.
3 Did the manager give Linda a chance to perform that evening?
   let   Did the manager _____ that evening?
4 She was afraid they would insist on her coming home.
   make   She thought they would try to _____ home.
5 You can talk all you want, but I will never believe you.
   make   Nothing you say will _____ you.
6 What is your reason for thinking I'm lying?
   makes   What _____ I'm lying?
7 Something in the drink caused me to fall asleep.
   made   Something in the drink _____ asleep.
8 Thank you for allowing me to use your dictionary.
   letting   Thanks for _____ dictionary.

WRITING

Article 1

If you are asked to write an article in Part 2 of Paper 2, you need to check what sort of audience you are writing for and choose a suitable style. For example, if it is an article for a magazine directed at young people, you will need to try and make it informal and chatty. Don't be afraid to use your imagination for what to include in your article!

A Sample Task

A magazine for young people is doing a feature on Chinese Horoscopes, which are based on the year in which you were born. You have been asked to write an **article** of between 120 and 180 words on the Year of the Snake.

Write your **article**.

B Read this answer.

CHINESE HOROSCOPES
THE YEAR OF THE SNAKE

If you're reading this, I suppose you were born in the Year of the Snake. You were probably secretly hoping that your Chinese sign would be a Dragon or a Horse. But don't feel too bad. As far as Chinese horoscopes are concerned, Snakes are great.

Above all, people born in the Year of the Snake are wise and have good organizational skills. You're attractive and sophisticated, and everyone admires your intelligence and charm. You're always calm and decisive, and people feel they can talk to you because you are sensitive and sympathetic too.

It must be said though, that you do have some faults. People born in the Year of the Snake are changeable and can be very spiteful and unforgiving under the wrong circumstances.

As far as romance is concerned, you're compatible with people born in the Year of the Ox, as they are quiet and have strong personalities. You also get on well with people born in the Year of the Rooster, as they are lively and amusing.

C Look at the words at the top of the next column, which are used to describe people's characters. Write a, b or c next to each word to show whether you think these qualities are:
  a good
  b bad
  c sometimes good and sometimes bad

When you have finished, compare your answers with your partner.

aggressive	enthusiastic	shy
rude	nervous	a sense of humour
careless	conceited	tense
tolerant	relaxed	frank
patient	easy-going	talkative
mean	competitive	quick-tempered
polite	kind	generous
ambitious	selfish	considerate

D Choose five qualities from C above. Write a paragraph to describe a person you know, using the words you have chosen and explaining what you mean. Below is an example.

Margaret was a wonderful person to go on holiday with. She was very *considerate* and *unselfish*, and never made us do anything we didn't want. She had a great *sense of humour*, and kept us amused the whole time with her stories. She was *easy-going*, and was always ready to come on trips with us even when she might have preferred to go elsewhere. Last but not least she was *generous*, and took us out to several meals at good restaurants.

E Writing task

An international magazine for young people has asked you to write an article about your star sign for a feature on horoscopes.

F Look through these notes before you write your article.

1 Think of the target audience. You are writing for young people, so keep the style friendly and chatty. Imagine you are talking to a friend you know well.
2 Paragraph 1: Think of an opening sentence that will catch the reader's attention. You can address the reader directly if you like.
3 Paragraph 2: Give details of the good points of this star sign, and try to give detailed examples that illustrate what you mean. Don't just give a list of adjectives! Look back at the sample answer if necessary.
4 Paragraph 3: Give details of some of the bad points of this star sign. Again, give more than just a list.
5 Paragraph 4: Give details of which other star signs are compatible or incompatible with yours as far as romance is concerned.
6 Write between 120 and 180 words. Remember to check your work for grammar, style, spelling and punctuation.

FOCUS FOUR

REVISION AND EXTENSION

Changing nouns to adjectives

A In English, nouns can often be changed into adjectives by putting -y or -ful on the end. Look at these examples.

a) *There is a lot of dirt in this room.*
b) *This room is very dirty.*
c) *Thanks for all your help.*
d) *You have been very helpful.*

1 Which of the words are nouns?
2 Which of the words are adjectives?

B Give the missing form of the words below.

NOUN FORM	ADJECTIVE FORM
1 care	_____
2 _____	cheerful
3 grass	_____
4 _____	noisy
5 health	_____
6 _____	funny
7 peace	_____
8 _____	smoky
9 hope	_____
10 _____	useful
11 salt	_____
12 _____	shameful

Adjectives to nouns

C But adjectives can also be changed back into nouns. Look at these examples.

a) *How high is that building?*
b) *What is the height of that building?*
c) *Be patient.*
d) *Patience is important.*

1 Which of the words above are adjectives?
2 Which words are nouns?

Complete these sentences.

1 How deep is the pool? – What is the _____ of the pool?
2 He is strong. – He has great _____.
3 It isn't important. – It has no _____.
4 Is it possible? – Is this a _____?
5 Be honest! – _____ is important.
6 You are very intelligent. – I'm impressed by your _____.

D Adjectives to adverbs

1 Most adjectives can be made into adverbs by adding -ly. Adjectives ending in -y add -ily.

quick – quickly   slow – slowly   easy – easily

2 Some adjectives and adverbs have the same form: fast, hard, late.
3 *Good* is an adjective. *Well* is the adverb.
4 Some adjectives already end in -ly. We cannot make an adverb. Instead, we use the phrase *in a … way*.
She gave me a friendly smile. (adjective)
She smiled at me in a friendly way.

Supply the missing words or phrases in the table.

ADJECTIVE	ADVERB OR PHRASE
good	_____
_____	heavily
nice	_____
_____	beautifully
hard	_____
_____	temporarily
lively	_____
_____	badly
fast	_____

E Complete this letter with the correct form of the word in brackets. Use nouns, adjectives and adverbs.

Dear Jack

I am staying in a very **1** (comfort) hotel in the south of France, near a **2** (sand) beach. Unfortunately it has been very **3** (wind) and the hotel itself is very **4** (expense).

Another problem is that the chef can't cook very **5** (good). The food is rather **6** (grease) and I have been **7** (hunger) most of the time because I have had great **8** (difficult) in finding anything **9** (suitably) on the menu.

However, I have been very impressed by the **10** (beautiful) of the surroundings and the **11** (kind) of the people. It is true that I have suffered a bit from **12** (boring) but I always do when I'm not **13** (full) occupied. Sometimes I feel **14** (sleep) in the middle of the day and have a short nap, which I am very **15** (thank) for. Unfortunately I sleep quite **16** (bad) at night because the people in the room next to me snore **17** (terrible).

Anyway, I'm leaving this Friday. The drive back will **18** (probable) take me two or three days, as long as the traffic isn't too **19** (badly). I'll get in touch **20** (immediate) I get home and maybe we can arrange to meet up for a meal.

See you soon,
Grace

SPEAKING

A Talking on your own
Work in pairs as Student A and B. Try to speak for about one minute.

Student A: Describe and compare what the people are doing in both pictures. Say whether you have ever taken part in occasions like these.

Student B: Describe and compare how the people might be feeling in both pictures. Say where you think the pictures were taken.

B Discussion
1 Describe other gestures you often see people making. Can you express their meaning in words?
2 Which do you think is better, expressing your feelings openly or keeping them to yourself? Why?

READING

A Seven sentences have been removed from this article. Choose from sentences A–H the one that fits each gap (1–6). There is one sentence you do not need. An example is given (0).

People use both words and gestures to express their feelings. Can you be sure you really know what these words and gestures mean? **0** *H*

It is true that a smile means more or less the same thing in any language, even though the things that make people smile may be very different. Laughter and crying also have universal meanings. It is equally true that there are many similarities in the ways in which humans and animals show their feelings. **1**

Fear and surprise are other emotions that are often shown in much the same way all over the world. A phrase like 'he went pale and began to tremble' suggests that the man was either afraid or had just had a nasty shock in any language. **2**

Nevertheless, even surprise is not always easy to recognize. In Chinese, this emotion can be described in a phrase like 'they stretched out their tongues'. In a language like English, however, sticking out your tongue usually has a different meaning. **3**

Even in the same culture, people differ in their ability to interpret and express feelings. **4** The same studies suggest that body language – the way we suggest our feelings in our physical movements and posture – is another problem. Older people in North America seem to find it easier to interpret than younger people.

In another famous experiment, there was clear evidence that the most difficult feeling of all to interpret is physical pain. **5** They could see only her face. She later died. However, more than ninety per cent of the audience believed she was experiencing great physical pleasure.

Psychologists such as E.G. Beier have also shown that some people often give completely the wrong impression of how they feel. **6** When they try to show interest, it seems to others that they are indifferent. This can happen even among close friends or members of the same family. In other words, what you think you communicate through words and body language may be the exact opposite of what other people actually understand.

FOCUS ONE

A In the same way, 'Her mouth fell open and she stared at me,' also suggests that something has just happened or been said which the woman did not expect.

B It suggests disgust, as if you had just tasted something unpleasant or seen something horrible.

C For example, they try to show affection but actually communicate dislike.

D University students were shown part of a film in which a woman in China was suffering while giving birth to a baby.

E When they are bored, they make it very clear by the way they look at you.

F Dogs and tigers, for instance, show their teeth in the same way we do when they are angry.

G Experiments in the United States have shown that women there are usually better than men at recognizing fear, anger, love and hate in people's faces.

H After all, they can be interpreted in many different ways.

B In pairs or groups, answer these questions. Then check your answers with other groups.

1 Give an example from the text of the way in which one emotion is expressed differently in two different cultures.

2 Give an example of how people can give other people the opposite impression of the feeling they are really trying to express.

3 Describe as fully as possible the experiment that showed which particular feeling is the most difficult to recognize.

SPEAKING

Talking about yourself
Work in pairs or groups. If you are working in groups of three or more, try to get at least two different answers to each question.

1 Name something that makes you feel depressed when you see or hear it, or when it happens to you.

2 Describe a moment in your life when you felt very happy.

3 Is there anything you are afraid of?

4 Describe something that someone you know finds exciting.

5 Describe your idea of a pleasant way to spend the weekend.

LANGUAGE STUDY

Comparisons ➤ GS 1.3

A Complete these sentences.

1 Some emotions _____ easier to express than others.

2 Women are better _____ recognizing emotions than men are.

3 I find it much easier to understand emotions _____ to express them.

4 Some feelings aren't as easy to describe _____ others are.

5 Everybody likes being happy _____ than being unhappy.

6 We all prefer happiness _____ unhappiness.

B Rewrite the second sentence in each pair. Use no more than five words including the word in bold. Do NOT change this word.

1 Is it easier for you to express anger than disgust?
find Do you _____ anger than disgust?

2 Can you understand words more easily than gestures?
better Are you _____ gestures?

3 Anger is easy to express. Disgust is difficult.
more Disgust is _____ anger.

4 You find it more difficult to express anger than I do.
harder It's _____ anger than it is for me.

5 Some rules are easy to understand. Others aren't.
difficult Some rules are _____ _____ others.

6 The last exercise was very difficult. This one is easy.
much This exercise is _____ the last one.

7 Do you think women are more careful drivers than men?
carefully In your opinion, do women _____ men do?

8 Japanese is difficult. Is Chinese, too?
as Is Chinese _____ Japanese?

9 I like this colour more than the other one.
prefer I _____ the other one.

10 I think you look better in blue than in red.
like I _____ than in red.

11 I don't like cooking food very much but I like eating it.
more I enjoy _____ cooking it.

12 The last exercise was difficult. Was this one difficult, too?
as Was this exercise _____ the last one?

SPEAKING

In the following pictures, each face is expressing a particular feeling. But is it clear from the expressions what the feelings are? People often disagree in their interpretation of such expressions. In pairs or groups, decide what you think each person is feeling.

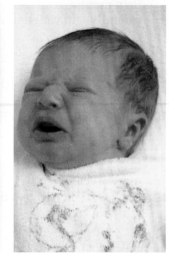

VOCABULARY

A Use the words in capital letters to form a word that fills each space. An example is given (0).

There is one particular (0) _feeling_ which I find difficult to express. When I am (1)_____ about something, I say nothing. Once, for example, after I had bought a very (2)_____ jacket, I met a friend in a café who said that the jacket didn't fit me very (3)_____. I was very (4)_____ but I said nothing. I didn't feel like continuing our (5)_____. My friend noticed my (6)_____ and asked me what was wrong. I couldn't tell him the (7)_____. I began to feel rather (8)_____ and left without giving him an (9)_____. Later I felt rather (10)_____ of my behaviour.

0	FEEL	6	SILENT
1	ANGER	7	TRUE
2	EXPENSE	8	EMBARRASS
3	GOOD	9	EXPLAIN
4	ANNOY	10	SHAME
5	CONVERSE		

B In pairs or groups, find out if there is a particular feeling your partners find difficult to express. Can they describe a situation in which they found it difficult to express this feeling?

C One word in each group does not belong with the other three. Can you explain why?

1 annoyed   angry   impatient   embarrassing
2 ashamed   frightened   worried   terrified
3 surprising   extraordinary   horrified   unbelievable
4 depressing   disappointed   sad   unhappy
5 wonderful   marvellous   satisfied   excellent
6 awful   terrible   horrible   satisfactory
7 pleased   adequate   cheerful   content
8 cool   indifferent   surprised   bored

D Which of the words in C can you use

a) to describe your own feelings?
b) to describe the events, things or people that cause those feelings?
c) if you feel you have done something wrong?
d) about people, events or things that you think are good?
e) to describe things you think are very bad?

SPEAKING

In pairs or groups, describe how you would probably feel in the following situations. Then describe what you would do and say in that situation.

Example: You invited someone you like to a party and they said they would come. Now that person has just told you that they can't come.

➤ *I think I'd be disappointed. I'd probably try to persuade them to come all the same. Perhaps I would say, 'Are you sure you can't come? I was really looking forward to seeing you again.'*

1 You took an important exam last month. The results have just come. You thought you had failed but your mark is excellent. A friend asks, 'How did you do in the exam?'

2 A friend is staying with you overnight. He or she went out after lunch to buy something, saying, 'I'll be right back.' It is getting dark and your friend hasn't come back yet.

3 You see a woman standing at a bus stop. Her back is turned but you are sure she's a good friend you haven't seen for a long time. You throw your arms around her. She turns. She's a total stranger.

4 A friend borrowed your dictionary an hour ago. The friend has just returned it. Some pages have been torn out of it.

5 It is evening. You have had a good meal at a reasonable price in a small restaurant. The waiter has just asked, 'Was everything all right?'

6 You have checked into a hotel. When you go to your room, you find dirty sheets on the bed. The toilet is filthy. You look under the bed. There is a dead rat there.

LISTENING 📼

A **Five different speakers describe their feelings now or in the past. Listen and decide which words (A–F) describe the feeling each speaker (1–5) is talking about. There is one letter you do not need.**

A very excited	Speaker 1	☐
B very depressed	Speaker 2	☐
C ashamed	Speaker 3	☐
D embarrassed	Speaker 4	☐
E very disappointed	Speaker 5	☐
F angry		

B **Now listen again and answer these questions about each speaker.**

Speaker 1
1 Who is the other person the speaker talks about?
2 What happened that Wednesday evening?
3 What did the speaker say to himself when it happened?

Speaker 2
1 Who were the two other people she talks about?
2 What had she planned to do with one of these people?
3 Explain why she didn't do what she had planned to do.

Speaker 3
1 How old do you think the speaker is?
2 Who is the other person he talks about?
3 What do you think has caused the speaker's feelings?

Speaker 4
1 When did the incident she describes happen?
2 Describe what happened after she went to her room.

Speaker 5
1 What is the event he describes?
2 Describe the most important thing that happened.

VOCABULARY

A Work in pairs. One of you reads out the start of each sentence in column A. Your partner reads aloud the part of the sentence in column B that goes with what you have read out.

A
1. A burglar broke
2. When she heard the terrible news, she broke
3. They were married for three years and then they broke
4. This terrible weather really gets me
5. How can you get
6. The poor man never got
7. Steel is a material that stands
8. He really stands out. I mean
9. In Chinese, they use symbols that stand

B
a) up to a lot of stress.
b) by on such a small salary?
c) for different words and ideas.
d) up and got a divorce.
e) into our house and stole some money and other things.
f) down. It's so depressing.
g) everybody notices him immediately.
h) down and began to cry.
i) over the shock of his wife's death.

B Rewrite the second sentence in each pair. Use no more than five words including the word in bold. Do NOT change this word.

1. I can just about live on this amount of money.
   get I can _____ this amount of money.

2. Some thieves managed to enter the bank illegally.
   broken The bank _____ some thieves.

3. You mustn't allow your troubles to depress you, you know.
   get You mustn't let your troubles _____, you know.

4. Her beauty attracted everyone's attention.
   stood She _____ because of her beauty.

5. If you mention his name to her, she begins crying.
   breaks She _____ whenever she hears his name.

6. This material resists wear and tear more than any other.
   stands No other material _____ wear and tear better than this one.

7. I'll never forget how rude he was to me.
   get I just can't _____ his rudeness to me.

USE OF ENGLISH

A Read the text below. Think of the best word for each space. Use only one word each time. An example is given (0).

Why do we like some people more than we do others? Why do we fall (0) _in_ love? Astrologers say it is determined (1)_____ the stars. Others believe in fate. However, psychologist Angela Hubbard, (2)_____ advises one of the biggest computer dating services in the country, rejects these explanations. 'The reasons people are attracted to each (3)_____ have been known for a very long time. There are four main reasons, and there's nothing mysterious about (4)_____,' she says.

The first reason is Frequency of Contact; the (5)_____ often we see a person, the more likely it is that we will become friends or lovers. Angela describes a well-known experiment that (6)_____ place in the 1960s. 'People were shown photographs of strangers and asked (7)_____ faces they liked most. They didn't realize it but they were shown (8)_____ photographs more frequently than others, and these were of the faces they later said they liked.'

The second reason is Similarity of Interests. The more interests we share (9)_____ another person, the more likely it is that we will not only become friendly with that person but that our friendship will not break (10)_____.

The third reason is called Complementary Qualities, which basically means that we are more likely to like or love people (11)_____ personalities balance our own in positive ways. If, for example you are a very quiet person, you may unconsciously look (12)_____ a friend or a lover who has a need to talk and who is more expressive than you are.

The fourth reason is Recognition and Reward. We tend to like people who (13)_____ us a feeling that they like and appreciate our good qualities (14)_____ than reject us because of our faults. However, most of us also tend to be suspicious (15)_____ people who flatter us – who say nice things about us but who we think are not really sincere.

B In groups or pairs, compare the words you chose for each space.

VOCABULARY

Complete the table. The first two examples have been done for you.

good	better	the best
bad	worse	the worst
happy	happier	the _____
sad	_____	the saddest
big	bigger	the _____
small	_____	the smallest
interesting	more interesting	the _____
boring	_____	the most boring
embarrassing	more embarrassing	the _____
wonderful	_____	the most wonderful
easy	easier	the _____
difficult	_____	the most difficult
cheap	cheaper	the _____
expensive	_____	the most expensive
terrible	_____	the most terrible
strange	stranger	the _____

USE OF ENGLISH

Rewrite the second sentence in each pair. Use no more than five words including the word in bold. Do NOT change this word.

1 I've never eaten food this good before.
   best This is the _____ ever eaten.
2 I've never had a meal that was so bad before.
   ever This is the _____ had.
3 I think that no city is more beautiful than Paris.
   most I think Paris _____ in the world.
4 I've never read an article as shocking as this before.
   ever This article is the most _____ read.
5 Nothing has ever embarrassed me this much before.
   so I've _____ before.
6 Very few cities are as expensive as Tokyo.
   one Tokyo is _____ cities in the world.
7 Few languages are as difficult as Chinese and Japanese.
   two Chinese and Japanese are _____ languages in the world.
8 I don't think anybody is as strange as Dan.
   one Dan is _____ men I've ever met.
9 Nobody has ever bored me so much before, either.
   most He's also one of the _____ ever met.

LANGUAGE STUDY

Preferences ➤ GS 14.2

A Are your preferences the same as Dan's? If they aren't, say what you prefer.

1 Dan prefers cool, cloudy weather to warm, sunny weather.
2 He'd rather sit inside than be outside when the weather is good.
3 He prefers watching films on television to seeing them in a cinema.
4 If his friends ask him about his marriage, he usually says, 'I'd rather not talk about it if you don't mind.'
5 For his next holiday, he'd prefer to stay at home rather than go to a foreign country.

B Rewrite the second sentence in each pair. Use no more than five words including the word in bold. Do NOT change this word.

1 Dan thinks English food is better than French food.
   prefers Dan _____ French food.
2 He likes eating meat more than anything else.
   rather He'd _____ than anything else.
3 If he has a choice between meat and fish, he always eats meat.
   rather He _____ fish.
4 Do you like meat more than fish?
   prefer Do _____ fish?
5 Which do you want to have, meat or fish?
   rather Which _____ have? Meat or fish?
6 Do you think eating in restaurants is better than cooking your own food?
   prefer Do you _____ cooking your own meals?
7 Do you want to go out rather than eat at home this evening?
   prefer Would _____ at home this evening?
8 Let's go out.
   rather I _____ go out.
9 Will you pay the bill?
   mind Would _____ the bill?
10 I don't want to answer that question.
   rather I'd _____ question.
11 We don't want to do this exercise, so let's read a story instead.
   rather We'd _____ do this exercise.
12 Isn't it better to stop instead of going on?
   prefer Wouldn't you _____ go on?

WRITING

Transactional letter 3

For the Part 1 transactional letter you need to be able to write different types of letter, for example, a letter of thanks, an apology for something, an invitation.

A Sample task

Here is part of a letter you have received from a friend, Richard. Read the letter and your notes and write a suitable reply.

> *Busy, but great.*
> So, how's your new job going? By the way, do you have any news about Stuart? I imagine he must be back from Nairobi by now, but I haven't got his new number. *Back last week. Staying for a year – course at LSE. 0171 844 9921*
> Let's try and arrange a date to meet up again.
> Hope to see you soon, *Party next Fri 8.30?*
>
> Yours, Richard

B Now complete the letter below by choosing the best alternative, A, B or C. Remember that this is an informal letter to a friend.

Dear (1)____

(2)____ for your last letter. I'm sorry I haven't written for so long, but I've been pretty busy with the new job. It's going really well – I've made lots of new friends, and I've been working on some very interesting projects.

(3)____ you asked if I had any news about Stuart. He came back from Nairobi a couple of weeks ago, and in fact he (4)____ me last Sunday. He's very well, and he'll be staying for a year, because he's arranged to do an MBA at the London School of Economics. He's (5)____with his parents at the moment, but he's moving to a flat in Wimbledon next week, and his number will be 0171 844 9921.

(6)____I'm having a party next Friday at 8.30, and I'd love you to come. I'm not sure who'll be there – I think it'll be people from work mainly.
(7)____let me know if you can make it.

(8)____,

James

1 A Richard   B Mr Richard   C Sir
2 A I would like to thank you   B I am grateful
   C Many thanks
3 A I shall get straight to the point   B Anyway
   C Furthermore

4 A got in touch with   B encountered
   C communicated with
5 A residing   B housed   C staying
6 A I would like to inform you that   B Finally
   C By the way
7 A Do   B I would be grateful if you could
   C Kindly
8 A Yours sincerely   B Love and kisses   C Yours

C Match the following sentences (1–6) with the sort of letters (a–f) they would come from.

1 Thank you very much indeed for the present.
2 I was so happy to hear your news. Well done!
3 I'm afraid that I won't be able to come.
4 I was very sorry to hear your news.
5 Would you like to have dinner on Sunday?
6 I'm writing to say sorry for being so rude.

a) apology
b) thanks
c) refusing an invitation
d) making an invitation
e) sympathy
f) congratulation

D Writing task

Below is part of a letter you have received from a friend who is in hospital after a minor operation. Write a suitable reply based on the letter and your notes.

> *so sorry*
> And they say I've got to stay here for another week or so. Anyway, do let me know your news – how was your holiday? If you have any time to spare, do come and visit. It isn't too bad, but as I said it's very boring. I haven't got anything to read or even a radio. It's a shame my parents are away, but I suppose that's just life, isn't it?   *okay, but* *terrible!* *not till next Monday*
> See you soon, *will bring radio – any requests for books, etc?*
> Sam   *visiting hours?*

E Read these notes before you write your letter.

Write in a suitably informal style. You can organize your letter as follows:

Say you're sorry to hear Sam is in hospital – no one told you.
Many thanks for your letter. I was so sorry...
Tell him briefly about your holiday.
Suggest a day to visit and ask about visiting hours.
I'm a bit busy for the next two days, but...
Suggest bringing a radio and offer to bring some things to read.
If you like, I'll...
Finish in a suitable way.

REVISION AND EXTENSION

Here is another part of the letter that Sam wrote. Choose the best word A, B, C or D, to fill spaces 1-15.

It all happened rather quickly – the doctor realized that I needed to have my appendix out immediately, to **(1)**_____ things from getting any **(2)**_____, and they operated **(3)**_____ me straight away. But I'm not feeling too bad and I'm getting **(4)**_____ all the time. The doctors say it will take about a week for me to **(5)**_____ the operation completely.

I'm in quite a large ward with about 20 other people, and **(6)**_____ I would **(7)**_____ to be somewhere a bit smaller, we all **(8)**_____ with each other quite well.

Still, I do find it a bit **(9)**_____ here – there's nothing to do. They say I **(10)**_____ get up unless it's absolutely necessary, so I can't even get to the TV room . Unfortunately I didn't have the **(11)**_____ to get home before coming in, so I haven't got any money. **(12)**_____ I'm sure one of the nurses would probably **(13)**_____ me enough to buy a paper, I'd **(14)**_____ not ask as I'd **(15)**_____ it a bit embarrassing.

1 **A** prevent   **C** block
   B forbid   **D** avoid
2 **A** bad   **C** serious
   B dangerous   **D** worse
3 **A** on   **C** at
   B up   **D** in
4 **A** improved   **C** finer
   B good   **D** better
5 **A** get at   **C** get over
   B get through   **D** get along
6 **A** although   **C** unless
   B despite   **D** except
7 **A** better   **C** more
   B want   **D** prefer
8 **A** get down   **C** get by
   B get on   **D** get out of
9 **A** annoying   **C** entertaining
   B irritating   **D** boring
10 **A** don't have to   **C** mustn't
   B needn't   **D** don't need to
11 **A** opportunity   **C** occasion
   B possibility   **D** permission
12 **A** In spite   **C** Unless
   B Despite   **D** Even though
13 **A** owe   **C** borrow
   B lend   **D** debt
14 **A** better   **C** prefer
   B rather   **D** want
15 **A** feel   **C** think
   B see   **D** find

LISTENING

Listen to the conversation about a swimming accident, and decide which of the following statements are true (T) and which are false (F).

1   Jenny thinks it might be useful to learn how to life-save. ☐
2   Peter was taught to life-save in the open sea. ☐
3   The hotel owner was very rude to everyone except Peter. ☐
4   The hotel owner told the group that swimming was dangerous. ☐
5   The friends were all longing to go for a swim. ☐
6   They had had a boring time in the mountains. ☐
7   Peter considered himself to be an experienced swimmer. ☐
8   Chris and Peter wanted to try out their surf-boards. ☐
9   A big wave dragged Chris under the water. ☐
10 Chris was unable to swim because he was injured. ☐
11 Peter held Chris's arm and pulled him back to the beach. ☐
12 In the end, Jenny changes her mind about life-saving. ☐

11 SCENES FROM A ROMANTIC NOVEL

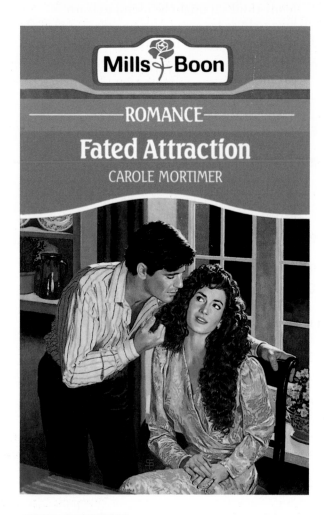

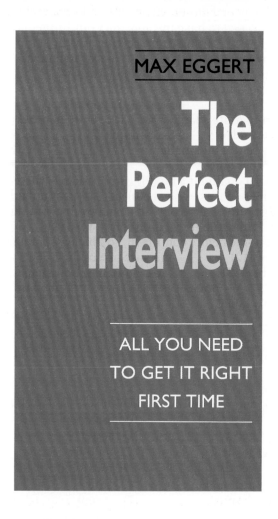

MAX EGGERT

The Perfect Interview

ALL YOU NEED
TO GET IT RIGHT
FIRST TIME

SPEAKING

A Talking on your own

Work in pairs as Student A and B. Try to speak for about one minute.

Student A: Describe and compare the book covers. Say who might read each book, and why.

Student B: Describe and compare what the books might be about and where you might find them. Say which book would interest you most.

B Finding out about each other

Ask your partners:
• what things they read in their own language.
• when they read these things.
• when they last bought a book.
• what kind of book it was and why they bought it.

READING

Study the summary which was printed on the back cover of a romantic novel. Then answer the questions.

Laura had worked for Carl Anderson for three years and had loved him since the beginning. But it was clear that he saw her as nothing but an efficient secretary – and when he announced his engagement to the beautiful Rosemary Carlton, that would seem to be that as far as Laura was concerned. However, shortly before the wedding, Carl was badly injured in an accident and told he might never walk again. Rosemary walked out on him. When Carl asked Laura to marry him, she gladly accepted. Had her chance of happiness come at last? But what if Carl still loved Rosemary? And what would happen if Rosemary came back into Carl's life again?

FOCUS ONE

1 Who is in love with whom?
2 How do you think Laura felt when Carl announced his engagement to Rosemary?
3 Explain why Carl did not marry Rosemary.
4 Describe what happened after Rosemary left.
5 Describe some of the things you think a typical reader would want to find out after reading the summary.

VOCABULARY

A Which word does not belong with the other three? Explain why not.

Example: love   like   hate   desire

➤ *Hate. It's the opposite of 'love' and very different in meaning from the other two words.*

1 beautiful   handsome   good-looking   ugly
2 dependable   reliable   attractive   earnest
3 efficient   lovely   capable   hard-working
4 lazy   dirty   dishonest   reliable
5 generous   jealous   kind   sincere
6 unreliable   sincere   frank   honest

B Answer these questions about the words above.

1 Which words suggest good characteristics?
2 Which words suggest bad characteristics?
3 Which words tell you how someone looks?
4 Which words do people tend to use more about a woman's looks than a man's looks?
5 Which words tell you only about a person's character or working-habits?
6 Which words suggest that a person usually tells the truth?

C Use the words in capital letters to form a word that fills each space. An example is given (0).

When Rosemary first saw Carl, she was strongly (0)*attracted* to him. He was one of the (1)_____ men she had ever seen. She knew that he felt a strong (2)_____ for her, as well, so it was only natural that they began seeing each other (3)_____. The (4)_____ of their engagement came a month later. When Laura heard the news, she tried very hard to hide her (5)_____. Then she realized that it was very (6)_____ of her to feel that way. She had always lived with the (7)_____ that Carl admired her only because of her (8)_____ as his secretary. The (9)_____ that she might be more than that had (10)_____ never occurred to him.

0	ATTRACT	6	FOOL
1	GOOD-LOOKING	7	KNOW
2	ATTRACT	8	EFFICIENT
3	REGULAR	9	THINK
4	ANNOUNCE	10	SIMPLE
5	DISAPPOINT		

LANGUAGE STUDY

Prepositions

A Complete this text with the correct prepositions.

Everyone knows the famous story (1)_____ Romeo and Juliet. When Romeo saw Juliet, he immediately fell (2)_____ love (3)_____ her. It was love (4)_____ first sight. He wanted to get married (5)_____ her but both his and her family were opposed (6)_____ the idea. Nevertheless, Romeo and Juliet could not forget their love (7)_____ each other. One evening Romeo took Juliet (8)_____ the hand. They gazed (9)_____ each other. Then he took her (10)_____ his arms and kissed her (11)_____ the lips. Soon afterwards, Romeo had a fight (12)_____ Juliet's brother and killed him.

B Discuss the story in pairs or groups. Ask your partners questions like these.

• Can you remember what happened after Romeo…?
• How do you think Juliet felt when Romeo killed…?
• Do you remember how the story…?

Question structures

C Study the difference in structure between the two questions in each pair.

1 Why did Romeo kill Juliet's brother?
   Why do you think Romeo killed Juliet's brother?
2 How did Juliet feel?
   How do you think Juliet felt?

D Rewrite the second sentence in each pair. Use no more than five words including the word in bold. Do NOT change this word.

1 In your opinion, is this an interesting story?
   think   Do you _____ interesting story?
2 Why were the two families opposed to the marriage?
   think   Why do you _____ opposed to the marriage?
3 Did Juliet love Romeo, too? Or have you forgotten?
   remember   Can you _____ Romeo, too?
4 Did they ever get married? Have you forgotten?
   remember   Can you _____ married?
5 Did the story have a happy ending? Can you tell me that?
   know   Do you _____ a happy ending?
6 In your opinion, did Romeo really love Juliet?
   think   Do you _____ Juliet?
7 When did you first hear this story? Can you tell me that?
   remember   Can you _____ this story?
8 In your opinion, was Shakespeare a great writer?
   think   Do you _____ a great writer?

READING

A Read this extract from a novel called *Never Say Never*.

'I look forward to meeting you on Monday, then.' Jane Winters spoke clearly and concisely, if not altogether truthfully, to the voice on the other end of the line.

'You can skip the formalities,' the voice barked. 'Just make sure you have all the information with you. I want to see copies of all the correspondence, understand?'

'Yes, Mr Francis.' She gave the telephone an angry look, not that it did any good. Adam Francis was totally unaware of her irritation, which was just as well, since he was the company's most important client. It certainly wouldn't do to offend the owner of Francisco Enterprises!

'And have you made a note of my other requirements?'

'Yes, Mr Francis.'

'Right. I'll see you at eight on Monday.' He'd hung up before Jane had a chance to say anything else.

She looked thoughtfully at the telephone receiver. Had Adam Francis been particularly curt today or was it just Jane's mood and her worries about her father which were making her less tolerant? She thought about this for a moment before carrying on with her work. No, there had been nothing out of place in her attitude towards Mr Francis; she never let her worries or any aspect of her personal life interfere with her work. The rudeness had been entirely on Mr Francis' part. He was always businesslike and curt at the best of times but he'd been particularly offensive today.

In the year that Jane had been with the company, she had had plenty of dealings with Adam Francis. She had written and sent fax messages to him frequently and had spoken with him on the telephone quite often when her boss, John Brinkman, was unavailable.

Brinkman, Clayton & Brinkman, Solicitors at Law, had offices in several countries. The London branch was the biggest and they had at least one specialist for every aspect of the law. John Brinkman's speciality was property matters – and Adam Francis was a property developer, an old-established client who gave the company a great deal of business. On Monday Jane would actually get to know the man. He was coming to London for a few days and because Jane's boss would then be away on a well-earned holiday, she had to meet Mr Francis at the airport.

B Choose the best answer.

1 During her conversation with Adam Francis, Jane was
   A worried.
   B annoyed.
   C bored.
   D embarrassed.

2 Why was Jane speaking to him?
   A She is his secretary.
   B She works for a company that does business with him.
   C She is a lawyer and had to give him advice.
   D She had to explain something she had written to him.

3 How well does she know him?
   A She has spoken to him once or twice on the phone.
   B She has never spoken to him before now.
   C She has often met him and has worked closely with him.
   D She has often communicated with him but has never met him.

4 What do we learn about Adam Francis in the last paragraph?
   A He is very important to the company Jane works for.
   B He is an old man with an important business.
   C He is a personal friend of Jane's boss.
   D He is a legal expert in property and property development.

5 How did Jane behave during the conversation?
   A She was very frank and sincere.
   B She was not always very polite.
   C She was businesslike and controlled her feelings.
   D She found it difficult to concentrate at times.

6 What is Jane's general impression of Adam Francis?
   A He is someone she is looking forward to meeting.
   B He is obviously a very good businessman.
   C He seems very easy to offend.
   D He is not a very pleasant man.

C Work in pairs or groups. Tell each other your answers. Read out the parts of the text which helped you to decide.

USE OF ENGLISH

Most lines in this text contain an unnecessary word. Underline these words and tick any lines that are correct. There are two examples (0) and (00).

0   I think an international property developer is first ✓
00 of all a man or woman who <u>they</u> has a lot of money
1   or can borrow it. Developing the property requires
2   a great deal of money and influence. I imagine me
3   that such a person travels all over in the world. I
4   suppose that a man like Adam Francis he probably
5   often travels in his own private jet and stays in the
6   most best hotels and spends a great deal of time
7   talking to clients in such places. People like as Adam
8   Francis always have a portable phone with them,
9   and are often get calls while they are sitting in
10 airports or those places at where they do business.
11 Of course, such people all them have big, expensive
12 cars. They don't drive them by themselves. Of
13 course not! They have chauffeurs for to do that.
14 Probably they don't get enough of exercise, and get
15 fat. At least, that is my impression.

Work in pairs or groups. Read the correct sentences aloud to your partners.

SPEAKING

A   In pairs or groups, choose one of the jobs below (1–3) and then spend about two minutes answering questions (a–c) about that job.

1   A secretary who works for an international law firm.
2   A pilot or stewardess who works for an international airline.
3   Someone who translates business letters and other documents from English into their own language and who also acts as an interpreter at international conferences.

a) What kind of knowledge, skills or qualifications does someone doing the job you have chosen need?
b) Describe some of the things this person does at work.
c) Would you like to do such a job? Explain why or why not.

B   Now work with a pair or group that has chosen a different job. Tell each other about the job you have chosen, using questions a–c as a guide.

LANGUAGE STUDY

Gerund (*doing*) or infinitive (*to do*)?
➤ GS 5.1, 5.2

A   Complete the following sentences with the correct form of the verb in brackets.

1   Jane enjoyed (work) for Brinkman.
2   However, she did not plan (be) a secretary all her life.
3   She didn't mind (be) a secretary for a few years.
4   But she couldn't imagine (do) the same job for years and years.
5   She hoped (become) a lawyer herself.
6   The only thing that prevented her from (study) law was a lack of time and money.
7   She often remembered (talk) to her father before he became ill.
8   She couldn't help (think) about him as she worked.
9   'I must remember (phone) the hospital,' she thought.
10 He had always urged her (think) of her future.
11 He used (talk) about the value of a good education when she was younger.
12 'Men will have to get used to (think) of women as equals, and not just as housewives or pretty faces,' he often said.

Infinitive with or without *to*?

B   Rewrite the second sentence in each pair. Use no more than five words including the word in bold. Do NOT change this word.

1   Jane never allowed her worries to interfere with her work.
    let   Jane didn't _____ her work.
2   I can't force you to do this if you don't want to.
    make   I can't _____ if you don't want to.
3   Adam hung up before Jane could reply.
    chance   Before Jane _____, Adam hung up.
4   I want to give my children a chance to get a good education.
    help   I want to _____ a good education.
5   Let me try to finish this exercise.
    chance   Give me _____ this exercise.
6   Doing this exercise may make it easier for you to pass the exam.
    help   This exercise may _____ the exam.

C   In two of the sentences you have just completed, it does not matter whether you use *to* or not. Which two sentences are these?

USE OF ENGLISH

Read this extract from the novel *Never Say Never*. Then decide which word A, B, C or D best fits each space. An example is given (0).

Adam Francis was nothing at all like the man Jane had **(0)** _expected_ to meet. During the year or two she had been with Brinkman's, from various conversations she had **(1)**____ with the client, she had gradually drawn up a mental **(2)**____ of the man.

She **(3)**____ not have been more wrong.

Not only was he years younger than she had expected but he was **(4)**____ attractive in a rugged sort of way. Handsome was not quite the **(5)**____ word for him. No, the **(6)**____ of the man who was approaching her were not handsome but they were exciting, interesting, and for one silly **(7)**____, Jane found herself wondering why John Brinkman had never **(8)**____ how attractive Adam Francis was – until it occurred to her that her boss obviously wouldn't **(9)**____ him attractive.

He was a big, tall man and there was something about him that **(10)**____ attention, a strength that was more than physical. His hair, **(11)**____ was a little too long, was **(12)**____ and straight and brushed carelessly from his face. Not only had Jane expected a much older man, but someone who would be dressed in a business **(13)**____. And there she was, looking **(14)**____ a man who seemed more like a film **(15)**____ than a property developer.

0	**A** anticipated	**C**	expected
	B attended	**D**	thought
1	**A** had	**C**	done
	B made	**D**	experienced
2	**A** drawing	**C**	painting
	B vision	**D**	picture
3	**A** would	**C**	should
	B could	**D**	can
4	**A** extremely	**C**	largely
	B greatly	**D**	mainly
5	**A** just	**C**	adequate
	B fair	**D**	right
6	**A** looks	**C**	look
	B appearances	**D**	appearance
7	**A** instant	**C**	second
	B moment	**D**	minute
8	**A** mentioned	**C**	told
	B talked	**D**	related
9	**A** remark	**C**	believe
	B regard	**D**	consider
10	**A** ordered	**C**	directed
	B commanded	**D**	requested
11	**A** that	**C**	who
	B which	**D**	what

12	**A** dense	**C**	fat
	B thick	**D**	heavy
13	**A** dress	**C**	clothes
	B costume	**D**	suit
14	**A** on	**C**	up
	B to	**D**	at
15	**A** conductor	**C**	leader
	B register	**D**	director

LANGUAGE STUDY

who, *which* or *that*? ➤ GS 11

A What is the missing word in each sentence? Sometimes more than one answer is possible.

1 The man in the picture is meeting Jane Winters, _____ works for a law firm in London.
2 The office in _____ she works is near St Paul's Cathedral.
3 The man _____ has just arrived is Adam Francis.
4 He is at Heathrow Airport, _____ is one of the biggest airports in the world.
5 Adam Francis, _____ is a property developer, was in New York last night.
6 Last year he was on a plane _____ crashed.
7 It was a crash _____ killed more than a hundred people.
8 Adam was one of the few people _____ survived the crash.

B In which of the sentences is it not possible to use *that*? Can you explain why it isn't possible?

FOCUS THREE

LISTENING 🔈

You will hear eight people talking in eight different situations. For questions 1–8, choose the best answer, A, B or C.

1 You will hear a man in a bookshop talking to a woman on the phone. What is the problem?
   A She can't remember the title of the book she wants.
   B The shop hasn't got the book but it can get it for her.
   C The woman is phoning the wrong kind of shop.

2 Jane Winters in *Never Say Never* has just met Adam Francis at the airport. What is it that surprises her?
   A He had nothing to eat on the plane.
   B He can't remember her name.
   C He doesn't want to discuss business at all.

3 You are going to hear an actor reading aloud from a novel. What kind of person is the woman in it?
   A A foolish woman in a typical romantic novel.
   B Someone who has a very unusual job.
   C A hard-working secretary like Jane Winters.

4 A man and a woman are talking on a train. What is their relationship?
   A He hardly knows her but wants to know her better.
   B They work together and know each other quite well.
   C It is impossible to guess from the dialogue.

5 A woman is talking about a book she bought recently. What is her opinion of it?
   A Reading it was a complete waste of time.
   B It was so interesting that she could hardly stop reading.
   C She lost interest in it after reading the first part.

6 A teacher is talking about romantic novels. What does she say about them?
   A She tells her students not to read them.
   B She thinks they can be useful for some students.
   C People think it is shocking that she reads them.

7 Two people are in a bookshop. What is the situation?
   A The man has just ordered a book.
   B He ordered the book some time ago.
   C He has decided to cancel his order.

8 A woman is talking to her son. What is she doing?
   A Forbidding him to read such terrible books.
   B Asking how much the book cost him.
   C Trying to persuade him to take better care of books.

LANGUAGE STUDY

More kinds of comparisons ➤ GS 1.3

A Complete the second sentence in each pair so that it has the same meaning as the first sentence. Then check with your teacher.

1 Jane had expected Adam to be older.
➤ Jane thought that Adam _____ be older.

2 I expected to get the book long before this.
➤ I didn't know it _____ going to take so long to get the book.

3 Everybody thought the weather would be colder.
➤ The weather _____ warmer than expected.

4 We had no idea that the bill would be so high.
➤ The bill _____ much higher than we thought it _____ be.

B Rewrite the second sentence in each pair. Use no more than five words including the word in bold. Do NOT change this word.

1 Jane was surprised because Adam was so young.
   going Jane had no idea Adam _____ _____ young.

2 Jane was more attractive than Adam thought she would be.
   expected Adam had _____ less attractive.

3 Did you expect this exercise to be so difficult?
   going Did you think this exercise _____ _____ easier?

4 I didn't expect them to fall in love.
   thought I never _____ in love.

5 Things are much more expensive here than we thought they would be.
   expected We had _____ cheaper here.

6 I had expected to get a much lower mark in the exam than I did.
   such I had no idea I _____ mark in the exam.

7 Jane was surprised because Adam was such a charming man.
   so Jane had never thought that Adam _____ charming.

8 She had no idea he would be so attractive.
   thought He was much more attractive than she _____ be.

9 I hope the next exercise won't be as difficult as this.
   easier I hope the next exercise _____ this.

10 Some exercises are easy and others aren't as easy.
   difficult Some exercises _____ others.

WRITING

Story 2

You may be asked to write a story ending with a particular sentence. You can use the simple past, past perfect and past continuous to help you make the order of events clear.

A Sample task and answer

> Write a short story of about 180 words ending with the following sentence:
>
> *Jake knew he was saved.*

It was already nearly six o'clock, and darkness was falling. Although Jake was quite high up the mountain, he couldn't see very far. The mist was getting thicker all the time, and the rain was coming down harder.

He couldn't understand where he had gone wrong. When he had set out that morning, the weather had been fine. Halfway through the morning, he had decided to take a short cut across the mountain. Now, as he sat down to look at the map, he realized that he must have taken the wrong path. He had no idea where he was. He stood up, feeling the cold rain trickling down his back, and set off down the side of the mountain.

Two hours later, it was completely dark. As he stumbled and fell, Jake knew he was really lost and began to wonder whether he would ever get back alive. Exhausted, he finally collapsed beside a large rock.

Some time later, he heard what sounded like a car engine. He hurried towards it and soon found himself on a rough track. He turned his head, and in the distance saw the car's headlights coming towards him. Jake knew he was saved.

B Put the events of the story in the correct order. The first one has been done for you.

- It got completely dark.
- He set out on the journey. *1*
- The weather changed.
- He saw the car.
- He found himself on a track.
- He noticed the weather was good.
- He decided to take a short cut.
- He collapsed by a rock.
- He heard a car.
- He realized he had gone the wrong way.

C Look at the story again. Find two examples where the same tense is used to:

1. set the scene at the beginning of the story and describe what was happening at the time.
2. describe what happened before the beginning of the story.
3. describe events that take place one after the other in the story and are all seen as complete actions.

D Complete this story with the correct form of the verb in brackets.

It was half past eight. Jennifer (**1** sit) alone in the restaurant waiting for Patrick to arrive. She (**2** pretend) to read the menu and (**3** try) very hard not to appear worried that he wouldn't come.

Suddenly he (**4** be) there beside her. He told her how lovely she looked, and she (**5** be) glad that she (**6** take) particular care that evening. She (**7** choose) his favourite dress and (**8** put) on the necklace that he (**9** give) her for her birthday.

Dinner was wonderful. They enjoyed the food and (**10** talk) happily throughout the meal. As they (**11** be) about to leave, Patrick (**12** take) a small package from his pocket and (**13** give) it to Jennifer. It (**14** be) a ring!

E Writing task

Write a short story ending with this sentence:

With a sigh of relief, he realized that he was going to be all right.

F You may use the following notes.

- Write about a friend in a car rally across the Sahara desert. Half way across, his car broke down.
- Paragraph 1: Imagine your friend and his car in the desert. Describe the scene – say what the weather was like, what he could see and hear, how he felt, and what he was doing at this moment. Use the past continuous form (*was doing*) for some of the verbs. For stative verbs like *see, hear,* use *he could see. . .* etc.
- Paragraph 2: Talk about how he got into this situation and about some of the events that took place from the beginning of the race until the car broke down. Use mainly the past perfect (GS 13.2.4) – for example: *The race had started very well, and he had made good progress at the start.*
- Paragraph 3: Talk about what happened next. Give details of what he did and how he managed to be rescued. Use mainly the past simple (GS 13.2.1) – for example: *In the distance, he saw a large sand dune and began to walk towards it.*
- Make sure you end the story with the sentence you are given.

FOCUS FOUR

REVISION AND EXTENSION

Infinitive with or without *to* ➤ GS 5.2

A Look at these examples.

a) *He did not want to study.*
b) *They made him study.*

The form of the verb *study* in example b is sometimes called the 'plain' or 'bare' infinitive. It is called this because it is used without *to*. Now read the letter below. Which of the infinitives (in brackets) need *to*?

Just a quick note and a few words of advice before you leave for England.

I think you should try (get) a nice family (stay) with. Some families let their guests (do) more or less what they want. But others make them (do) all sorts of unpleasant things, such as housework and the washing-up. I have even heard of one family that forced a student (take) the dog for a walk and (look after) the children.

This is why I would advise you (stay) with the Jacksons, in Wimbledon. Mrs Jackson is a wonderful person. If you can get a room there, you needn't (worry) about anything! She'll allow you (do) almost anything you like – and she really knows how (cook), as well!

Gerund (*going*) or infinitive (*to go*)? ➤ GS 5

B Complete this letter by putting the verbs in brackets into the *-ing* form where necessary.

How right you were! I'm afraid to (say) that things haven't been going too well. I didn't manage to (get) a room with the Jacksons, as I arrived a bit late. As a result, I got sent to the Smiths, and although I objected to (go) there, there was nothing else available. Anyway, I thought I might get used to (live) with them, so I decided not to (make) a fuss. But it hasn't been a success – in addition to (be) a long way from the school, the Smiths go out a lot, so I don't get much of a chance to (practise) my English.

The course has been OK, but I'm looking forward to (come) back home next week. Hope to (see) you then.

C Complete the following conversation by putting the verbs in brackets into the gerund (*going*) or the infinitive (*to go*).

A Oh, I forgot (tell) you, Jane's got married.
B Not to that dreadful man? What was his name?
A Peter. Yes, she has.
B Oh no. What ever made her decide (do) a thing like that?

A It's impossible (say). Can you imagine (be) married to him?
B No, but I can't help (feel) sorry for her, though. She seemed (be) such a nice girl. She really deserved (have) someone better.
A I know, I did my best to stop her. I told her (give) up (see) him, but she just refused (listen).
B So did I. I asked her several times (consider) (put off) (get) married, but in the end I realized it wasn't worth (try).
A Oh well, she chose (marry) him and she's got (learn) (live) with it. Anyway, we mustn't go on (talk) all day. I've arranged (meet) Janet for tea, and I don't want (be) late.

Changes in meaning ➤ GS 5.3

D Complete these sentences by putting the verb in brackets into the gerund (*going*) or the infinitive (*to go*).

1 On the way to London, he stopped (get) some petrol.
2 I'm so sorry I forgot (send) you a birthday card.
3 She stopped (eat) chocolate because she wanted to lose some weight.
4 I hope you will remember (do) all these things I have asked you.
5 Why don't you try (open) the tin with a coin?
6 I'm sure he's a doctor. I remember (talk) to him about his work the other day.
7 He always regretted not (go) to university.
8 I regret (say) that I won't be able to come to the wedding.

E Rewrite the second sentence in each pair. Use no more than five words including the word in bold. Do NOT change this word.

1 I don't really want to go to Scotland.
   rather I _____ to Scotland.
2 Our lessons were held in a very cold classroom.
   which The classroom _____ held was very cold.
3 Could you please open the window?
   mind Would _____ the window?
4 It is more dangerous to ride a motorbike than to drive a car.
   more Riding a motorbike _____ a car.
5 The exam was so difficult that I couldn't finish it.
   such It was _____ I couldn't finish it.
6 I am not as good a tennis player as John.
   at John is _____ than I am.
7 Even though they disliked him, they agreed to help.
   of Despite _____, they agreed to help.
8 I hadn't realized the meal would be so expensive.
   much The meal _____ I had expected.

12
A STUDY IN CONTRASTS

READING

Aaron Spelling is said to be the richest and most successful television producer in Hollywood and, in a city famous for its wealth, his wife Candy is the biggest spender. They recently paid more than $10 million for the huge house the famous American singer, Bing Crosby, used to live in. Then they had it torn down so that an even bigger, more wonderful mansion could be built. Not only will it have a more luxurious swimming pool, but there will be an indoor ice-skating rink and a private zoo as well. The final bill will come to at least $25 million.

They say that a few years ago, on a typically warm Californian Christmas Eve, Candy had a huge amount of real snow delivered to the Spelling mansion and spread all over the green lawns so that their children could enjoy 'a white Christmas'.

Not long ago Candy decided she needed a few more clothes. She had a whole fashion show flown out to her from New York, along with the designer and three models. Not only did she buy the entire collection but – so the story goes at least – the bags and hats the models travelled with, as well. A lot of people in Hollywood wonder what she is going to buy next.

'What more can she possibly want?' others ask.

Martin and Rebecca Granger used to teach in a tough secondary school in London. Two years ago, they moved to a small cottage in Cornwall, in the extreme south-west of England. 'We got tired of trying to make kids learn things they had no interest in,' Martin says. Martin's mother died, leaving the cottage to them. 'It was in a terrible state when we came. There were leaks in the roof. There wasn't even an indoor loo.* Rebecca and I have rebuilt the place with our own hands.'

It is a pleasant, small place by the sea. In their large garden they grow most of their own vegetables and keep a goat. They also make all their own clothes. 'Money is still a problem, but we've learned to get by on very little,' Rebecca says. She does some part-time teaching in a school in a village nearby. Martin paints water-colours of the wild Atlantic and the brilliant sunsets they see almost every day. He has sold a few recently.

They both say that what they value most is their freedom from the rat race and the pressures of life in a big city. Only one thing really bothers them, and that is the invasion of tourists every summer.

'We've been happy here, but we might emigrate to New Zealand, where we'd be even further away from it all,' Rebecca says.

*lavatory

FOCUS ONE

Choose the best answer.

1   Aaron and Candy Spelling are now living in
    A   the house that belonged to Bing Crosby.
    B   a house they paid more than $10 million for.
    C   a more luxurious house than the one they
        bought.
    D   a house that needed a lot of repairs.

2   The real snow Candy wanted for Christmas was
    A   brought to her home from elsewhere.
    B   placed on the edge of the lawns.
    C   manufactured at her own home.
    D   more than she needed to cover her property.

3   A short while ago, Candy decided to
    A   fly to New York to buy some clothes.
    B   run a clothing company herself.
    C   employ a fashion designer and fashion models
        permanently.
    D   purchase every single item in a fashion show.

4   Martin and Rebecca Granger moved to a small
    cottage in Cornwall because they
    A   couldn't find a teaching job in London.
    B   wanted to teach outside London.
    C   found teaching salaries too low in London.
    D   wanted a change from their life in London.

5   The cottage they moved to in Cornwall
    A   had belonged to a distant relative.
    B   was bought for them by Martin's mother.
    C   was in a dreadful condition.
    D   was in a small village.

6   After Martin and Rebecca had moved to the
    cottage, they spent some time
    A   creating a large garden.
    B   renovating the building themselves.
    C   looking for suitable work.
    D   finding help to make the place habitable.

7   They are thinking of emigrating to New Zealand
    because
    A   they are seeking freedom from the rat race.
    B   they cannot manage on what they earn.
    C   they are no longer happy where they are.
    D   they want to live in an even more remote place.

8   By contrasting the two families, the writer suggests
    that people
    A   are rarely satisfied with their houses.
    B   do not need a lot of money to be happy.
    C   need to be kept busy.
    D   often find living in the country unpleasant.

SPEAKING

Talking on your own

Work in pairs as Student A and B. Try to speak for
about one minute.

Student A: Describe and compare the houses shown
             in the pictures on page 90. Say what you
             think they might look like inside and
             which you would prefer to live in.

Student B: Describe and compare the settings of the
             houses in both pictures. Say what kind of
             people might not enjoy living in these
             surroundings, and why not.

VOCABULARY

**Which is the word in each group that does not
belong?**

1   elegant   marvellous   luxurious   shabby
2   mansion   castle   cottage   palace
3   partial   whole   entire   complete
4   tough   hard   relaxing   demanding
5   repair   leak   hole   crack
6   loo   shower   lavatory   toilet

LANGUAGE STUDY

A   **Study the following pairs of sentences. Is there a
    difference between them?**

1   a)   She bought the clothes and the hats and bags as
         well.
    b)   Not only did she buy the clothes, but the hats
         and bags as well.

2   a)   I can speak Chinese, and I can read it as well.
    b)   Not only can I speak Chinese, but I can read it
         as well.

B   **Which sentences suggest most clearly that there
    is something unusual and surprising in the
    statement?**

C   **Rewrite the following sentences using *Not
    only...***
Example: Bill can sing and dance.

➤   *Not only can Bill sing, but he can dance as well.*

1   I can sing and dance.
2   He is a thief and a killer.
3   He lies and he steals.
4   You will pass your exam and get a good mark.
5   The room I live in is cold and it smells.
6   The roof leaks, and there is a ghost in the house.
7   This computer is expensive and it's useless.
8   We had to clean the house and repair the roof.

SPEAKING

A Talking on your own

Work in groups of three as Student A, B and C. Try to speak for about one minute.

Student A: Choose two of the pictures. Describe and compare them, saying what type of holiday you could have in the two places, and which place you would prefer.

Student B: Choose two different pictures. Describe and compare them, saying what type of holiday you could have in the two places, and which place would be more expensive.

Student C: Talk about the two remaining pictures. Describe and compare them, saying what type of holiday you could have in these places, and which place would be more exciting.

B Discussion

1 Is it better to discover new places for holidays, or to go back to a place you know well?
2 What things are important to you when you go away on holiday?
3 What good or bad changes has tourism brought to your area?

FOCUS TWO

LANGUAGE STUDY

have something done ➤ GS 15.1.1

A What's the difference?

1 The old lady delivered the food.
   The old lady had the food delivered.

2 I'm going to repair my car.
   I'm going to have my car repaired.

3 You should cut your hair.
   You should have your hair cut.

B Read the sentences and answer the questions, using the correct form of the verb in brackets.

Example: An old lady is having trouble with her TV set. What is she going to have done? (repair)

➤ *She's going to have her TV set repaired.*

1 Candy doesn't like the house she has just bought. What is she going to have done? (tear down)

2 A businessman has lots of suits, but never buys them from a shop. What does he have done? (make)

3 A film actress is at the hairdresser's at the moment. What is she having done? (cut)

4 A man went into a chemist's with a roll of film yesterday. Today he has just come out with some photos. What has he just had done? (develop)

5 A large hotel has a '12-hour laundry service'. What can you have done? (wash)

6 Candy employed decorators at her house last year. What did she have done? (paint)

C Rewrite these sentences with the correct form of *have something done.*

1 I take my car to Bowen's Garage for servicing.
   serviced
   ➤ I _____ at Bowen's Garage.

2 Someone can repair your shoes in an hour.
   have
   ➤ You _____ in an hour.

3 The designers have made a dress for Candy's party.
   had
   ➤ Candy _____ for her party.

4 We've arranged for someone to fix the washing machine next week.
   have
   ➤ We're going _____ next week.

5 Someone in London is printing the wedding invitations for us.
   printed
   ➤ We are _____ in London.

6 Candy organized a delivery of snow on Christmas Eve.
   some
   ➤ Candy _____ on Christmas Eve.

VOCABULARY

lie or *lay*?

A Study these dictionary definitions.

lie[1] (make a) statement that one knows to be untrue: *tell ~s. He ~d to me. He's lying. What a pack of ~s!* ⇨ pack[1] (3) also white lie.

lie[2] **1** be, put oneself, flat on a horizontal surface or in a resting position: *~ on one's back/side. He lay on the grass enjoying the sunshine. (not) take sth lying down,* (not) submit to a challenge, an insult without protest. *lie-in,* stay in bed after one's usual time. Hence, *lie-in n: have a nice ~-in on Sunday morning. lie low,* ⇨ low[1] (1). **2** (of things) be resting flat on something: *The book lay open on the table.* **3** be kept, remain, in a certain state or position: *money lying idle in the bank. The snow lay thick on the ground.*

lay[2] **1** put on a surface; put in a certain position: *He laid his hand on my shoulder.* **2** (of non-material things, and *fig*) place; put. *lay (one's) hands on sth/sb,* (a) seize; get possession of: *He keeps everything he can ~ (his) hands on.* (b) do violence to: *How dare you ~ hands on me?* (c) find: *The book is somewhere, but I can't ~ my hands on it just now.*

Now study the forms:
lay/laid/have laid
lie/lied/have lied
lie/lay/have lain

B Complete these sentences with the correct form of *lie* or *lay*.

1 Don't _____ the table yet. Wait until they get here.

2 If you _____ a hand on me, I'll call the police!

3 There was a tree _____ across the road.

4 I fell asleep as soon as I _____ down.

5 He came in and _____ all the books on the table.

6 I've never _____ eyes on that man before.

7 Those things have just _____ there for weeks; nobody has even touched them.

8 She _____ to me about her age.

bring, take, fetch, carry or *wear*?

C Complete each of the following sentences with one of the above words.

1 Will you _____ this letter to the post office for me, please?

2 Do you have to _____ a shirt and tie at work?

3 Waiter! Please _____ me a menu.

4 You're very ill. I think I'd better go out and _____ a doctor immediately!

5 How much weight can you _____ on your back?

6 Please remember to _____ your books with you.

LISTENING 🙁

A You are going to hear part of a radio programme about Linda de Vere Hardy. Listen to it at least once, and then choose the best answer, A, B or C.

1 What was Linda most interested in when she was at school?
   A French and History
   B boyfriends
   C cars

2 She decided to fly to India because she
   A knew Lindberg was going to do the same thing.
   B couldn't find the right plane to cross the Atlantic.
   C wanted to be the first woman pilot in Europe.

3 What happened during the flight?
   A She thought about giving up and returning.
   B She had to land in the desert but got some petrol from a camel-driver.
   C She crashed in the desert and finished the journey by camel.

4 The architect who knew her never married her because
   A he was not very fond of her.
   B she was not very fond of him.
   C she did not want any children.

5 Diana Cusard thinks the stories about Linda and Clark Gable
   A may have been true.
   B were not true.
   C were definitely true.

B Now listen to the second part at least once. Complete the notes below.

She flew bombers to Britain during
[1]_____.

Later she married Angus Hardy who worked in
[2]_____.

The marriage was unusual because he was
[3]_____ than her.

Both Linda and her husband were interested in
[4]_____.

Angus encouraged her to develop her talents as a
[5]_____.

Her books were popular
[6]_____.

In 1962, her husband died
[7]_____.

For the remainder of her life, she lived alone on
[8]_____.

Her son Ian stopped visiting her because he felt
[9]_____.

Linda and her son
[10]_____ relationship.

Donald Winstone feels proud
[11]_____.

He admired her [12]_____.

VOCABULARY

The following article appeared in a newspaper a few days after Linda de Vere Hardy's death. Use the words in capital letters to form a word that fills each space. An example is given (0).

Linda de Vere Hardy, who died last week, was not at all a (0) _conventional_ woman of her generation. In the 1920s she was (1)_____ to learn to fly, and became the first woman to become a fully (2)_____ pilot. Her solo (3)_____ from London to Delhi was one of the greatest (4)_____ of the early days of aviation. Her (5)_____ to Angus Hardy took place after the end of the Second World War. With his (6)_____, she wrote a number of (7)_____ stories in the 1950s that achieved great (8)_____. In 1962, her husband's tragic (9)_____ in a car crash ended her literary career, and she spent the rest of her life on an (10)_____ island off the coast of Scotland.

0	CONVENTION	6	ENCOURAGE
1	DETERMINE	7	DETECT
2	QUALIFY	8	POPULAR
3	FLY	9	DIE
4	ACHIEVE	10	ISOLATE
5	MARRY		

FOCUS THREE

LANGUAGE STUDY

What is the meaning of *they*?

A Study the example. Who could *they* be?

a) They gave Linda a prize for one of her books.
b) They say her books are still popular.
c) They used to say that she was a bit crazy.

1 In which two sentences does *they* mean people in general?
2 In which sentence does it mean something like 'whoever the people are who decide such things'?

The passive ➤ GS 8.1

B Rewrite these sentences without using *they*, *people* or *someone*. Use the word in bold.

Example: They gave Linda a prize for one of her books.

➤ *Linda was given a prize for one of her books.*

1 They will give me a prize if I can learn this.
be   I will _____ if I can learn this.

2 Perhaps someone will find a cure for this disease one day.
found   Perhaps a cure for this disease _____ one day.

3 Will they find an easier way to learn English one day, too?
be   Will an easier way to learn _____ one day, too?

4 Someone has told me you could learn English in your sleep.
been   I _____ you could learn English in your sleep.

5 People learn English easily.
is   They say that English _____ to learn.

6 People speak it all over the world.
is   It _____ all over the world.

7 They sell English books in that shop.
sold   English _____ in that shop.

8 Someone is repairing my car at the moment.
repaired   My car _____ at the moment.

VOCABULARY

Verb and noun combinations: *make* and *do* ➤ GS 15.2

A Which of these things below can we *make*? Which can we *do*? Read each one aloud. Then say if they need *make* or *do*.

- someone a favour
- your homework
- French
- money
- a phone call
- military service
- something/nothing/anything
- friends
- a course
- the washing-up
- a mistake
- an appointment
- a noise

B Rewrite the second sentence in each pair. Use no more than five words including the word in bold. Do NOT change this word.

1 Let's clean the dishes in the morning.
washing-up   Let's _____ in the morning.

2 My sister is studying French at university.
course   My sister is _____ at university.

3 His books are very profitable.
money   He _____ from his books.

4 Have you made any arrangements for this weekend?
anything   Are _____ this weekend?

5 Joachim's composition was very inaccurate.
mistakes   Joachim _____ in his composition.

6 The protesters were very noisy at the meeting.
noise   The protesters _____ at the meeting.

7 Young people in England don't have to spend any time in the army any more.
service   Young people in England don't have _____ any more.

8 You can ring your mother from my office.
make   You can _____ to your mother from my office.

9 Could you be quieter, please.
noise   Could you stop _____, please.

10 Could I arrange a time to see the dentist?
appointment   Could I _____ to see the dentist?

WRITING

Letter of application 2

In addition to writing a letter of application for a job (see Unit 3), you may also be asked to apply for something else, such as a scholarship or a grant.

A Sample task

The Green Foundation is offering grants of up to £5000 to fund new projects at schools and universities which are aimed at improving the environment. If you would like to be considered for a grant, please write to us, telling us what you will do in your project, how much money you will need and how you plan to spend the money.

B Read the following answer. There are ten extra words that should not be there. Can you find them?

Dear Sir or Madam

I am writing with reference to your announcement and would like to apply me for a grant.

I am a seventeen-year-old student at Brandon School in London. I am studying science because I intend to do medicine at the university. I have always been interested in the environment. I feel that we should to make people more aware of the benefits of re-cycling.

Last year, as part of our chemistry course, we did a project on re-cycling. The project had two aims. The first aim it was to study the problem of disposing of ordinary household products such as like bottles and plastics. We worked out which products were enough safe to throw away, and which ones could be re-cycled. Our second aim was to give this information out.

We produced leaflets for students and parents and at the weekends we handed more leaflets out in supermarkets. The cost of this it came to about £1000. We also spent £500 in writing to local shops near, supermarkets and other businesses asking them to provide re-cycling facilities.

I hope you will consider us for a grant for £1500, and am look forward to hearing from you.

Yours faithfully,

Paul Porritt

C Analysis

1 Is the letter written to the right person?
2 Is it written in the right style?
3 Are the paragraphs clear?
4 Read the question again. Why (apart from the mistakes) is this a bad answer?

D Writing task

Write a letter of about 180 words applying for one of the grants mentioned in this announcement.

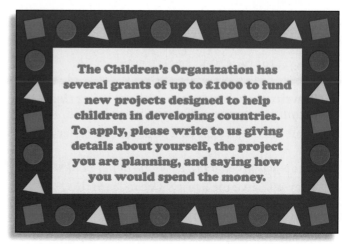

The Children's Organization has several grants of up to £1000 to fund new projects designed to help children in developing countries. To apply, please write to us giving details about yourself, the project you are planning, and saying how you would spend the money.

E Plan your answer, using these notes. The letter can be answered in five paragraphs:

1 Refer to the announcement and say why you are writing.

2 Give a few details about yourself and what you do. Keep this part fairly short – they just want an idea of who you are, how old you are, etc.

3 This is the main part of the letter, and you must use your imagination. Think of a project that would help children in developing countries. You may use any of your own ideas or any of the following:
   • collecting second-hand clothes
   • giving children presents for Christmas
   • supplying food and medicine

4 Explain how much you need and what you would spend the money on. It would be a good idea to make it clear that you will be doing a lot of the work for free.

5 Finish appropriately and say you look forward to hearing from them.

Remember to write in a formal style.

REVISION AND EXTENSION

Complete the text by choosing the best answer, A, B, C or D.

A YEAR WITH OVERSEAS VOLUNTEERS

I was with Overseas Volunteers (OV) for a year after leaving university, and I was sent to an isolated village in Chad, about 500 kilometres from the capital N'Djamena. Coming from a **(1)____** country, I got quite a shock, as conditions were much harder than I had **(2)____**. But after a few days I soon got used to **(3)____** there. The people were always very friendly and helpful, and I soon began to appreciate how **(4)____** the countryside was.

One of my jobs was to supply the village with water. The well was a long walk away, and the women used to **(5)____** a long time every day **(6)____** heavy pots backwards and forwards. So I contacted the organization and arranged to **(7)____** some pipes delivered. We built a simple pipeline and a pump, and it worked first time. It wasn't perfect – there were a few **(8)____**, but it made a great difference to the villagers, **(9)____** had never had running water before. And not **(10)____** did we have running water, but in the evenings it was hot, because the pipe had been **(11)____** in the sun all day.

All in all, I think my time with OV was a good experience. Although it was not well-paid, it was well **(12)____** doing, and I would recommend it to anyone who was **(13)____** working for a charity.

Finally, there's one more reason why I'll never **(14)____** working for OV. A few months before I left, I met and fell in love **(15)____** another volunteer, and we got married when we returned to England.

1	**A** rich	**C** well-paid	
	B comfortable	**D** luxurious	
2	**A** felt	**C** found	
	B planned	**D** expected	
3	**A** live	**C** living	
	B lived	**D** lives	
4	**A** beautiful	**C** handsome	
	B good-looking	**D** sweet	
5	**A** spend	**C** spends	
	B spent	**D** spending	
6	**A** fetching	**C** carrying	
	B wearing	**D** holding	
7	**A** make	**C** have	
	B let	**D** allow	
8	**A** breaks	**C** splits	
	B leaks	**D** punctures	
9	**A** which	**C** they	
	B that	**D** who	
10	**A** hardly	**C** only	
	B scarcely	**D** also	
11	**A** lied	**C** laying	
	B lay	**D** lying	
12	**A** worth	**C** cost	
	B value	**D** price	
13	**A** considering	**C** going	
	B thinking	**D** planning	
14	**A** regret	**C** miss	
	B feel sorry	**D** lose	
15	**A** at	**C** for	
	B to	**D** with	

LISTENING

You will hear an interview about why conservation groups, such as Greenpeace, are interested in protecting whales. For questions 1–9 fill in the missing information in the advertisement below.

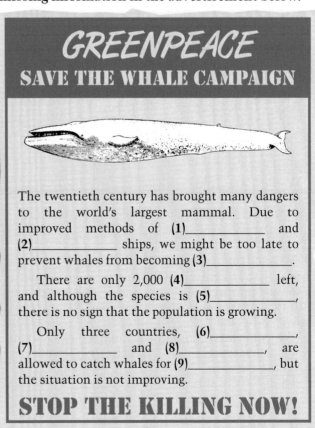

GREENPEACE

SAVE THE WHALE CAMPAIGN

The twentieth century has brought many dangers to the world's largest mammal. Due to improved methods of **(1)_____** and **(2)_____** ships, we might be too late to prevent whales from becoming **(3)_____**.

There are only 2,000 **(4)_____** left, and although the species is **(5)_____**, there is no sign that the population is growing.

Only three countries, **(6)_____**, **(7)_____** and **(8)_____**, are allowed to catch whales for **(9)_____**, but the situation is not improving.

STOP THE KILLING NOW!

£13
A SHOPPER'S NIGHTMARE

READING

A **Eight sentences are missing from this article. Study sentences A–I on the next page. Choose the one that fits each gap (1–7). There is one sentence you do not need. An example is given (0).**

The jumper I had been given for my birthday was too small for me and I wanted to exchange it for a larger one. One day some friends with a car came to visit me. They suggested dropping me off near the department store where the jumper had been originally bought. **0** *I* I jumped out of the car and they drove off, saying they would be back in ten minutes.

The girl I spoke to at the counter was extremely helpful. Unfortunately, however, they had no other jumpers in my size and I decided to leave with the original gift. **I** I was standing there, looking for my friend's car, when someone suddenly grabbed one of my arms from behind.

I tried to turn around to see who it was but a man shouted 'Don't try to run away!' I caught a glimpse of a man with a moustache behind me. As I turned, the jumper fell out of the bag. Then a woman suddenly appeared in front of me and told me she and the man were store detectives. She picked up the jumper. **2**

I was so shocked I could hardly concentrate.

'Don't try to deny it!' she whispered.

Just at that moment, my astonished friends arrived in their car. One of them jumped out and asked the woman who she was and what was going on. She ignored him.

'You'd better come with us,' she told me. **3**
They took me up some stairs and into an office.

'What am I supposed to have done?' I demanded when they asked me to give them my name and address. The woman smiled.

'Why don't you admit what you've done?' she said. I had realized by this time that they thought I had stolen the jumper, so I began to explain that it was a gift. **4** The woman smiled again when I showed it to her.

'Why did you try to throw the jumper away if you didn't steal it and if this is really the receipt for it?' she asked.

'I didn't try to throw it away. It fell out of my bag when your friend here grabbed me,' I protested.

The next person I spoke to was another man who was obviously the boss of the two store detectives. **5** I insisted that he should go and find the shop assistant I had spoken to earlier. Eventually, he and the woman reluctantly agreed to do so.

'Keep an eye on her,' the woman said to the man with the moustache as she left. The woman came back a few minutes later, looking very embarrassed. She asked the man with the moustache to step outside with her. **6** Then the manager of the store arrived, and apologized for what had happened. I told him that nothing he could say or do would compensate for the rudeness and insensitivity of his employees.

My friends later urged me to sue the store, but for some reason I never did. **7**

FOCUS ONE

A   I heard them whispering in the corridor.

B   Luckily, or so I thought, the friend who had given me the jumper had also given me the receipt for it, and I had it with me.

C   If I had done so, I might have received a lot of money, but I just didn't want to be reminded of what had happened.

D   Without thinking, I put it and the receipt back in my bag, and dashed outside.

E   My astonished friends stared as she and the man with the moustache marched me back into the store.

F   He seemed totally uninterested in what I had to say.

G   It was dark green, which happens to be my favourite colour.

H   'Do you admit that you had this in your bag when you left the store?' she said accusingly.

I   It seemed like an excellent idea.

B   Match the words or phrases (1–8) with the explanations (a–h) below.

1   drop someone off   5   receipt
2   grab   6   reluctantly
3   catch a glimpse   7   compensate
4   astonished   8   sue

a)   proof that you have bought something
b)   demand money from someone who has hurt you in some way
c)   take someone in a car and let them out
d)   see only for a moment
e)   unwillingly
f)   very surprised
g)   suddenly put your hands around
h)   pay money to or do something for someone after you have done something wrong

C   Explain these things to your teacher or your partners.

1   Why did the writer leave without exchanging the jumper?
2   How did the writer try to prove that she had not stolen the jumper?
3   Why do you think the woman detective didn't believe her?
4   Why did the woman whisper to the man with the moustache later – and what do you think she probably said to him?
5   What do you think the manager of the store actually said to the writer?

SPEAKING

Finding out about each other

Work in pairs. Find out:
1   what things your partners have bought recently.
2   where they bought these things.
3   when was the last time they bought something special.
4   why they bought it.

LANGUAGE STUDY

Leaving out relative pronouns ➤ GS 11.1.2

A   You can transform two of these sentences without using *who*. But you must use *who* in the other two. Try to explain why.

1   I spoke to a shop assistant. She was very helpful.
➤   The shop assistant I spoke to was very helpful.
2   I stopped a man. He was a detective.
➤   The man I stopped was a detective.
3   A woman spoke to me. She was very helpful.
➤   The woman who spoke to me was very helpful.
4   A man stopped me. He was a detective.
➤   The man who stopped me was a detective.

B   Transform these sentences in the same way. When can you leave out *who*, *which* or *that*?

1   I spoke to a shop assistant. She was very young.
➤   The shop assistant _____ .
2   A shop assistant spoke to me. She was very young.
➤   The shop assistant _____ .
3   A man grabbed me. He had a moustache.
➤   The man _____ .
4   I grabbed a man. He had a beard.
➤   The man _____ .
5   I went into a shop. It was in Oxford Street.
➤   The shop _____ .
6   A shop sells these things. It's in Oxford Street.
➤   The shop _____ .
7   A dictionary is a book. It explains words.
➤   A dictionary is _____ .
8   You've got a book. It's mine.
➤   The book _____ .

LISTENING

You are going to hear a store detective talking about three different types of shoplifter. Complete the notes below (1–9) so that they summarize what he says.

The speaker says that the first type of shoplifter steals, even though he or she usually has

[1] _____ buy the thing they steal.

Shoplifters of this first type often steal because they have [2] _____ with their husbands or wives.

The second type, whom he calls 'petty thieves', have already decided [3] _____ before entering the store.

These are usually things that cost so [4] _____ they can't buy them.

The third type consists of professional gangs consisting [5] _____ people.

The 'spotter' is the person who decides [6] _____.

He or she also looks around to see if any [7] _____ what the gang is doing.

The 'hand' is the person who [8] _____.

The job of the 'catcher' is to [9] _____.

SPEAKING

In pairs or groups, choose ONE of the two questions below. Discuss it for about 3 minutes. Then tell the whole class your answer.

1. Shoplifters are sometimes well-off people who have never stolen before and who could afford to buy the things they steal. Do you think these people should be punished? If so, describe what you think would be a proper punishment. If you don't think they should be punished, what do you think should be done when they are caught?

2. Large department stores often have to hire trained 'store detectives'. Smaller, family-owned shops, on the other hand, don't need store detectives. It also seems that the danger of shoplifting in such shops is not as great as in department stores. Think of a possible reason for this.

VOCABULARY

A Is the meaning of the word in *italics* the same in both sentences? If it is different, can you explain the difference?

1. a) The thieves *used* hand signals to communicate with each other before they stole the diamonds.
   b) I have a friend who *used* to be a store detective.

2. a) Have you ever had a sudden *urge* to do something that you couldn't resist?
   b) Why do parents often *urge* their children to get a good education and to think of the future?

3. a) Two members of the gang usually *help* another member to get the stolen goods out of the store.
   b) I can't *help* thinking there is something wrong here.

Which of the words in *italics* above not only has two different meanings but also two different pronunciations?

B How many words in English do you know that are spelled the same way but have at least two different meanings? In pairs or groups, write down at least three such words.

C Which word in each group does not belong with the other three? Explain why.

1. impulse   decision   desire   urge
2. help   aid   assist   participate
3. urge   encourage   stop   persuade
4. resist   fight   surrender   struggle
5. help   stop   resist   assist

If you aren't sure which word doesn't belong with the other three in group 5, decide which three you can use to complete the sentence below.

I know I shouldn't do this, but I just can't _____ it.

SPEAKING

Talking on your own

Work in pairs as Student A and B. Speak for about one minute.

Student A: Describe and compare the types of shop shown in the pictures below. Say how shopping would be different in both places and which place you would prefer to shop in, and why.

Student B: Describe and compare what is being sold in the pictures below. Say who might shop in each place and what kind of clothes you like to buy, and why.

USE OF ENGLISH

A Complete each space below with one word only. Sometimes you will use the same word to complete more than one space.

A fire broke out yesterday afternoon in Mason's department store in River Street. Nobody knows yet **(1)**_____ caused it, but it may have been an accident. However, the police are looking for two young men **(2)**_____ were seen running out of the store shortly before it began. They jumped into a car **(3)**_____ was waiting for them. A witness **(4)**_____ was walking past the car at the time says he overheard **(5)**_____ one of the men said to the driver.

'I didn't hear everything but I'm sure one of the words **(6)**_____ he said was "bomb" or something like that,' the witness told the police.

The police have said they are looking for a young man between 19 and 24 **(7)**_____ hair is red and **(8)**_____ was seen with two other men in a yellow car **(9)**_____ was being driven at high speed along River Street at 4.30 p.m. yesterday. Anyone **(10)**_____ saw him or has information about the other two men should contact the police immediately. **(11)**_____ you tell the police will be treated confidentially. Luckily the fire **(12)**_____ began in Mason's was quickly put out by the fire-fighters **(13)**_____ arrived at the scene. However, **(14)**_____ happened at Mason's yesterday could happen again with results **(15)**_____ might be far more serious.

B Go back over each space that you filled with *who, which* or *that*. Which one of the sentences would still be correct even if you didn't fill the space at all?

LANGUAGE STUDY

what clauses

A The sentences below can all be completed with the same word. What is that word?

1 Can you see _____ the people in the picture are doing?
2 Did you understand _____ I said a moment ago?
3 Was _____ I said a moment ago clear?
4 _____ you said a moment ago suggests you didn't really understand my question.

B Complete the second sentence in each pair using the word in bold. Do NOT change that word.

1 We don't know the cause of the fire.
   caused We have no idea _____ _____ the fire.
2 Perhaps a bomb caused the fire.
   what Perhaps _____ was a bomb.
3 The man with red hair may have caused it.
   whose It may have been caused by _____ _____ was red.
4 The police want to contact people if they saw him.
   anyone The police want to talk to _____ _____ him.
5 He jumped into a car waiting in front of the store.
   was The car he _____ waiting in front of the store.
6 The driver of the car had a beard.
   was The man _____ the car had a beard.
7 Luckily the fire didn't cause serious damage.
   very Luckily, the damage the _____ _____ serious.
8 Sudden fires often cause very serious damage.
   is The damage _____ often very serious.
9 The thing that happened at Mason's must be prevented from happening again.
   what We have to _____ at Mason's from happening again.
10 How should people be punished if they start a fire?
    someone What should we do with _____ _____ a fire?
11 If people deliberately start a fire, they should be punished.
    anyone I think _____ a fire should be punished.
12 Just think if they start a fire and someone is killed.
    kills What if a fire _____ someone?

READING

A In pairs or groups, discuss the meaning of each of the public notices below. Where could you see such a notice? Who do you think is supposed to read it? For example, which one do you think is for guests in a restaurant?

A WE BELIEVE OUR PRICES TO BE UNBEATABLE. IF YOU CAN FIND THE SAME GOODS AT A LOWER PRICE ANYWHERE ELSE, WE UNDERTAKE TO MAKE UP THE DIFFERENCE.

B DOCUMENTS ENCLOSED. CHECK CONTENTS BEFORE SIGNING FOR RECEIPT.

C Once you have signed, you will have fourteen days in which to cancel this contract. You can do this only by sending a WRITTEN notice of this intention to the address below.

D PLEASE NOTE THAT SECURITY CAMERAS OPERATE IN THIS STORE. ALL SHOPLIFTERS WILL BE PROSECUTED.

E THESE SPACES ARE RESERVED. UNAUTHORISED VEHICLES WILL BE TOWED AWAY. RECOVERY FEE MINIMUM OF £40 PER DAY.

F INTEREST-FREE CREDIT AVAILABLE ON ALL FULL-PRICED MERCHANDISE. ASK OUR STAFF FOR DETAILS.

G REFUNDS IN EXCESS OF £15 CANNOT BE MADE WITHOUT PROOF OF PURCHASE BY PROPER RECEIPTS.

H PLEASE WAIT TO BE SEATED. A WAITER WILL CONDUCT YOU TO YOUR TABLE.

I THIS GARMENT WILL FADE WITH REPEATED WASHING. TO MAINTAIN OPTIMAL APPEARANCE, TURN INSIDE OUT AND WASH SEPARATELY. DO NOT RUB ISOLATED STAINS.

J SMOKING KILLS. EVERY YEAR MILLIONS DIE FROM SMOKING-RELATED ILLNESSES.

K FOR SECURITY REASONS, ANY LUGGAGE OR OTHER PARCELS LEFT UNATTENDED WILL BE REMOVED AND MAY BE DESTROYED.

L IF YOU ARE UNABLE TO FIND THE GOODS YOU ARE SEEKING, PLEASE REQUEST THE ASSISTANCE OF OUR SALES STAFF.

B Now match the letter (A–L) that identifies each notice with the questions (0–11). Question 0 is an example.

Which of the notices:

would you see in a restaurant?	**0**	*H*
advises you what to do if you need help?	**1**	
warns you not to park in the wrong place?	**2**	
guarantees good value?	**3**	
would you find only on an article of clothing?	**4**	
warns people about a health risk?	**5**	
warns you that you are being watched?	**6**	
says what you need to get your money back?	**7**	
advertises a way to borrow money?	**8**	
could be a warning for air or rail travellers?	**9**	
could you see on a parcel being delivered?	**10**	
informs you of your right to change your mind?	**11**	

VOCABULARY

Phrasal verbs

A What is the phrasal verb in each example (a–e)? Explain its meaning to your partners.

a) Where can I try these jeans on?
b) Let's go into the shop and look around.
c) Take this agreement and look it over for me.
d) They won't take the goods back unless you have a receipt.
e) Don't miss out on this wonderful opportunity.

B Use the same phrasal verbs above to complete these sentences.

1 Before you buy anything, you should always _____ it _____ carefully.
2 I don't want to buy anything. I just want to _____ _____.
3 This sale is the chance of a lifetime. Don't _____ _____ _____ it.
4 Aren't you going to _____ the dress _____ before you buy it?
5 I'm sorry, sir, but you've already worn these shoes. That's why we can't _____ them _____.

WRITING

Article 2

You may be asked to write a descriptive article about a place you know well. You must make sure that the style of the article is suitable for the people who are going to read it.

A Sample task

An international magazine is doing a feature on favourite childhood memories. Write an article of about 180 words describing a place you liked as a child.

B What is wrong with this article? Why would it get a poor mark?

> I remember that there were a lot of rooms in the house. Downstairs there was a kitchen. The sitting room was next to the kitchen. There were three bedrooms upstairs. The dining room was next to the sitting room, opposite the kitchen. There was a dining room table in the dining room, and there were six chairs round the table. In the garden there was a tennis court and a swimming pool. The garden was big. My best friend used to live in this house, and it was about fifty miles from London. There were two bathrooms upstairs. I used to visit the house during my school holidays. It was nice.

C Compare what you have just read with the article below.

> As time has passed, many of my childhood memories have faded, but the memory of one place is still as bright as ever. It was my best friend's house and it was very important to me when I was young. It was about an hour's drive from London, and because I only ever visited in the school holidays, I always associated it with being free.
>
> The house itself was set in a large garden. Here we used to play tennis on warm summer days or enjoy lazy barbecues by the side of the cool swimming pool. Beautiful pale pink roses seemed to grow everywhere, and even now, the scent of roses takes me back to those happy days.
>
> Inside the house it was always warm. The kitchen, which was where the family spent most of their time, was heated by a large cast-iron stove. The old wooden table, comfortable chairs and red floor tiles gave the kitchen a homely atmosphere.
>
> They say your schooldays are meant to be 'the best days of your life'. For me, the days away were far better.

D Analysis

1 Paragraphs: What is the topic of each paragraph in the second article?
2 Use of adjectives: How many descriptive adjectives are there in the first article? How many are there in the second paragraph of the second article?
3 Which article shows how and why the place was important to the writer? What are some of the words and phrases that describe the writer's feelings about the place?

E Look at these examples in which two or more sentences with different ideas are joined as one sentence.

a) He was a man. He was nasty. He had a terrible temper.
➢ He was a nasty man with a terrible temper.
b) I lived in a house. It was old. It was always cold.
➢ I lived in an old house which was always cold.
c) I have three brothers. They are older than me. They live in London.
➢ I have three older brothers who live in London.

Now join these sentences in the same way.

1 There is a beach. It is sandy. It has a good restaurant.
2 The hotel is run by a woman. She is old. She makes everyone feel at home.
3 There are a lot of shops. They are wonderful. They stay open till late at night.
4 The Ramada is a hotel. It is first class. It has a marvellous swimming pool.
5 The resort has an airport. It is small. It is only open in the summer.

F Writing task

Write an article for a travel magazine about a holiday destination you know well. The article should make readers want to visit this place.

G Use this paragraph plan.

1 Introduction: You could say you have found a perfect place for holidays. Give an overall description of the place – where it is, how big it is, etc.
2 A closer look: Describe one or two of the special features of the place – the beaches, the countryside, the shops, etc. Use descriptive adjectives to give a feeling of the place (don't just list the number of hotels, etc.).
3 More detail: Describe one thing you remember well or particularly liked in more detail – perhaps a hotel, someone the readers may meet, or the town at night. Try to paint a picture with adjectives.
4 Ending: Say how you feel about the place, and suggest to the readers that they should visit it.

FOCUS FOUR

REVISION AND EXTENSION

The passive ➤ GS 8.2

A Read passages a and b below. Which style would be better in a newspaper report? Why?

a) Yesterday evening, at Hepelworth's Department Store in London, an explosion occurred which killed three people and injured forty others. People believe that a bomb caused the explosion and police later arrested a young man in connection with the incident.

b) Yesterday evening three people were killed and forty others were injured in an explosion at Hepelworth's Department Store in London. It is believed that the explosion was caused by a bomb and a young man was later arrested in connection with the incident.

1 Which passage draws attention immediately to the people who were killed and injured in the explosion? How is this done?
2 If you don't know who the 'people' are, is it better to say *People believe . . .* or *It is believed . . .*? Why?
3 Is it really necessary to say '*police* arrested a young man'? Give reasons for your answer.

B Rewrite the following sentences as if you were reporting them in a newspaper.

1 Yesterday afternoon a fire occurred at a café in George Street which killed two people and injured three others.
2 People believe someone started the fire deliberately.
3 Someone saw a young man running from the café shortly before the fire began.
4 People have reported a number of other fires in the area in the last month.
5 People believe that the same young man may be responsible for all these fires.

Forming opposites

C Study these definitions. How do the prefixes *dis-* and *mis-* and *un-*, *in-* and *im-* change the meaning of a word? With what kind of words can we use these prefixes?

> **spell** write or name the letters of a word.
> **misspell** write or name the wrong letters for a word.
> **obey** do what you are told to do.
> **disobey** not do what you are told to do.
> **aware** in a state of knowing.
> **unaware** in a state of not knowing.

> **accurate** careful, exact.
> **inaccurate** not careful or exact.
> **probable** likely to happen.
> **improbable** not likely to happen.

Give the opposite of the words in the tables below. The first few have been done for you.

VERB	OPPOSITE
like	*dislike*
spell	*misspell*
agree	
believe	
understand	
cover	
dress	
connect	
please	

ADJECTIVE	OPPOSITE
able	*unable*
possible	*impossible*
capable	*incapable*
necessary	
patient	
proper	
correct	
conscious	
complete	
polite	

• The prefixes *il-* and *ir-* are also used to form the opposite of some adjectives (*illegal*, *irregular*, etc.).

> **il·legal** /ɪˈliːgl/ *adj.* not legal.
> **ir·regu·lar** /ɪˈregjʊlə(r)/ *adj.* **1** contrary to rules, to what is normal and established: ~ *attendance.* **2** uneven; not regular in shape, arrangement, etc: *a coast with an ~ outline.* **3** (*gram*) (of words), not having the usual endings or forms in a sentence: '*Child*' *has an ~ plural.* '*Go*' *is an ~ verb.*

SPEAKING

A Problem solving

In pairs or small groups, look carefully at the photos above and decide what could or must have happened to the woman between the time the first and the last photos were taken.

B Discussion

1 Why do you think photographs like the ones above are so important?
2 Which would you rather have to remind you of a special event: a video tape or photos? Why?
3 What are your earliest memories as a child?

READING

A Read this text quickly. Then choose the sentence (A–G) that best summarizes each paragraph (1–5). There is one sentence that you don't need to use. An example is given (0).

0	C

One day, more than sixty years ago, a young man had an accident in which he was knocked off his motorbike. He was taken to hospital but the doctors who examined him found no injuries apart from a few bruises and some slight bleeding from one ear. The young man couldn't remember being knocked off his bike, but that often happens in such accidents.

FOCUS ONE

| 1 |

This accident happened when the young man was 22 years old. The date was August, 1933. A few days later, he was examined again and at first seemed to be normal. Then he was asked how old he was. To the doctor's astonishment, he claimed to be 11 years old. He also insisted that the date was February, 1922. What is more, he was unable to remember anything that had happened in the previous 11 years.

| 2 |

As time went by, the young man began to recall some of his lost memories. He even remembered living in Australia between the ages of 15 and 20. However, the two years before he had the accident were still a total blank. He was unable to recall ever being in the village he had lived in since his return from Australia. He couldn't even remember the names and faces of his friends or colleagues at work.

| 3 |

Despite these serious problems, he was able to take up his old job in the village again. For a time, however, he often got lost while walking around, and often found it difficult to remember what he had done during the day. Nevertheless, he eventually recovered all his memory except for one important detail. He was never able to remember the last few minutes just before the accident, or the actual accident itself.

| 4 |

Since 1933, many more such cases have been recorded. The cause is either an accident involving injuries to the head or a certain type of illness in which the brain is affected. At first, nothing seems to be seriously wrong. The patients appear to talk normally. Then it turns out that they are convinced they are years younger. They have no memory of the 'missing years'.

| 5 |

The young man who was knocked off his motorbike in 1933 was able gradually to recover the missing years. Some people, however, never do so. This permanent loss of important memories is often accompanied by serious and unpleasant changes in their personalities. As a result, their relationship with their families, friends and loved ones can be badly damaged.

A He managed to make almost a complete recovery.

B The pattern is the same in other cases.

C At first nothing seemed to be very wrong.

D Not everyone is so lucky.

E The mystery of what caused the accident remains.

F Essential parts of his memory were still lost.

G A simple question revealed something serious.

B Work in pairs or groups. Read out the parts of each paragraph which helped you to decide on your answers.

Example: Paragraph 0: C

➤ *The doctors who examined him found no injuries apart from a few bruises and some slight bleeding from one ear. The young man couldn't remember being knocked off his bike, but that often happens in such accidents.*

LANGUAGE STUDY

A Explain the difference in meaning.

1 I can't remember doing all these things.
2 I can't remember to do all these things.
3 Can you remind me to do these things?
4 Can you remember me doing these things?

Which sentence means

a) Tell me later that I have to do these things.
b) I'll probably forget I have to do them.
c) Are you sure I did them?
d) Perhaps I did them, but I can't remember.

B Complete the sentences below using the word in bold. Do NOT change this word. Use the gerund form (-ing) or the infinitive with to.

1 I hope you won't forget to pay these bills.
   remember   I hope you'll _____ these bills.

2 Tell me tomorrow that I have to pay them.
   remind   Will you _____ I have to pay them?

3 Are you sure you paid those bills yesterday?
   remember   Do you _____ yesterday?

4 Yes, of course I'm sure I paid them. Aren't you?
   remember   Don't you _____ them?

5 You did another exercise like this. Do you remember?
   remember   Do you _____ like this?

6 I remember that you did it even if you don't.
   remember   I _____ even if you don't.

7 Tell me so that I don't forget to give you a break.
   remind   Please _____ you a break.

8 Don't forget that you have to do this homework.
   remember   Please _____ this homework.

LISTENING 📼

A You will hear five people talking about an accident. Match the number of the speaker (1–5) with the letter (A–F) that describes the person speaking. There is one letter you don't need.

A The person that had the accident

B Someone who lives with the person who had the accident

C Someone who deals with people with possible brain damage

D The person that caused the accident

E Someone who saw the accident

F Someone who works in a hospital

Speaker 1 ☐

Speaker 2 ☐

Speaker 3 ☐

Speaker 4 ☐

Speaker 5 ☐

B Now listen a second time. This time work in pairs or groups of three. Discuss answers to the questions below.

1 From what the first speaker says, whose fault do you think the accident was?

2 Whose car do you think the second speaker is talking about?

3 Describe what happened to the second speaker at that time.

4 Who do you think the third speaker is talking about?

5 Describe what happened in hospital after the accident.

6 Whose problem is the fourth speaker talking about?

7 Describe the problem itself.

8 What does the fifth speaker think will happen in regard to this problem?

SPEAKING

Think about these questions. Then tell each other your answers to them.

1 How do you remember new words you learn in English?

2 Imagine you are preparing for a long trip. You have to get a passport, buy tickets and plan what to take with you. What would you do to make sure you don't forget anything?

3 Some people are better at remembering people's faces than their names. Others are very good at remembering numbers but not so good at remembering new words. What about you? What are you good and not so good at remembering?

VOCABULARY

A What is the correct preposition?

1 My friend, Barbara, was almost killed _____ an accident.

2 She was taken _____ hospital afterwards.

3 There were some injuries _____ her head and face.

4 They kept her _____ observation overnight.

5 Since then, she has complained _____ her memory.

6 She says there are gaps _____ it.

7 She was later examined _____ a specialist.

8 He thinks that _____ any luck, she'll be all right soon.

9 In other words, her memory will return _____ normal.

B Now use the words in capital letters to form a word that fills each space. An example is given (0).

Barbara saw a doctor who is a (0)_*specialist*_ in such cases. Her powers of (1)_____ aren't as good as they used to be and at times she is very (2)_____ but the doctor has (3)_____ predicted that in time she will make a complete (4)_____. He believes she is making very (5)_____ progress in this direction. Of course, not all such (6)_____ come true, but the doctor is usually very (7)_____. As for the cuts and bruises she had, they have healed almost (8)_____. Barbara herself is very (9)_____ to be alive. As one of the people who examined her at hospital said, she was (10)_____ lucky.

0 SPECIALIZE	6	PREDICT
1 CONCENTRATE	7	RELY
2 FORGET	8	COMPLETE
3 CONFIDENT	9	THANK
4 RECOVER	10	EXTRAORDINARY
5 SATISFY		

C Complete the sentences below with one of the following words. Use each word only once.

injure   damage   wound   hurt   spoil   ruin

1 I hope I didn't _____ your feelings when I said that.

2 A few bad stains can _____ your clothes.

3 The food will _____ unless it is kept cool.

4 The storm didn't _____ the house.

5 Guns _____ and kill thousands of people every year.

6 Cars _____ and kill even more people every year.

LANGUAGE STUDY

should have, *must have* or *might have*?
➤ GS 7.4, 7.5, 7.8

A Complete the sentences below with *should*, *must*, or *might*. Use each word only once.

1 What do you mean you didn't see the red lights? You _____ have seen them! It's impossible not to see them!

2 The policeman _____ have seen you, but I don't think he did.

3 You really _____ have stopped at the red lights. It's the law!

B Rewrite the second sentence in each pair. Use no more than five words including the word in bold. Do NOT change this word.

1 Barbara wasn't wearing a safety-belt, despite regulations.
should Barbara _____ a safety belt.

2 It was the other driver's fault. He didn't stop at the red light.
should He _____ at the red light but he didn't.

3 It's surprising that her injuries weren't far more serious.
might Barbara's injuries _____ far more serious.

4 In such situations, people often are badly injured or killed.
might She _____ or killed in the accident.

5 I can imagine how worried Barbara's husband was.
must Her husband _____ very worried.

6 I'm sure she looked terrible after the accident.
must She _____ after the accident.

7 It's surprising how quickly the cuts healed.
might The cuts _____ far more slowly.

8 I'm surprised you didn't visit her after the accident.
should You _____ after the accident.

9 I suppose the explanation is that you were very busy.
must You _____ busy.

C Complete each space with one word only. If you think another word is also possible, choose the one you think fits best.

Amnesia is a condition in **(1)**_____ people lose their memories. There are a number of things **(2)**_____ may cause this. Scientists **(3)**_____ have studied the condition say there are different types of amnesia. For example, once a woman **(4)**_____ mother had just died refused to believe the fact, even **(5)**_____ she was actually with her mother **(6)**_____ the time. This type of amnesia,

(7)_____ is usually 'hysterical amnesia', is caused **(8)**_____ the patient's refusal to face an unpleasant fact. Traumatic amnesia is far **(9)**_____ common than hysterical amnesia. It is usually the result **(10)**_____ a head injury.

SPEAKING

A Study the facts below carefully.

A young man whose name is Mike Harris cannot remember what happened to him in an accident one evening last month. There are, however, a few clues. The numbers (1–3) refer to where important events occurred. The locations are shown above.

1 Another accident happened here at about 6 p.m. on the same evening. There was oil and broken glass on the road as a result.

2 Mike's motorbike was later found here, by the side of the road. He was on his way to Oxford.

3 Mike was found wandering in the forest after midnight. He had serious head injuries. His wristwatch, which was broken in the accident, had stopped at 7.48 p.m.

B In pairs or groups discuss these questions.

1 What do you think might or must have happened when Mike passed the scene of the earlier accident?

2 A man in a car saw Mike's motorbike around 8 p.m. Instead of informing the police, he went to a pub where he was overheard talking about the motorbike. What do you think he might or must have thought when he saw the motorbike?

3 What do you think he should have done?

4 What do you think Mike might or must have done between 7.48 p.m. and the time he was found in the forest?

5 Mike was not wearing a safety helmet. It was found strapped to his motorbike. What do you think of this?

USE OF ENGLISH

A Read the passage quickly to get an idea of what it is about. Ignore the spaces.

There are a great **(1)**_____ mistaken ideas about memory. One of the **(2)**_____ common of these is the belief **(3)**_____ you can lose your memory completely and still survive physically. There is only one way to **(4)**_____ this: you can fall into a coma **(5)**_____ which you never recover. However, **(6)**_____ a condition is for all practical purposes the same **(7)**_____ death.

Human memory actually consists **(8)**_____ different memory systems, which interact with **(9)**_____ other. **(10)**_____ memory systems are usually referred **(11)**_____ as the long-term, short–term and sensory memory systems. People said to **(12)**_____ lost their memory are people **(13)**_____ have something wrong with one or more of these systems. If they **(14)**_____ lost all three types of memory, they would be either unconscious **(15)**_____ dead.

```
┌──────────────┐   ┌──────────┐   ┌──────────┐   ┌──────────┐
│ Information in│→ │ Sensory  │→ │Short-term│→ │Long-term │
│              │   │ memory   │   │ memory   │   │ memory   │
└──────────────┘   └──────────┘   └──────────┘   └──────────┘
                                        │
                                        ↓
                                  ┌──────────┐
                                  │Information│
                                  │recalled years│
                                  │ later    │
                                  └──────────┘
```

B Fill in the missing words. Then discuss these questions in pairs or groups.

1 What are the three types of memory system?
2 Which type do you think we use when we

a) remember a smell or a taste?
b) repeat a new word or a phone number we have just heard for the first time?
c) use the grammar system of a language we know well, play a musical instrument we have often played before, or find our way around a city we have lived in for a long time?

VOCABULARY

Word combinations

A Explain the meaning of the word combinations in 1–8 below.

Example: short-term memory
➤ *memory that lasts only for a short time*

1 a long-winded speech
2 a short-sighted person
3 a four-legged animal
4 a user-friendly computer
5 a green-eyed monster
6 a five-hour lecture
7 a twice-yearly event
8 a sweet-smelling flower

B What are the word combinations in English that express the following ideas?

1 a book that publishers say sells better than any other book
2 an athlete that breaks a record
3 a loan which you have to pay back in a short time
4 the opposite of this kind of loan
5 a man or woman whose age is somewhere between 45 and 60
6 a shirt with short sleeves
7 a man with blue eyes
8 a monster with four arms, three eyes and long teeth
9 a book with 112 pages
10 an English lesson that goes on for two hours
11 a fruit that tastes very bitter
12 a recipe that is easy to prepare

FOCUS THREE

SPEAKING

A In pairs or groups of three, find out how good your partners' memories are. First, fill the spaces in the 15 questions (A–O). When you have done this and all agree that the questions are correct, ask each other the completed questions. Keep a record of each answer on a separate piece of paper by writing one of the numbers (1–6) below next to the letter of each question.

B Before you look at the answer key in the box below, discuss these questions with your partners.

1 Which of the things in the questions do people sometimes seem to forget not because they really 'forget' – but for some other reason? What is that reason?

2 Which things do you think it is most serious to forget? Why?

How good is
your memory?

1 **never**
2 **very rarely** – say once every six months
3 **only now and then** – say once every two or three months
4 **sometimes** – say once a month
5 **fairly often** – say once a week
6 **very often** – almost every day

A How often _____ you forget where you have put something; let's say a letter, a bill or something you have bought?

B How often _____ it happen that you don't remember being somewhere where you have been before?

C How often do you forget to _____ a bill or do something someone has asked you to do?

D How often do you forget when something happened even though it _____ happened quite recently?

E How often do you forget someone's name not long after meeting that person and being _____ his or her name?

F How often do you forget a new word you _____ learned recently?

G How often do you forget important details of something? For example, how _____ money you paid not long ago for something expensive.

H How often do you forget the name of someone you _____ to know very well but whom you haven't seen in a long time?

I How often do you forget _____ important information as your telephone number, address, date of birth or where you live?

J How often do you get lost in a place in _____ you have often been before?

K How often do you get lost somewhere you have been only once or _____ before?

L How often do you forget information you have only recently learned? For instance, the time you are _____ to arrive at a party or meet a friend.

M How often do you get confused about _____ someone has told you? For example, a friend said you promised to meet at 5.15 but you thought it was 5.50.

N How often do you forget what you have just said? For instance, you stop and say, 'What was I _____ about?'

O How often do you forget what people have just told you? For instance, someone says 'My friend, Mary, is coming tomorrow.' Then, a few minutes later when they _____ the name 'Mary' again, you ask 'Who's Mary?'

SCORES

85–90 Very bad, especially if you scored more than one point in answer to question I.

70–84 Not very good but don't worry. Perhaps you're just tired, or did you get a score of more than 1 to question I, too?

50–70 A little below average, or perhaps you're just not very interested in what people tell you?

40–50 Pretty average.

25–40 Above average.

15–25 Congratulations, is your name 'Supermemory'?

WRITING

Transactional letter 4

You may have to write a letter asking someone for information. You will need to know some useful phrases and pay special attention to word order.

A Sample task

You are thinking of renting a holiday farmhouse. Read the advertisement and your notes, and then write a letter to Mrs Sorrento.

> **Charming farmhouse between Rome and Naples. Most dates available.**
> **Sleeps 5. Pool.**
> **Contact Mrs Caroline Sorrento, Box 140.**

Available July? *Prices & extras?*
No. of bedrooms? *Anything for children to do?*
Pool private? *Local airport + car hire?*
Where exactly? *Rome or Naples easier?*

B Read this letter.

Dear Mrs Sorrento

I am replying to your advertisement in The Times on March 11 for the farmhouse, and there are a number of things I would like to ask.

I am interested in renting the farmhouse for the last two weeks of July for myself, my wife and two children aged 7 and 9. Could you let me know whether it would be free then, how much it would cost, and what the price includes?

Could you also send me some more details about the farmhouse itself? It would be useful to know exactly where it is, how many bedrooms it has, and whether the pool is private. I would also be grateful if you could give me an idea of what sort of activities we could organize for the children.

Finally, I would be grateful if you could let me know if there is a local airport and whether it is possible to hire a car there. If not, could you tell me whether it would be easier for us to fly to Rome or to Naples?

I look forward to hearing from you.

Yours sincerely,

C Rewrite these questions. An example is given.

1 When does the last train leave?
Could you tell me *when the last train leaves?*

2 Is there a good bus service?
Do you know _____

3 What did he tell you?
I need to know _____

4 How much did it cost?
Could you tell me _____

5 Did they enjoy their holiday?
Do you know _____

6 Will the house be free in June?
I would be grateful if you could tell me
_____

Now find five examples of indirect questions in the letter in B.

D Writing task

Below is part of an advertisement for a language school. Using your notes, write to the Principal telling him a little about yourself and including the questions you want to ask.

> **LAKELAND LANGUAGE SERVICES**
> Easter and summer courses. All levels.
> Accommodation arranged.
> **Fees from £150 per week.**

August – wks 1 and 2. Any places left? Course dates? How far from family to school? Family to provide meals? Collection from airport? Bus / train details please. Accommodation included or extra? How long from airport to school? Possible to change families if necessary?

E Use this paragraph plan.

1 Introduction: Say why you are writing.
2 Tell the Principal about yourself; say when you would like to come, and ask about the course dates.
3 Cover the notes that refer to questions about the host family and accommodation.
4 Include the questions about transport.
5 Finish in a suitable way.

F Useful phrases for asking questions

I would be grateful if you could tell me/ let me know
Could you please (also) tell me/ let me know
It would be useful to know
Could you please send me details of

REVISION AND EXTENSION

Complete the text by choosing the best answer, A, B, C or D.

Amazing mice

Researchers in the United States have discovered a powerful drug, pregnenolone, that can improve **(1)**_____ in mice.

In the laboratory, mice were trained to associate a sound with a shock a few seconds later. They had to **(2)**_____ their way through a maze to avoid the shock. Then some of the mice were given pregnenolone. The mice that had been injected with the drug showed such a **(3)**_____ improvement in memory that the researchers were astonished.

It was already known that pregnenolone can help people **(4)**_____ from spinal cord **(5)**_____ after car crashes or falls, but **(6)**_____ this new research shows is that it plays an even more important role. The results suggest that it may one day be possible to treat people **(7)**_____ memories have been affected by old age or disease.

Scientists have already tried out the drug on a number of patients **(8)**_____ had been **(9)**_____ affected by Alzheimer's disease and who were **(10)**_____ of **(11)**_____ members of their own family. **(12)**_____ they only showed a **(13)**_____ improvement, if any, but the scientists believe that the doses they used **(14)**_____ have been either too high or too low. They are confident that they will reach their **(15)**_____ aim of producing a drug that will be safe and effective for humans.

1 **A** recollection **C** reminder
   B recognition **D** memory

2 **A** remember **C** review
   B remind **D** realize

3 **A** grand **C** decisive
   B significant **D** important

4 **A** recover **C** rescue
   B return **D** regain

5 **A** harm **C** hurt
   B damage **D** injury

6 **A** which **C** who
   B what **D** that

7 **A** who **C** whose
   B their **D** which

8 **A** who **C** which
   B they **D** whom

9 **A** badly **C** hardly
   B wrongly **D** heavily

10 **A** disabled **C** unaware
   B incapable **D** unconscious

11 **A** reviewing **C** reminding
   B recognizing **D** realizing

12 **A** Improbably **C** Unlikely
   B Unfortunately **D** Importantly

13 **A** petty **C** poor
   B mean **D** small

14 **A** should **C** will
   B ought **D** might

15 **A** long-distance **C** long-sight
   B long-time **D** long-term

LISTENING

Listen to the telephone conversation in which Jane gives Harry directions to her new house. Then complete the notes that Harry made about how to get to Jane's house.

Take A34 to Peartree Roundabout. Turn

(1)_____. Go to Kidlington, take

(2)_____ exit. Down

(3)_____ Road, over flyover. Turn left

50 m after **(4)**_____. Sign to

(5)_____. Down drive for one mile,

past first farm with **(6)**_____.

Continue another half mile to Middle Farm (with

(7)_____). Watch out for

(8)_____ ramps between farms.

15
THE MAN IN THE PARK

SPEAKING

A Talking on your own

Work in pairs as Student A and B. Speak for about one minute.

Student A: Describe and compare what the man looks like in each picture. Say what you think might have happened to him.

Student B: Describe and compare the situations in both pictures. Say how you would feel if you were in situations like these.

B Discussion

1 What do you think can be done to help people who have no jobs or money?

2 Why do you think people are often unwilling to help those less fortunate than themselves?

3 How do you think richer countries can help poorer ones?

READING

A A man is talking to his girlfriend on the phone. Read what he says. Can you guess what she is saying to him in the numbered gaps?

Example **(0)** ➤ *You mean the man you used to work for?*

I've told you about Kevin Rogers before, haven't I? **(0)**_____ That's right. He used to be my boss. He was a real slave-driver. Never satisfied. Kept telling us we had to work harder. I got another job as soon as I could. **(1)**_____ Oh? Have I told you all that before? Well, you know it's been at least five years since I last saw him. I mean, that's what I thought until last week. Did I tell you what happened then? **(2)**_____ Yes, last week. You see, I was on my way back to the office just after lunch. There's this small park there and **(3)**_____ Near the restaurant where I had lunch, of course. Anyway, I decided to have a little stroll. And

FOCUS ONE

there was one of those beggars there. Shabby and unshaven. You see so many of them now, don't you? And I had a good look at him. There was something familiar about him. **(4)____** Yes, that's what I've just said. He asked me for some change. He said something like, 'It's been a long time since I had a good meal.' So I gave him a few coins.

Well, it wasn't until I got back to the office that it dawned on me. **(5)____** Where I'd seen him before, of course. But it just didn't seem possible. Then today – I still can't get over this – I ran into this old friend of mine. Someone I'd worked with when Rogers was our boss. **(6)____** No, I'm sure you've never met him. And would you believe it, he asked me if I'd heard about Rogers. So I said to him, 'What do you mean? Heard what?' And then he said, 'I thought you knew.' That's when he told me. **(7)____** What happened to Rogers, of course. You see, apparently it had been in all the papers, though I never saw the article. **(8)____** The story about Rogers, of course. He'd stolen a lot of money from the company and they sent him to prison. **(9)____** No, no. He was in prison. This all happened about four years ago. But guess what my friend said then? Listen. These were his exact words. 'They won't give him a job, not after what happened. He's probably sleeping in parks and begging money from people now.' So, you see, it must have been him.

(10)____ Rogers, of course. Kevin Rogers. Haven't you been listening?

B Work in pairs or groups. Read the text aloud and stop each time you come to any of the words in *italics* below. Ask your partners who the speaker is talking about (1–5).

I	The speaker means
me	1 himself
my	2 his girlfriend
You you	3 the man in the park
they	4 the friend he saw later
He he	5 somebody who is not identified
him	exactly
his	

C Now listen to the complete conversation on cassette. Then answer these questions.

1 How did the speaker get on with his boss six years ago?
2 When does he think he last saw his ex-boss?
3 Describe what the speaker was doing when he saw him.
4 What did he notice about his ex-boss when he saw him again?
5 When was he absolutely certain it was his ex-boss?
6 Explain what had happened to his ex-boss since the speaker had last seen him.

VOCABULARY

Find a word or phrase in the text that means

1 someone who forces others to work very hard
2 a slow walk for pleasure
3 someone who asks others for money
4 worn-out or cheap-looking
5 coins or money of no great value
6 it became clear
7 to recover from an illness, a shock or a great surprise
8 answer a question when you have very little information

LANGUAGE STUDY

Talking about the last time you did something

A Complete the sentences below.

1 It's _____ a long time _____ I last heard from Roger.
2 The last time I _____ a letter from him _____ a long time ago.
3 I _____ heard from him _____ a long time, either.
4 It _____ more than a year _____ that I last _____ a letter from him.

B Rewrite the second sentence in each pair. Use no more than five words including the word in bold. Do NOT change this word.

1 The last time I saw Dan was five years ago.
   ago   It was five years _____ Dan.
2 I haven't heard from him for ages.
   since   It's been _____ from him.
3 The last time I heard from Mary was more than a year ago.
   more   It's been _____ I last heard from Mary.
4 I last saw her a year ago.
   for   I _____ a year.
5 Mary hasn't seen Dan for a long time.
   been   It's _____ Mary last saw Dan.
6 I haven't seen either of them for years.
   last   The _____ either of them was years ago.
7 When was the last time you saw Mary?
   long   How _____ you last saw Mary?
8 I'm sure it was more than a year ago.
   least   It must _____ a year ago.

'Partner in crime' did it all for love

A property expert who was described (0)___as___ a man who would have had a bright future if he had not fallen for a mysterious and beautiful woman, was (1)_____ to five years in prison yesterday.

Kevin Rogers, 39, of Hurst Road, Horsham, Sussex, was employed by Selford Holdings, a London company with a broad (2)_____ of investments in hotels, golf courses and shopping centres. His downfall began when he met someone (3)_____ as 'La Contessa'.

'I was completely in her (4)_____. I did everything she asked me to do. It didn't matter to me how dangerous it was or that I was (5)_____ the law,' he told the court.

'La Contessa', whose real name was Pilar Gutiérrez, (6)_____ as an agent for Rogers' employers. She found property in Spain and Portugal that was about to be (7)_____ down or needed extensive repairs and then (8)_____ Selford Holdings to buy them. The London company did not realize that the prices they were paying were considerably more than the real (9)_____ of these properties. The original owners paid her very large (10)_____ of money each time this happened.

Rogers, whose job it was to estimate how much the property was really worth, admitted that he accepted a large (11)_____ of the profits Gutiérrez made in this way. Rogers claimed that at first he wasn't (12)_____ of what she was doing. 'When I finally (13)_____ through it all, I warned her not to do it. However, I was already in love with her, so instead of telling my employers what was really going on, I became her partner in crime,' he said.

Gutiérrez, who has been (14)_____ of accepting illegal payments of money and other crimes was last seen in England on the same day Rogers was arrested. She is believed to be (15)_____ somewhere in South America.

USE OF ENGLISH

A **Read the newspaper article above. Then decide which word, A, B, C or D, best fits each space. An example is given (0).**

0 **A** like   **C** how
   B for   **D** as
1 **A** punished   **C** subjected
   B sentenced   **D** ordered
2 **A** range   **C** extent
   B width   **D** number
3 **A** referred   **C** spoken
   B called   **D** known
4 **A** command   **C** power
   B strength   **D** use
5 **A** breaking   **C** smashing
   B cutting   **D** crashing
6 **A** handled   **C** treated
   B behaved   **D** acted
7 **A** pulled   **C** put
   B brought   **D** taken
8 **A** advised   **C** suggested
   B recommended   **D** proposed

9 **A** cost   **C** value
   B expense   **D** quality
10 **A** sums   **C** totals
    B numbers   **D** figures
11 **A** size   **C** degree
    B share   **D** area
12 **A** sensible   **C** aware
    B sensitive   **D** apparent
13 **A** saw   **C** glimpsed
    B looked   **D** watched
14 **A** criticized   **C** accused
    B attacked   **D** doubted
15 **A** hiding   **C** covering
    B concealing   **D** escaping

B **In pairs or groups, discuss your answers to the questions below.**

1 What kind of job did Rogers have and what did he do in this job?
2 Explain how 'la Contessa' made a lot of money.
3 How was Rogers able to help her to do this and to make money himself?

LANGUAGE STUDY

suggest doing or *suggest that ... should do*
➤ GS 12.5

A Imagine that a woman said the first four things (a–d) to you yesterday. Match them with the sentences (1–4) to report her suggestions today.

a) Why don't we go for a walk?
b) Why don't you go for a walk?
c) Let's go for a walk in the park.
d) Why don't you go for a walk in the park?

1 Yesterday she suggested going for a walk in the park.
2 She suggested that I should go for a walk in the park.
3 She suggested that I should go for a walk.
4 Yesterday she suggested going for a walk.

B One of these rules is incorrect. Which one?

1 If you suggest something that you and someone else are going to do, you can talk about it later by saying 'I suggested ...ing'.
2 If you suggest that someone should do something that you aren't going to do, you can't use 'suggest ...ing' to talk about it later. You have to say 'I suggested that ... should...'.
3 If you suggest something that you and someone else are going to do, you can't use 'suggest that ... should' to talk about it later.

C Yesterday Mary said the things below to you. Report her suggestions today. If there are two different ways of doing this, say both.

Example: Let's meet for lunch.

➤ *She suggested meeting for lunch.* or
She suggested that we should meet for lunch.

1 Let's do this exercise.
2 Why don't you do this exercise?
3 Wouldn't it be nice to go on holiday together?
4 Let's see a film.
5 Why don't you buy some new clothes?
6 What about having a party tomorrow?
7 Why don't you take a taxi home? It's much quicker.
8 Why don't you phone me later?
9 Wouldn't it be a good idea to meet for lunch?
10 What about going to that new Italian place?

VOCABULARY

cost, value, expense, price or *worth*?

Complete the following sentences with one of the words above.

1 What? You paid £30 for this? It's not even _____ £10!
2 The _____ of living increased by 3% this year.
3 You can see the _____ of the book on the back cover.
4 The _____ of the dollar against the D mark and Yen has fallen.
5 He travels everywhere at the company's _____.

Phrasal verbs

A How many phrasal verbs can you find in the following examples?

1 She made up all sorts of untrue stories but eventually he saw through them.
2 She saw to it that he got half the money.
3 They kept on breaking the law.
4 Now he says he wants to make up for his crimes.
5 How did she talk him into breaking the law?

B Say the phrasal verb in the examples above that means

a) make sure that something happens   d) invent
b) compensate for   e) persuade
c) not be deceived by   f) continue

C Complete these sentences using the word in bold.

1 I don't think anybody will be taken in by that story.
   see I'm sure that everybody _____ story.
2 It isn't possible to compensate for the harm you've done.
   make You can't _____ harm you've done.
3 These things must be done, so make sure that they are!
   see You must _____ these things are done.
4 How did she persuade you to spend so much money?
   talk How did she _____ so much money?
5 It's important to do these exercises again and again.
   keep You have to _____ these exercises.
6 Don't invent excuses in order not to do them.
   make Don't _____ in order to get out of doing them.

D There are two additional phrasal verbs in the exercise you have just done. What are they and what do they mean?

LISTENING 😐

A **You are going to hear a conversation between a man and a woman. Answer questions 1–8 below by writing:**
   M: (for Man)
   W: (for Woman)
   N: (for Neither)

Who seems very friendly at first?	**0**	*W*
Who is looking at a written record of an earlier conversation?	**1**	
Who claims not to understand the purpose of the other's questions?	**2**	
Who has some embarrassing information about the other's finances?	**3**	
Who urges the other to do something?	**4**	
Who wants to talk to someone else?	**5**	
Who wants to leave?	**6**	
Who accuses the other of having lied?	**7**	
Who has the means of letting the other person go?	**8**	

B **Listen to the conversation once more. Then explain to each other the answers to the questions below.**

1 What do you think the woman's job is?
2 Where do you think the two people are as they are talking?
3 What exactly is the information that one of them has and which the other person didn't want anybody to know about?
4 What was the lie one person told earlier?
5 What exactly does one of the speakers advise the other person to do or not to do?

USE OF ENGLISH

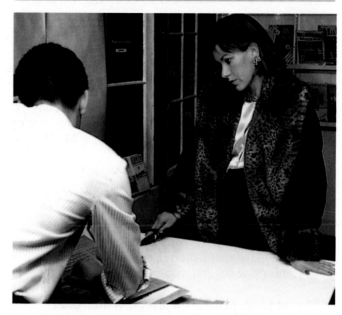

A **Put a tick (✓) next to each line that you think is correct. If you think a word should not be in a line, underline that word.**

 0 Pilar Gutiérrez, who <u>she</u> was known as la Contessa,
00 and Kevin Rogers were both criminals. Before his trial ✓
 1 took a place, he had always insisted that he had not
 2 known that what she was doing, but the police did not
 3 believe in him. They told him so, but Kevin kept
 4 saying that he was an innocent. Shortly before his trial
 5 began, one of the detectives, whose name was
 6 Sally Kennedy, interviewed him in the jail. The day
 7 before, she had found out that he had very much more
 8 money in his bank account than which he should have
 9 had. She was very polite and friendly at the first but
10 Rogers didn't want to talk. She said him that she
11 wanted to discuss about what he had said the day
12 before. Then she showed to him a bank statement. This
13 statement was proof that he had lied to the police. It
14 showed that Gutiérrez had been paid thousands of
15 pounds into his bank account.

B **Now work in pairs or groups. Go through the text above sentence by sentence and do the following things.**

1 Find the one complete sentence in the text that has no mistakes in it. Read that sentence aloud.
2 How many sentences can you find that have only one mistake in them? Correct them and then read aloud the corrected sentences.
3 How many sentences have two mistakes in them? Again, correct them and read the corrected sentences aloud.
4 One sentence has three mistakes in it. Correct all three mistakes and read the corrected sentence aloud.

LANGUAGE STUDY ➤ GS 12

A Work in pairs. One of you reads aloud the beginning of each sentence (1–6). The other reads the second part of each sentence.

Example:

➤ **Student 1** *She urged*
Student 2 *him to tell the truth.*

1	She wondered	a)	of lying.
2	She criticized him	b)	that he should tell the
3	She urged him		truth.
4	She accused him	c)	if he was telling the truth.
5	She warned him	d)	not to lie.
6	She suggested	e)	to tell her the truth.
		f)	for not telling the truth.

B Now complete the second sentence in each pair. Use no more than five words including the word in bold. Do NOT change this word.

1 'Am I using the correct form?' students often ask.
wonder Students often _____ the correct form.

2 'Don't translate word for word,' teachers often tell students.
warn Teachers often _____ word for word.

3 'Try harder,' teachers often tell students.
urge Teachers often _____ harder.

4 'You're breaking the law,' a policeman once told me.
accused Once a policeman _____ the law.

5 'You're late again,' my teacher said to me.
criticized My teacher _____ late again.

6 'If I were you, I'd get a haircut,' my friend told me.
suggested My friend _____ a haircut.

7 'Oh, you've made the same mistake,' my teacher often tells me.
criticizes My teacher often _____ the same mistake.

8 'You can't park there,' the policeman said to us.
warned The policeman _____ there.

9 'Where can I park?' I thought to myself.
wondered I _____ park.

10 'It's important to get a good job,' my father told me.
urged My father _____ a good job.

11 'Why don't you go to bed early?' my mother often says.
suggests My mother often _____ to bed early.

12 'You're lazy,' parents sometimes tell children.
criticize Parents sometimes _____ lazy.

VOCABULARY

Verb and noun combinations: *have* and *make*

A Which of the things below can we *have* in English? Which can we *make*? Read them aloud. Then say if they use *have* or *make*.

- progress
- a good time
- an argument with someone
- a conversation
- a suggestion
- a good look at someone

- a mess of something
- a good night's sleep
- a word with someone
- a promise to someone
- the right decision
- a full confession

B Complete the second sentence in each pair. Use no more than five words including the word in bold. Do NOT change this word.

1 I hope you enjoy yourself at the party.
time I hope _____ at the party.

2 Do you feel that your English is getting better?
progress Do you think you _____ in English?

3 I don't want to argue with you about this.
argument I don't want to _____ you about this.

4 I'd like to suggest something to you.
suggestion Do you mind if I _____ to you?

5 I'd like to talk to you very briefly about this.
word Could I _____ you about this?

6 The thief confessed to everything he had done.
full The thief _____ confession.

7 He did the job very badly.
mess He _____ the job.

8 In the exam, you'll probably talk about this.
conversation You'll probably _____ this in the exam.

9 We have to decide quickly about this matter.
decision We have to _____ about this matter.

10 Would you look at this carefully, please?
careful Please _____ at this.

11 Dan promised sincerely that he wouldn't watch so much TV.
sincere Dan _____ not to watch so much TV.

12 Did you sleep well last night?
good Did you _____ sleep?

C Work in pairs or groups. One of you reads aloud a first sentence from 1–12 above. The others, with books closed, try to remember what the complete second sentence was.

WRITING

Report 2

You may be asked to write a report that is like a survey, for example on how people in your country spend their leisure time, where they go on holiday, etc. You will probably not have this information, but you can use your imagination. If you are simply reporting 'factual' information, the style should be neutral. Avoid emotional, poetic or informal language.

A Sample task

You have been asked by your careers teacher to find out what happened to people from your school after they left. Write a report of about 180 words for the careers department, explaining what you found out.

B In the following sample answer there are eleven extra words that you do not need. Find these.

This report looks at the careers of students who have left from St Anthony's, and is based on questionnaires were received from over 300 former students.

Over the past few years, the majority of students (63%) have continued on with their education after they leaving school. Most of these have gone to the university, and the others have done vocational courses at Colleges of Further Education.

About a quarter part of the students have found jobs after leaving school. Some of these jobs are with employers in the local area, but others are in London or even in abroad. About half of the students said that they were unemployed for several of months before finding work. A small minority of students (1.5%) went straight into their family businesses.

About 12% of the students were been unable to find work and have been unemployed for over a year. Most of these were students who were failed their examinations, although a few had passed with reasonable grades.

In general, more and more leavers are going on to university or further education, and this trend will probably continue as long as the unemployment is high.

C Look at some of the words and phrases we can use when presenting the results of a survey.

All of	Some of
Most of	(Just over) a quarter of
The majority of	A minority of
Over 90% of	A small number of
Three quarters of	A few of
A significant number of	Very few
Many of	None of
Half of	

Rewrite the following sentences using the word in bold. An example is given (0).

0 60% of people go abroad once a year.
   majority
   The majority of people go abroad once a year.

1 3% of people go to the same place every year.
   very _____

2 26% of families with children stay in England.
   over _____

3 49% of travellers hire a car when they are abroad.
   half _____

4 75% of families with children travel by car.
   three _____

D Writing task

You have been asked by your local tourist office to carry out a survey of where people who live in your area go for their summer holidays. Write them a report giving your findings.

E Write a paragraph on each of the following points. The paragraph order can be changed, so that what the majority of people do comes in the first paragraph after the introduction.

1 Introduction: Say what your report was meant to find out and what your information is based on.
2 Say how many local people go abroad. You could mention some of the destinations – for example, the Far East.
3 Explain how many people stay in your country, what sort of people they are, and where they tend to go on holiday.
4 Talk about people who do not fall into the two categories above – for example, people who have to work or cannot afford to have holidays.
5 Write a short conclusion, saying what general patterns or trends you have found.

Remember to keep the style fairly neutral, as you are simply reporting 'facts'.

REVISION AND EXTENSION

Further forms of the future ➤ GS 13.3

A Read the following notes about Jennifer's year.

March 15-30	Stay with Chris in Spain.
June 1-7	Half-term – revise for exams.
July 20	Take final exams.
August 1	Move to London.
August 1-30	Look for a job and somewhere to live.
September-December 15	Live and work in London.
December 20	Travel to Paris for Christmas.

Now put the verbs in brackets into the correct tense. Here are two examples.

On March 20th, she will be staying in Spain.
By April, she will have come back from Spain.

1 On June 5th, she (revise) for her exams.
2 By June 8th, half-term (finish).
3 On August 1st, she (move) to London.
4 During August, she (look) for a job.
5 By the end of August, she hopes she (find) a job.
6 She thinks she (find) somewhere to live by September.
7 In November, she (live and work) in London.
8 On December 20th, she (travel) to Paris.

Four types of infinitive

B Look at these examples.

a) He is said to live in London.
b) He is said to have lived in London.
c) He is said to be living in London.
d) He is said to have been living in London.

Which sentence can be rephrased as follows?

1 They say that he is living in London.
2 They say that he lives in London.
3 They say that he has been/was living in London.
4 They say that he has lived in London.

C Read the following passage.

SUNKEN TREASURE

EXPERTS FROM THE BRITISH MUSEUM have announced the discovery of a Spanish ship which sank in a storm off the Scottish coast over 400 years ago. Divers have found gold bars on the sea bed near the wreck, which the experts believe are only a small part of the ship's precious cargo. According to the British Museum, the ship is in good condition and the cargo is worth millions of pounds.

Now write out the following sentences using an appropriate infinitive form (*to do, to have done, to be doing, to have been doing*).

1 Divers are reported (find) a Spanish ship.
2 Experts are reported (study) objects from it.
3 The ship is thought (sink) 400 years ago.
4 The ship is thought (return) to Spain.
5 The ship is believed (carry) gold bars.
6 The gold is believed (lie) on the sea bed.
7 The ship is said (be) in good condition.
8 The gold is said (be) worth millions of pounds.

Review of tenses

D Put the verbs in this extract from a letter into the correct tense.

I'm sorry I (not write) for so long, but we (be) very busy recently with the new house, and we (not have) any time at all to ourselves.

Luckily, the worst part is over now. We (have) to stay in a hotel until we could move in, and we (be) there for three months. Still it (give) us a chance to do lots of major repairs; a few weeks ago we (have) the roof mended, and we (put) in central heating too.

We (live) in the house since last Monday, and I (be) very busy redecorating. We (do) all the rooms downstairs, and they're very nice. We (buy) all the furniture we need, and (lay) new carpets. Last week, I (make) the curtains, so now everything looks lovely.

Upstairs, it's a different story. I (paint) the bedrooms this week, but I (not finish) yet. The bathroom is in a terrible mess too, as I (put) up wallpaper, and there's still paper and glue everywhere. Anyway, with a bit of luck, we should be finished by the weekend.

E Complete the second sentence in each pair. Use no more than five words including the word in bold. Do NOT change this word.

1 I mustn't forget that I have to buy some cheese.
   remember I _____ some cheese.
2 It's possible that he went to London.
   might He _____ to London.
3 I haven't seen such a good film for ages.
   since It's _____ such a good film.
4 The last time he wrote home was two months ago.
   for He _____ two months.
5 He said to me, 'Let's have a Chinese meal.'
   suggested He _____ Chinese meal.
6 She said to him 'If I were you I'd ring your lawyer.'
   suggested She _____ ring his lawyer.
7 If it doesn't stop snowing we won't get home.
   unless We won't _____ snowing.
8 You were supposed to give the letter to Peter.
   should You _____ to Peter.

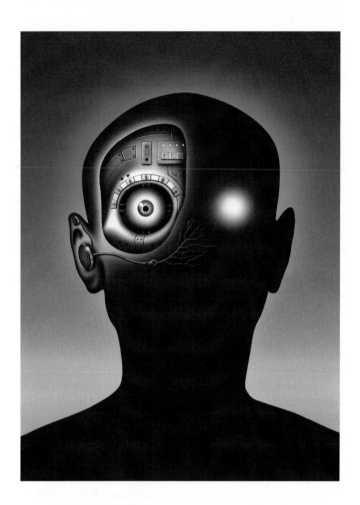

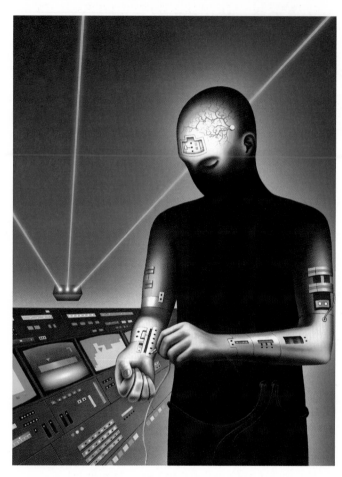

SPEAKING

A Talking on your own

Work in pairs as Student A and B. Student A should speak for about one minute and Student B for about 20 seconds.

Student A: Describe and compare the images in the pictures. Say how you think they show us the future.

Student B: Say whether you would enjoy living in a future like this.

B Discussion

1 What things do you think could be done by robots in the future?
2 Will robots ever replace people completely? Why? Why not?
3 What two predictions would you make about what the world will be like in the year 2050?

READING

A Read the sentences (A–H) on the next page and decide which sentences fill each gap in this text. There is one sentence you do not need.

A famous philosopher once said, 'The one thing the study of the past teaches us is that the future is never how people imagine it will be.' **0** *F* Only twenty years earlier, it had been predicted that wars between nations would be 'a thing of the past' and that in the future 'disputes will be settled only through 'reason and good will by people sitting around a table.'

In 1946, physicists predicted that within twenty years, most of the world's energy would be supplied by nuclear power. **I** In 1951, a famous surgeon said that he and his colleagues were confident that 'by the end of the 1950s, a cure for most if not all cancers will have been found.' In 1954, an American economist predicted Americans would go on getting

FOCUS ONE

richer and richer. **2** [ ] In the year 1963, a German politician said that 'within twenty years, a full-scale atomic war between the United States and the Soviet Union will have been fought, mainly in Germany.' **3** [ ]

In the year 1969, an automation engineer working for Max Factor Cosmetics in Britain said that 'within twenty or twenty-five years factories that today employ hundreds of workers will need only five or ten computer technicians to run them.' **4** [ ]

In the same year, an astrophysicist in Texas predicted that 'now that man has at last set foot on the moon, other space voyages will soon take men to Mars and other planets.' In the early 1970s, there were many predictions that before the end of the century most homes in the United States, Europe and Japan would have computers in them. **5** [ ]

Long before 1980, it was predicted that instead of letting nature and luck choose their children's characteristics, people would have to decide which characteristics they wanted their children to inherit from them and previous generations in their families. **6** [ ] We may be able to have 'undesirable' characteristics changed or destroyed through genetic therapy. Perhaps we may even begin to wish that Bertrand Russell was right when he said that history teaches us that the future is never like the future we imagine.

A 'By the end of the century,' he said, 'there will be no poverty anywhere in the country.'

B According to the same predictions, this would result in 'an information explosion' as well as 'radical and revolutionary changes in the way we work, learn and do business.'

C He added that this 'will lead to enormous social problems for unskilled manual workers in particular, who will be unable to find work.'

D He claimed that the scale of destruction would be far greater than in World War Two.

E When this prediction came true, more people were killed than ever before.

F The philosopher, Bertrand Russell, said this in 1944, while the worst and most devastating war in history was still being fought.

G If this prediction comes true, we will be faced with a much greater responsibility than ever before.

H They were certain that this would not only be 'far cleaner than coal and other fossil fuels but far safer and much cheaper.'

B Go through the text again. This time, read each paragraph aloud with the missing sentence in place. Then discuss these questions.

1 Which of the predictions have come true?
2 Which predictions have not, as far as you know, come true?
3 Which predictions do you think may come true in the future even if they have not come true so far?

LANGUAGE STUDY ➤ GS 13.3

A Explain the difference between the two sentences in each pair (1–4).

1 I'll do this tomorrow.
  I'll have done this by tomorrow.
2 They will happen in the year 2050.
  They will have happened by the year 2050.
3 We will be able to do this soon.
  We may be able to do this soon.
4 We may be able to change this.
  We may be able to have this changed.

B Complete the second sentence in each pair. Use no more than five words including the word in bold. Do NOT change this word.

1 It's possible that this prediction will come true.
  may This prediction _____ true.
2 It's possible that this prediction has already come true
  may This prediction _____ true.
3 This prediction will come true before the end of the year.
  have This prediction _____ by the end of the year.
4 We will have the ability to do these things in the future.
  able We _____ these things in the future.
5 Perhaps I can see you tomorrow, but I'm not sure.
  may I _____ you tomorrow.
6 Perhaps we will have the ability to do these things in the future.
  may We _____ these things in the future.
7 Perhaps it will be possible for an expert to do this for us.
  have We may be able to _____ _____ by an expert.
8 Perhaps you didn't understand something in this exercise.
  may You _____ everything in this exercise.
9 An expert will do this job for me tomorrow.
  by I'll _____ an expert tomorrow.
10 An expert will have done it for me before you come back
  by I'll _____ an expert before you come back.

ALP 357

THE ALL-PURPOSE WONDER ROBOT

Does life ever seem to (1)_____ getting you down? Do you ever get tired of doing the cooking, the housework or all those other jobs that prevent you (2)_____ enjoying life? Do you ever find yourself putting off writing letters (3)_____ your friends because you simply haven't got enough time? Do you ever find yourself washing clothes or ironing them when you'd rather be doing something (4)_____? If so, what you need (5)_____ our new ALP 357, the all-purpose wonder robot.

Once you buy one, you'll wonder how you ever did (6)_____ it. In no time at all you'll feel (7)_____ if the ALP 357 is not only a reliable assistant but your best friend, as well. It will listen to your problems, take care of your home (8)_____ even write routine letters for you. (9)_____ can look after your pets, prevent burglars from stealing things (10)_____ you're out of the house and remind you of all the things you have to do every day. The ALP 357 is more than a robot. It's your cook, cleaner, secretary and friend all (11)_____ the same time.

The ALP 357 is programmed to understand spoken instructions as (12)_____ as each word is clearly pronounced. It will also translate simple phrases from your language (13)_____ 100 other foreign languages, including Russian, Chinese, Japanese, Swahili, French, Italian, German and Spanish. 'Before I had an ALP 357, life seemed to be almost impossible. (14)_____ I bought it, all my troubles seem to (15)_____ disappeared,' one of our typical customers says. Get an ALP 357 yourself and you'll see what she means.

USE OF ENGLISH

Read the advertisement above to get a general idea of its meaning. Then discuss with your partners which word best fills each of the spaces.

SPEAKING

A Find out how many different kinds of machines your partners use at home, at work or at school.

B Suppose they could keep only three of these machines. Find out which they would keep and why.

C Think of a machine that has not yet been invented which would be useful to you. Explain how it would be useful to you and describe the things you would want it to do for you.

FOCUS TWO

LANGUAGE STUDY

A Explain the difference.

1 Life is getting you down.
   Life seems to be getting you down.
2 All my troubles have disappeared.
   All my troubles seem to have disappeared.
3 Life was impossible for me.
   Life seemed to be impossible for me.
4 You haven't understood this.
   You don't seem to have understood this.
5 You don't know the answer.
   You act as if you don't know the answer.
6 You didn't understand what I told you.
   You acted as if you didn't understand what I told you.

Repeat only the sentences above which suggest you are talking about *impressions* and not facts.

B Complete the second sentence in each pair. Use no more than five words including the word in bold. Do NOT change that word.

1 I have the impression that you are having a good time.
   seem You _____ a good time.
2 I have the impression that you've had a good time.
   seem You _____ a good time.
3 I have the impression that this prediction has come true.
   seems This prediction _____ true.
4 I have the impression that this prediction isn't accurate.
   seem This prediction _____ accurate.
5 I have the impression it hasn't come true.
   seem It _____ come true.
6 There was something here you didn't understand.
   seemed There _____ something here you didn't understand.
7 I have the impression you aren't enjoying this very much.
   seem You do _____ this very much.
8 Is it your impression that this exercise is difficult?
   be Does this exercise _____ difficult?
9 You don't seem to have studied this before.
   as You act _____ never studied this before.
10 I mean, you don't seem to know what to do.
    as You act _____ know what to do.
11 Yesterday you didn't seem to know what to do.
    as You acted _____ know what to do.
12 You're acting now as if you're having difficulty with this.
    seem You _____ difficulty with this.

LISTENING

You are going to hear people talking in eight different situations. For questions 1–8, choose the best answer, A, B or C.

1 Listen to part of a radio programme. What is the man talking about?
   A a new kind of food
   B a new use for certain kinds of animals
   C a new method of selling meat
2 Listen to another part of the same radio programme. What is the woman talking about now?
   A a traditional type of meat
   B a completely new type of vegetable
   C a new variety of a traditional food
3 Two people are talking on the phone. What form of communication does the man want the woman to use?
   A the normal post office service
   B computer to computer
   C fax transmission
4 A woman is talking to someone on the phone. What does she want to do?
   A sell something
   B buy a house
   C find out about heating
5 The presenter of a TV 'chat show' is introducing her next guest. What is unusual about the guest?
   A She plays tennis even though she is seventy.
   B She has lived a long and active life.
   C She is a computer and electronics expert.
6 Listen to this radio advertisement. Who do you think the advertisement is designed to interest?
   A people who suffer from common colds
   B people who work too hard
   C anyone who has had too much food or alcohol
7 A travel agent is talking to a client on the phone. Which form of transport is the client going to use?
   A a plane
   B a surface vehicle
   C a spaceship
8 Someone has an ALP 357 robot. What is the problem with it?
   A It couldn't tell the difference between two words that sound almost the same.
   B It's impossible for robots like this to understand even very simple speech.
   C The man spoke too quickly to the robot.

SPEAKING

A Problem solving

These inventions have been entered in a competition to find 'The Inventor of the Year'. In pairs or groups, decide which invention should win the first and second prizes, giving reasons for your choices.

Kwikcool the opposite of a microwave oven; it rapidly cools down food and drinks

CommunicAnt automatically translates from your language into spoken English

Autostylist automatically cuts your hair to the best style

Motorblades motorized rollerblades with remote control; top speed of 40km per hour

B Discussion

1 What other inventions have helped to make our lives more comfortable in modern times?
2 Do you think the human race could survive without technology? Why? / Why not?
3 What other sources of power could replace coal, oil and gas in the future?

READING

A Read the text quickly to get a general idea of what it is about.

Until recently, the 'science of the future' was supposed to be electronics and artificial intelligence. Today it seems more and more likely that the next great breakthroughs in technology will be brought about through a combination of those two sciences with organic chemistry and genetic engineering. This combination is the science of biotechnology.

Organic chemistry enables us to produce marvellous synthetic materials. However, it is still difficult to manufacture anything that has the capacity of wool to conserve heat and also to absorb moisture. Nothing that we have been able to produce so far comes anywhere near the combination of strength, lightness and flexibility that we find in the bodies of ordinary insects.

Nevertheless, scientists in the laboratory have already succeeded in 'growing' a material that has many of the characteristics of human skin. The next step may well be 'biotech hearts and eyes' which can replace diseased organs in human beings. These will not be rejected by the body, as is the case with organs from humans.

The application of biotechnology to energy production seems even more promising. In 1996 the famous science-fiction writer, Arthur C. Clarke, many of whose previous predictions have come true, said that we may soon be able to develop remarkably cheap and renewable sources of energy. Some of these power sources will be biological. Clarke and others have warned us repeatedly that sooner or later we will have to give up our dependence on non-renewable power sources. Coal, oil and gas are indeed convenient. However, using them also means creating dangerously high levels of pollution. It will be impossible to meet the growing demand for energy without increasing that pollution to catastrophic levels unless we develop power sources that are both cheaper and cleaner.

It is tempting to think that biotechnology or some other 'science of the future' can solve our problems for us. Before we surrender to that temptation we should remember nuclear power. Only a few generations ago it seemed to promise limitless, cheap and safe energy. Today those promises lie buried in a concrete grave in a place called Chernobyl, in the Ukraine. Biotechnology is unlikely, however, to break its promises in quite the same or such a dangerous way.

FOCUS THREE

B **Choose the best answer. Then read aloud the sentence or sentences from the text that show your choice is correct.**

1 According to the text, the science of the future is likely to be
  A electronics.
  B biotechnology.
  C genetic engineering.
  D nuclear technology.

2 Organic chemistry helps to produce materials that are
  A almost as strong, light and flexible as an insect's body.
  B almost as good as wool.
  C not as good as natural materials.
  D stronger, lighter and better than natural materials.

3 According to the text, it may soon be possible
  A to make something as good as human skin.
  B to cure certain diseases that damage human organs.
  C to take an organ from one human and give it to another human.
  D to make useful substitutes for human hearts and eyes.

4 In 1996, Arthur C. Clarke predicted
  A new and better ways of heating and lighting homes, offices and factories.
  B newer and better ways of using oil, gas and coal.
  C that using oil, gas and coal would lead to very high levels of pollution.
  D that we may not be able to meet future demand for energy.

5 What does the text say is one of the worst problems caused by the use of coal, gas and oil?
  A They are no longer as easy to use as they once were.
  B They are so cheap that people waste them.
  C They are too expensive for poorer people in many parts of the world.
  D They are very bad for the world around us.

6 Which of these statements do you think best summarizes what the text is about?
  A We have good reasons for hoping that biotechnology will help us to solve some but not all our problems.
  B Science has promised to solve our problems in the past but has often created even worse problems for us.
  C Because of biotechnology, nuclear power and other scientific achievements, the future will be much better.
  D Despite the problems we have had with nuclear technology, it is still the best way to produce power.

VOCABULARY

Say the word or phrase in each group that doesn't belong with the others. Explain why it doesn't belong.

1 artificial synthetic genuine false
2 combine separate mix blend
3 replace construct manufacture produce
4 enable prevent make possible give a chance
5 previous earlier future former
6 water oil gas coal
7 power energy fuel waste
8 tempt persuade reject attract

USE OF ENGLISH

Complete the second sentence in each pair. Use no more than five words including the word in bold. Do NOT change that word.

1 With the help of biotechnology, we can do many things.
  enables Biotechnology _____ many things.

2 Unless you study it, you won't understand it.
  without You won't understand it _____ _____ it.

3 To find new fuels it is necessary to spend a lot of money.
  means Finding new fuels _____ _____ money.

4 It will be impossible to avoid pollution if we don't find other fuels.
  unless We can't avoid pollution _____ _____ other fuels.

5 People said that nuclear energy was safe.
  supposed Nuclear energy was _____ _____ safe.

6 People say that nuclear energy has caused lots of problems.
  supposed Nuclear energy _____ _____ lots of problems.

7 It will be necessary for us to use it more often.
  have We will _____ more often.

8 I'm not as capable of concentrating now as I was earlier.
  capacity My _____ isn't as strong as it was earlier.

9 These biotech tablets will enable you to concentrate a little longer.
  if You'll be able to concentrate longer _____ these biotech tablets.

10 You won't concentrate without using them.
  unless You won't concentrate _____ _____ them.

WRITING

Informal letter 2

You may be asked to write an informal letter giving someone advice.

A Sample task
This is part of a letter you have received from a friend who is coming to your country for a month's holiday.

> *Anyway, I'd appreciate your advice on the best way of getting to your country, as I haven't got much spare cash. And could you tell me what I should bring?*
> *All the best,*
>
> *Jason*

B Read the answer below. Underline each sentence or part of a sentence in which you think the writer is giving her friend advice. An example is given.

> Dear Jason
>
> It was great to hear that you're coming over.
>
> You can travel by plane or ferry. <u>Why not contact a few travel agents?</u> They sometimes offer cheap flights. Whatever you do, don't book a seat on a scheduled flight, because it's very expensive. If I were you, I'd take the ferry. It's very cheap and reasonably fast.
>
> It would be worth bringing another form of identification, like an ID card, because you won't want to carry your passport round all the time. You ought to bring a little English currency with you, in case the banks are shut when you arrive. However, it's a good idea to have mainly traveller's cheques, as they're much safer. By the way, you'll probably find it's well worth getting a student card – you'll be able to get all sorts of discounts, particularly when it comes to travelling around.
>
> There's just one other thing – you'd better remember to get in touch with us when you're over here, or we'll be very upset!
>
> Love
>
> Martha

C Analysis

1 Notice that the writer gives an explanation for each separate piece of advice. Look again at the letter and say why Martha advises her friend:
  - to go round some travel agents
  - to bring mainly traveller's cheques
  - to take the ferry
  - to get in touch
  - not to book a scheduled flight
  - to get a student card
  - to bring an ID card

2 Write down the words the writer uses to link the reason to the advice.

Example: *because (it's very expensive).*

D Writing task

Here is part of a letter you have received from a pen friend. Write a suitable reply of about 180 words.

> *Anyway, it means that I've now got two months free to learn your language. I'm really looking forward to being able to write to you in your language rather than mine. Can you give me some advice on how to learn your language quickly?*

E Read these notes on planning.

1 Before writing your answer, spend a few minutes thinking of at least four pieces of advice you could give your friend. Then make notes on each piece of advice.

2 Look again at the ways of giving advice in the sample answer. Use a different one for each piece of advice in your letter.

3 Organize your letter like this:
  - Introduction – thank your friend for the letter, etc.
  - Main part of the letter: give your advice, with reasons. Start with the most important points and use paragraphs to separate your ideas.
  - Remember to include an informal ending.

REVISION AND EXTENSION

Complete the text by choosing the best answer, A, B, C or D.

This year's *Innovations and Inventions Fair* has just opened, and has attracted inventors from all over the world who need **(0)** *to show* their new ideas to the public.

The fair always provides a wonderful **(1)**_____ of inventions, and this year is no exception. One inventor is demonstrating a way of making it impossible to copy documents **(2)**_____ as passports and tickets. So far, the only person who has offered to buy the patent is said **(3)**_____ a member of the Mafia, but it is not clear what he wants to do **(4)**_____ it. The inventor will have to go ahead with the sale **(5)**_____ he can find a more normal buyer **(6)**_____ the end of the show. There are plenty of new gadgets too to help the disabled. The youngest inventor, fourteen **(7)**_____ old Jane Watson, has come up with a battery-powered device for people who cannot clean their teeth **(8)**_____. One of its special features is that it never needs **(9)**_____, because it runs on solar power.

A new feature of this year's show is the Helpcentre, which has been **(10)**_____ up to give new inventors **(11)**_____ on how to make the most of their ideas. According to the show's organizers, many inventions fail because inventors spend **(12)**_____ much time developing the product and don't pay **(13)**_____ attention to the business side of the project.

The fair is open from 9 a.m. to 6.30 p.m. every day and runs **(14)**_____ March 11. Tickets are **(15)**_____ at £3.50.

0	**A** a show	**C** showing	
	B to show	**D** shows	
1	**A** choice	**C** difference	
	B variation	**D** range	
2	**A** so	**C** such	
	B like	**D** how	
3	**A** had been	**C** to being	
	B to be	**D** was	
4	**A** by	**C** in	
	B with	**D** without	
5	**A** unless	**C** without	
	B if	**D** except	
6	**A** until	**C** since	
	B by	**D** ago	
7	**A** age	**C** year	
	B ages	**D** years	
8	**A** itself	**C** herself	
	B himself	**D** themselves	
9	**A** re-charge	**C** to re-charge	
	B re-charged	**D** re-charging	
10	**A** set	**C** started	
	B established	**D** founded	
11	**A** advice	**C** recommendation	
	B suggestion	**D** directions	
12	**A** too	**C** over	
	B extra	**D** far	
13	**A** enough	**C** complete	
	B plenty	**D** full	
14	**A** by	**C** for	
	B until	**D** since	
15	**A** priced	**C** worth	
	B valued	**D** cost	

LISTENING

Listen to the recording. Then answer questions 1–8 by writing one of the following letters:
J = Jenny   **K** = Katie   **S** = Steve
An example is given (0).

Who has been to the Lake District before?	**0**	*S*
Who asks for a favour?	**1**	
Who has no experience of camping?	**2**	
Who has little money to spend?	**3**	
Who says camping can be expensive?	**4**	
Who likes to be independent?	**5**	
Who knows about a self-catering apartment?	**6**	
Who is not enthusiastic about camping?	**7**	
Who agrees to phone the owner of the flat?	**8**	

DEATH TRAP

SPEAKING

A Talking on your own

Work in pairs as Student A and B. Speak for about one minute.

Student A: Describe and compare the buildings in both pictures. Say what is happening and what damage has been caused.

Student B: Describe and compare the people in both pictures. Say what they could be thinking or feeling.

B Discussion

1 What might have caused the fire?
2 What would you do if there was a fire now?
3 What sort of places are particularly dangerous when a fire breaks out? Why?
4 What can be done to prevent fires breaking out?

READING

Read the following newspaper article which appeared the day after a terrible fire. Put the headings (A–G) in the correct place in the text. There is one heading which you do not need to use.

A HEROES IN FLAMES
B DESPERATE SEARCH
C AN EXPLOSION OF FIRE
D DEATH TOLL RISES
E LESSONS LEARNED
F DEATH TRAP
G A TRAGEDY WAITING TO HAPPEN

1

The number killed in the Bradford City football ground disaster has increased to 52; more than 70 police and spectators have also been detained in hospital, making this one of the worst tragedies in football history.

2

The match was being recorded by Yorkshire TV when the fire began. When it first broke out, a few tongues of flame could be seen under the wooden seats in the G block of the stand. Some of the spectators walked away casually from the smoke. Then suddenly the fire spread with terrifying speed, and within minutes the whole stand suddenly burst into flames.

3

Most of the spectators rushed forwards onto the pitch to avoid the blaze. In the panic, several spectators were crushed, and police and other fans ran back to the stands to help them. The rescuers' clothes and hair caught fire in the intense heat, but their bravery saved many lives.

FOCUS ONE

4

Most of the dead were found piled up at the back of the stand, where they had run to try and escape from the fire. However, the gates at the back of the stand had been locked before the start of the match. This had been done to prevent people from entering without paying. Eye-witnesses spoke of fans being crushed beneath the turnstiles in a desperate attempt to escape. There was no way of putting out the fire because extinguishers had been removed because they had been used in the past by fans as missiles.

5

Throughout the day, weeping relatives trailed into hospitals and police stations looking for missing members of their families. The police are faced with the problem of identifying the victims, and dental records and jewellery are being collected to help with the task.

6

The alarmingly quick spread of the fire was of serious concern to police and fire brigade investigators last night. They believe the fire was started by a dropped cigarette, and that paper and other rubbish that had accumulated over the years beneath the wooden stands provided ready-made fuel for the inferno. One officer commented 'It is incredible that no one did anything about the stand. It was obvious that it was only a matter of time before there would be a disaster like this.'

VOCABULARY

Choose the word or phrase which is closest in meaning to the word in *italics*.

1 have also been *detained*
   A arrested   B imprisoned   C kept

2 it first *broke out*
   A cracked   B escaped   C started

3 walked away *casually*
   A quickly   B calmly   C nervously

4 to avoid the *blaze*
   A argument   B fight   C fire

5 beneath the *turnstiles*
   A large crowds   B spectators' feet
   C special gates

6 identifying the *victims*
   A the dead   B the injured   C the fans

7 that had *accumulated*
   A grown   B been lost   C dropped

8 had been used as *missiles*
   A things to steal   B things to throw
   C things to break

LANGUAGE STUDY

More about the passive ➤ GS 8.2

A Look at these sentences.

1 a) They could see flames under the wooden seats.
   b) Flames could be seen under the wooden seats.

2 a) Most of the dead were found at the back of the stand.
   b) They found most of the dead at the back of the stand.

Repeat the sentences you would probably use if you didn't know who *they* were.

B Rewrite the following sentences using the word in bold.

1 People were watching the match on TV.
   being   The _____ on TV.

2 The intense heat burned many of the rescuers.
   were   Many of the _____ the intense heat.

3 They had taken away the fire extinguishers on purpose.
   been   The fire extinguishers _____ _____ on purpose.

4 They have set up an investigation to look into the tragedy.
   set   An investigation _____ to look into the tragedy.

5 Doctors have treated many people for burns and shock.
   treated   Many _____ for burns and shock.

6 The police know the identity of one of the victims.
   to   The identity of one of the victims _____ police.

7 Fire officers regularly inspect stadiums.
   inspected   Stadiums _____ fire officers.

8 They will have to rebuild many existing stands because of this.
   rebuilt   Many existing stands _____ _____ because of this.

9 The fire destroyed the stand in a matter of minutes.
   was   The _____ in a matter of minutes.

10 A dropped cigarette probably started the fire.
   by   The fire _____ a dropped cigarette.

LISTENING

You will hear two people talking about how the fire affected them. Listen and choose the best answer, A, B or C.

1   The first speaker says that going to a football match these days is
    A good family entertainment.
    B better than staying at home.
    C like being in a war.

2   The first speaker says he
    A won't allow his children to go to football matches.
    B will only go to football matches by himself.
    C has lost interest in football.

3   The second speaker realized there was a fire when she saw
    A the smoke.
    B the flames.
    C the fire engines.

4   She couldn't get close to the main entrance because of the
    A heat from the fire.
    B people standing outside.
    C people coming out.

5   When she saw the children again they were
    A in the police station.
    B watching TV.
    C in hospital.

LANGUAGE STUDY

could or *managed to*?

A What's the difference? Look at these four sentences and answer the questions below.

a) The men could escape.
b) The men managed to escape.
c) The police couldn't catch them.
d) The police didn't manage to catch them.

*   Which two sentences are so close in meaning that it is impossible to be sure what the difference is?
*   Which sentence clearly tells us that the men actually escaped?
*   Which two sentences have very different meanings?

could, managed to and *couldn't*

PARTICULAR ACTION	GENERAL ABILITY	
They *managed* to get away.	They *could* feel the heat.	POSITIVE
They *couldn't* get away. feel the heat.		NEGATIVE

B Complete the following sentences with *could, managed to* or *couldn't*.

1 The smoke was so thick that you _____ breathe.
2 The man in front of me fell down. He was heavy but somehow I _____ help him to stand up.
3 The doors at the back were locked, so at first we _____ open them.
4 We tried to break the doors down, but we _____ do it.
5 Then someone broke the lock on the doors on the other side and a few fans _____ escape.
6 I was one of them. I just _____ get out alive.
7 When I got out, I turned around and looked. I _____ see a lot of fire-engines, police cars and ambulances.
8 The firemen worked all night and finally _____ put the fire out early the next morning.
9 You _____ smell the smoke for days after the fire.

Two meanings of *must* ➤ GS 7.8

C What's the difference?

a) In future, stadiums must be inspected regularly.
b) The fire must have been started by a cigarette.
c) Someone must have dropped one.
d) The families must be feeling terrible.
e) We must improve safety regulations.
f) The football clubs must take some responsibility for this.

• In which sentences is the speaker making a guess?
• Which sentences sound like an order or recommendation?

Give two possible meanings for this sentence.

You must work hard.

D Rephrase these recommendations using *must* or *must not*.

Example: Keep emergency exits open at all times.
➤ *Emergency exits must be kept open at all times.*

1 It's important to provide protective clothing.
You _____ protective clothing.
2 It's important to check the fire extinguishers regularly.
You _____ fire extinguishers.
3 Clear rubbish away from under the stands.
Rubbish _____ from under the stands.
4 Don't lock the doors when there are people in the stadium.
Doors _____ when there are people in the stadium.
5 It's essential that such a tragedy does not happen again.
Such a tragedy _____ again.
6 It would be awful if we forgot this terrible lesson.
We _____ this terrible lesson.

E Rewrite the following sentences using *must do, must be doing, must have done,* or *must have been doing.*

1 I'm sure people are worried about their friends and families.
People _____ about their friends and families.
2 I'm sure John knows some of the people who were there.
John _____ some of the people who were there.
3 I'm sure some of the fans are feeling very angry.
Some of the fans _____ very angry.
4 I'm sure your parents are looking for you.
Your parents _____ for you.
5 I'm sure somebody realized how dangerous it was.
Somebody _____ how dangerous it was.
6 I'm sure someone has seen my son.
Someone _____ my son.
7 I'm sure someone was smoking in the stands.
Someone _____ in the stands.
8 I'm sure John was watching the match on TV.
John _____ the match on TV.

F Read through the following sentences. Then write down what each speaker might say next, using *must*.

Example: We haven't got much time to get to the airport.
➤ *We must leave now.*
Sarah usually leaves home at 8.30 and it's 9.30 now.
➤ *She must have left home an hour ago.*

1 This exam is important but you don't study enough.
_____

2 If you go on smoking so heavily, you'll ruin your health.
_____

3 Sarah was all alone in that dark house when she heard the burglar break in. Can you imagine it?
_____

4 She got up this morning at 6, took the children to school, worked all day, cooked supper for her family, did the washing-up and now it's midnight and she's still working.
_____

5 I was driving along the road, and I was tired, and the next thing I knew I was upside down in a field.
_____

6 Look, Mr Simpkins is getting into a police car. And he's got handcuffs on.
_____

7 Now, you're going away for three months, and you know how much your mother will miss you.
_____

8 All right. Your father and I will let you go to the party tomorrow evening but remember what we've told you.
_____

Read the article _Close Calls_. For questions 1–16, choose the part of the article (A, B, C or D) in which you can find the answer. One question requires two answers (15 and 16) from different parts.

Which story or stories mention someone who:

got uncomfortably close to a dangerous animal?	**0** D
was seriously injured?	**1**
was delighted to have rescued someone?	**2**
expected to be eaten?	**3**
has saved people before?	**4**
decided to be very calm and patient?	**5**
was too interested in something else?	**6**
was very grateful to the rescuer?	**7**
could smell and feel that something was wrong?	**8**
was very impressed by a colleague's strength?	**9**
did not realize that someone else was in trouble?	**10**
had to show great courage in the rescue?	**11**
was too tired to be interested in a problem?	**12**
risked dying in the cold?	**13**
worked with a colleague during the rescue?	**14**
must have been surprised to be in danger ?	**15** **16**

CLOSE CALLS

As the New Year is nearly upon us, we look back at some of the stories and interviews that made the headlines this year. Here are some of the stories about people who can count themselves lucky to be alive.

A   Quick thinking by two Park Rangers in the Rocky Mountains saved the lives of two Canadian teenagers. Timothy Beck and Marc Dubois were driving near the Fraser River when they saw the two girls and realized they were in trouble.
Mr Beck said 'The river was flowing incredibly fast because of the rain and melting snow; we were about to tell them to get out when their canoe crashed into a rock and broke up. We knew we had to work quickly to save them, because they couldn't last long in such freezing water.'
Mr Dubois ran downstream and climbed over some rocks. He caught the first girl as she was being swept past, and Mr Beck took care of her on the river bank. The second girl was further over, so Mr Dubois had to swim across to her.
Mr Beck added 'Marc was super-human the way he got her out of the raging water as if she weighed nothing. She was under the water, and all we could see was her fingers poking out. But Marc managed to get her before it was too late.'
The men drove straight to the nearest hospital, where the girls made a quick recovery. The men said they were delighted at being able to help with yesterday's rescue. Mr Dubois has rescued several people in the past. 'It is always a fantastic feeling. In this case we were lucky to be on the spot when the accident happened. It was a job well done.'

B   The Eiger is one of the most dangerous and feared mountains in the Alps, and last week it nearly claimed another victim. Johann Bauer and Klaus Schumann were near the peak when a rock came loose and Klaus fell over 100 metres and crashed into the side of the mountain.
'I feared the worst,' explained Johann. 'I called out, but there was no reply. Then, a few minutes later, Klaus shouted that he was OK, but thought he had broken his arm. He was still tied to the rope, and he managed to find a ledge to sit on. But it was clear that I would have to go and get help. Then I saw that my rope had been badly cut, and I realized that I would have to try and get to the top on my own and try to find an easier way down. I have never liked free-style climbing, but I didn't have any choice. In the end, I managed to get to the top after about three hours, but I have never been so terrified in my life.
After the rescue, Klaus said 'When Johann said he was going to climb without his equipment, I didn't think he had a chance – it's like going up a wall. But I am full of admiration for what he did. When the rescue party arrived, I was shaking because I had lost a lot of blood. There's no doubt that he saved my life.'

C Eva Larsen had seen plenty of snow in her native country of Norway, but she'd never seen quite so much of it before. Eva, 28, was trapped on Wednesday afternoon for more than 2 hours after a pile of snow dropped onto the car from a roof three floors above.

At 3:30 p.m. on Wednesday, Eva and her husband Sven had just come back from a shopping trip. Her husband was in a bad mood because he had missed most of an important football match on TV, and he went straight inside to see the end.

Eva was just about to get out of the car when the avalanche occurred. 'I couldn't believe it. All of a sudden I was buried under a mountain of snow. I couldn't get the doors open, and there was no point shouting, so I had to wait.'

In the end, she had to wait longer than she had expected. Sven waited until the end of the match, and then came out to see what had happened to his wife. 'At first I was very worried, because I thought someone had stolen the car. I couldn't see it anywhere. But then I realized what had happened and began to dig the snow away. I knew Eva would be all right. We had had the heater on, and I knew snow would help to keep the warmth in. And there was plenty to eat, because we'd been to the supermarket.'

D Sir David Attenborough has spent a lifetime filming animals. This can be dangerous.

Sir David recalls 'I was flying to East Africa in the old days to meet Joy Adamson and Elsa, the famous lioness from the film *Born Free*. When I met up with Joy Adamson, she was terribly upset. 'Oh David, it's the end of the world. Elsa is dying. She has been attacked by a strange lioness and she has run away.'

I was exhausted after my long journey and decided I wasn't going to worry about the lioness, and I certainly wasn't going to look for her late at night. All I wanted was some sleep and I finally got out a camp-bed and fell asleep in my tent.

When I woke up, there was a terrible weight on my chest and a frightful smell of bad breath! It was Elsa – and she was sitting on me. She had long hair around her chin, and I could see those yellow teeth. I thought I was about to be her breakfast. And then Joy came around the corner and said 'Ah Elsa, my darling,' and ran over to hug the lioness. Never mind me, who was about to be her 'darling's' breakfast!' And then Elsa got up and went off. It was quite an awakening, I can tell you!'

VOCABULARY

Words with many meanings

A **Each of these words (1–6) has at least three different meanings (A–C). In pairs or groups, decide which one of the three meanings each word has in the article you have just read. The part of the article where the word is used is given in brackets.**

1 *clear* (B)
   A not cloudy
   B obvious
   C easy to hear
2 *party* (B)
   A group of people
   B social event
   C political organization
3 *just* (C)
   A very recently
   B only
   C fair
4 *match* (C)
   A a small piece of wood
   B to have the same pattern as
   C a game
5 *strange* (D)
   A peculiar
   B not familiar
   C not at ease
6 *ran over* (D)
   A repeated
   B drove over with a car
   C moved quickly towards

B **Use the words above in another of their meanings to complete these sentences.**

1 This rule isn't very _____ to me.
2 What a _____ bird. I've never seen one like it before.
3 That's a nice tie but it doesn't _____ your shirt.
4 Drive carefully or you'll _____ somebody _____.
5 The Conservative _____ are worried about the next election.
6 I never have much for breakfast; _____ some toast and tea.

WRITING

Composition 3

The *for and against* composition is one method of answering a question that asks for your opinion on a subject or asks whether you agree with a particular statement. Like the *advantages and disadvantages composition* (see Unit 1), you can make a list of the important points on both sides of the question and then make your decision at the end.

A Sample task

You have been asked by your teacher to write a composition on the following topic:

The fur trade should not be allowed to continue. Do you agree?

B Read the following answer. There are ten words in the text that should not be there. Can you find them?

The fur trade is an issue which it arouses strong feelings. On the one hand, fur farmers are fighting to continue producing their goods, and, on the other hand, animal rights groups are trying to get the trade stopped.

The fur traders say that they do not cause an unnecessary suffering to animals and that there is no difference between killing an animal for its fur and killing it for its meat. They also claim that banning the trade would mean more of unemployment and less choice for the fashion industry.

Opponents take up a different view. They say us that animals do suffer and to prove it they have made many horrifying films. They consider the killing of animals for fur a luxury, whereas they regard the killing of animals for meat as a necessity. Finally, they point out that the manufacturing of artificial fur would create jobs and satisfy the demands of the fashion.

In conclusion, it is clear that opponents of the fur trade are beginning to have got some success. For example, consumer opinion is changing itself, as more people refuse to buy fur products. In addition, people connected with the fur trade are changing. Some famous supermodels they have refused to wear fur at fashion shows. If these trends will continue, it may be possible to stop the trade without making it illegal.

C Analysis

1 Repeat the arguments the writer gives for the fur trade.
2 Repeat the arguments the writer gives against it.
3 Look again at the question in A. Do you think the writer's answer is successful? Give one reason for your answer.

D In pairs or groups, discuss the following statement, carefully considering the four aspects below.

Old people should be looked after by members of their family.

1 The emotional side
   FOR: How might an old person feel about going into a home? What bad effects might it have?
   AGAINST: Aren't some old people sometimes happier in an old people's home? Do they have company all day? How might a carer feel about having to give up work to look after someone?

2 The practical side
   FOR: How expensive are these old people's homes? Is it a good way to spend money?
   AGAINST: How easy is it to look after an old person? What happens when they need special equipment? How easy is it in a small house or flat?

3 The moral side
   FOR: Do you have a duty to look after your parents, since they spent so long looking after you?
   AGAINST: Do some parents want to avoid being a burden?

4 Your own experience
   Say what has happened or will happen with your own family. What would you like to happen when you get old?

E Now write your composition, arguing for and against the statement in D. Use the notes below to help you.

Introduction: Look back at the answer in B. Introduce the subject in the same way and say what the argument is about.

Arguments FOR: Write one paragraph covering the points that support the statement. If you can, give examples.

Arguments AGAINST: Keeping if possible to the same order as the previous paragraph, list and contrast the points that oppose the statement.

Conclusion: Say which of the two arguments you accept and why. If appropriate, suggest any possible solutions.

REVISION AND EXTENSION

A Complete the dialogue with the best option, A, B, C or D.

A: **(1)____** you like to come round on Saturday for dinner?

B: I'm sorry, but I'm afraid I **(2)____**. I **(3)____** to go to my grandmother's for the weekend. She's getting old and there are a few things that **(4)____** doing around the house.

A: I think you **(5)____** get your brother to do something.

B: I know, I wish he **(6)____** . I've asked him several times but he just **(7)____** help at all.

A: Oh well. Anyway, when **(8)____** you get back?

B: Wednesday, I think, but I **(9)____** get back earlier.

A: OK, well, **(10)____** we fix a date now? **(11)____** you come on Friday?

B: I **(12)____** just have a look in my diary. Yes, that's fine. **(13)____** I borrow a pen? I just **(14)____** to make a note or I **(15)____** probably forget. You know what it's like.

A: Yes, of course. Here you are.

	A		B		C		D	
1	**A** Would	**B** May	**C** Shall	**D** Will
2	**A** won't	**B** can't	**C** might not	**D** needn't
3	**A** must	**B** should	**C** have	**D** would
4	**A** will	**B** might	**C** must	**D** need
5	**A** ought	**B** need	**C** should	**D** shall
6	**A** would	**B** should	**C** might	**D** ought
7	**A** won't	**B** mustn't	**C** shouldn't	**D** needn't
8	**A** will	**B** shall	**C** need	**D** ought
9	**A** would	**B** might	**C** shall	**D** need
10	**A** must	**B** shall	**C** will	**D** ought
11	**A** Should	**B** Could	**C** May	**D** Shall
12	**A** can	**B** would	**C** will	**D** need
13	**A** Shall	**B** Would	**C** Will	**D** Could
14	**A** should	**B** must	**C** need	**D** could
15	**A** will	**B** might	**C** must	**D** should

B Complete this letter by filling the spaces with *must, mustn't* or *needn't*.

Dear Parent

Please read through these notes to make sure that your child is prepared for the school trip to Scotland next Saturday.

We leave at 7.30 from the school, and all children **(1)_____** arrive before that time or they will be left behind. They **(2)_____** bring more than one case, as space on the coach is very limited. Please note that children **(3)_____** bring sheets or towels as these will be provided by the hostel.

Children **(4)_____** bring a packed lunch, but can if they want to. Children without packed lunches **(5)_____** bring enough money to buy their own sandwiches and drinks. However, they **(6)_____** bring more than £5 for security reasons.

C Now complete this letter with the correct form of *have to, don't have to,* or *can't.*

I tell you, this health farm is almost as bad as being in prison. We **(1)_____** get up at about 5.30 and go for a short run. Then we have breakfast, which is usually just a few slices of toast, but we **(2)_____** have any butter or jam. They give us lemon tea, which I can't stand, but at least we **(3)_____** drink it if we don't want to. Then we have to do various forms of exercise until lunchtime, which again is usually not much more than a lettuce leaf. The afternoon is better because we **(4)_____** run around, and we're allowed to rest and watch TV. Then we **(5)_____** do another aerobics class before dinner, but of course we **(6)_____** have anything to drink with it because alcohol is fattening. Then it's time for bed. Oh well, only five more days to go!

D Rewrite the second sentence in each pair. Use no more than five words including the word in bold. Do NOT change this word.

1 He is not old enough to vote.
   too He _____ to vote.

2 Remembering vocabulary is never easy.
   difficult It is _____ vocabulary.

3 They have found the stolen money in the park.
   been The stolen _____ in the park.

4 Someone almost certainly broke the window on purpose.
   must The window _____ on purpose.

5 He is too short to join the police.
   tall He _____ to join the police.

6 They say Charles is a very rich man.
   supposed Charles _____ very rich man.

7 Someone must tell him the truth.
   told He _____ the truth.

8 If I were you, I wouldn't tolerate his behaviour.
   put If I were you, I _____ his behaviour.

9 I wish you had told me about this before.
   should You _____ about this before.

10 It is possible that one of the men died on the mountain.
   may One of the men _____ on the mountain.

11 I'm sure you're very tired after working so hard.
   must You _____ after working so hard.

12 I'm sure you were surprised when you heard the news.
   must You _____ when you heard the news.

13 It wasn't necessary for you to do all this work.
   needn't You _____ all this work.

14 It was possible for me to do it instead.
   could I _____ it instead.

15 You caused the accident because you were driving too fast.
   so If you _____ fast, the accident would not have happened.

THE WOMAN WITHOUT A NAME

SPEAKING

A Talking on your own

Work in pairs as Student A and B. Speak for about one minute. Briefly say whether you agree with what your partner has said.

Student A: Describe and compare the people in both pictures. Say what kind of food they might be eating and why they might have gone for a meal.

Student B: Describe and compare the restaurants in both pictures. Say which place you would prefer to eat in, and why.

B Discussion

1 What kind of food is healthy and what is unhealthy? Why?
2 How can people be encouraged to have a healthy diet?
3 How have people's eating habits changed over the last ten years or so?

READING

A The following passage has been taken from a novel called *The Dark Side of the Street*, which takes place in Los Angeles. Seven sentences have been removed. Choose the one (A–H) which fits each gap (1–7). There is one extra sentence you do not need.

A It was hard to tell how old she was in the candle-light.

B The waiter pronounced the last word as if he didn't quite understand it.

C Even though it was candle-lit, I could see the inside of the place was as empty as the car park.

D I wondered if it could be hers.

E I called the waiter over and asked for the bill.

F Not that I'm hard of hearing, it's just better that way.

G Then she took out a photograph of a man and a woman on a beach.

H Her voice suggested someone in her early 30s.

FOCUS ONE

'At Antoine's. At seven,' the woman's voice said at the other end of the phone.

'At Antoine's, at seven,' I repeated. I always repeat such information on the phone in case I haven't heard correctly. [1]

'Very well, then. I'll be expecting you,' she replied.

'Just a moment. How will I recognize you?' I asked. I was trying to imagine what she looked like. [2] There was something smooth but at the same time hard about that voice, something that goes with diamonds and an expensive education.

'You won't have to. Just don't be late!' she said curtly. Then she hung up.

Antoine's was one of those new-style French places that specializes in very small portions and very high prices. I left my old Ford in the car park. There was only one other car there, a white Mercedes. [3]

'Yes, sir? Have you got a reservation?' the headwaiter asked as soon as I came through the door. I looked around. [4]

'No, but I don't think I'll need one,' I answered.

The waiter smiled. But his eyes didn't. He looked at my well-worn sports jacket and not very new shoes.

'I'm afraid we're fully booked this evening,' he said.

'It's all right. I think the gentleman is looking for me.'

It was the same voice I had heard on the phone and it came from a table in the corner. The waiter's manner suddenly changed.

'You should have said she was waiting for you,' he said in a low voice as he showed me to the table. I looked down. She had red hair and was dressed casually in denims. But they were the sort of denims you can't buy in most shops. [5] But it was obvious she was beautiful. Very beautiful.

'Sit down, Mr Nelson. What would you like to drink?' she said.

'Beer.'

'Excuse me, sir. Did you say … beer?'
[6]

'Perhaps you'd better have a glass of champagne instead,' the woman said and nodded to the waiter before I could refuse. She waited for him to leave.

[7] The woman's face was famous, but I had never seen the man with her before. He was middle-aged, tanned, and had his arm around her.

'I'll get straight down to business if you don't mind,' she said. She looked around and then laid some neatly-typed notes on the table, too.

'Go ahead. Read them. I thought I'd better put it all in writing just in case someone was listening.'

She looked around the empty restaurant again.

'You can never be too careful, even in a place like this,' she said.

B In pairs or groups, discuss these questions.

1 What kind of job do you think the writer has?
2 Who could the woman in the restaurant be? Why do you think she wants to see the writer?
3 What do you think happens next in the novel?

LANGUAGE STUDY

in case and *if* ➤ GS 6.6

A Match each sentence in the first group (a–d) with the sentence in the second group (1–4) that is closest in meaning.

a) I always repeat information in case I haven't heard it correctly.
b) I always repeat information if I haven't heard it correctly.
c) We'd better meet again somewhere more private in case people notice us together.
d) We'd better meet again somewhere more private if people notice us together.

1 When I think I haven't heard information correctly, I always repeat it.
2 I always repeat information because there is always a chance I haven't heard it correctly.
3 We should meet in a different place next time because there's a chance people will notice us together.
4 We can meet here again unless someone notices us together.

B Rephrase these sentences using *in case*. Notice that *will* is never used after *in case*.

1 It might rain later, so you'd better bring your raincoat.
   You'd better bring your raincoat _____ later.
2 There's a chance there will be a war, so I'm building a bomb shelter.
   I'm building a bomb shelter _____ war.
3 In America, a lot of people carry guns because there is always a chance someone will try to rob them.
   In America, a lot of people carry guns _____ them.
4 There's a chance I won't see you again, so let me say goodbye now.
   Let me say goodbye now _____ you again.
5 Don't talk so loud! The boss may be listening.
   Don't talk so loud _____ listening.
6 Get to the restaurant early. It may be crowded.
   Get to the restaurant early _____ crowded.
7 Remind me again. I might forget to call her.
   Remind me again _____ to call her.
8 Perhaps someone is watching us. You'd better leave by the side door.
   You'd better leave by the side door _____ us.

Student A: Describe and compare the woman's clothes in both pictures. Then say which image you prefer.

Student B: Describe and compare the woman's physical appearance in both pictures. Then say why you think the changes might have taken place.

B In groups ask each other these questions.

1 Who is your favourite pop/film star?
2 Describe the star physically and say why he/she is famous.
3 Has he/she changed since he/she became famous?
4 Do you know anyone whose character has been spoiled by becoming famous?
5 Would you like to become famous? Why?/Why not?

LISTENING 😐

A You are going to hear a scene from a radio play. The play is based on the novel *The Dark Side of the Street*. After listening at least once, decide which of these statements are true (T) or false (F).

1 One of the people the two speakers are talking about is a famous person. ☐
2 They are also talking about a man who knew this famous person very well. ☐
3 The woman who is talking says she knew both the man and the woman very well. ☐
4 The man called Earlham died in 1962. ☐
5 The woman says that before Earlham died he gave her some letters. ☐
6 She says the letters are from the woman in the photograph. ☐
7 The woman speaker believes the letters are worth a lot of money. ☐
8 In the end the man who is speaking decided to buy the letters. ☐

B Now discuss these questions.

1 Why is the woman talking to the man?
2 What do you think is going to happen next?

VOCABULARY

Phrasal verbs with *make*

A Complete these sentences with *up*, *out* or *for*.

1 Are you telling the truth? Or are you making this story _____?
2 I can see two people down there in the street but I can't make _____ what they are doing.

SPEAKING

A Talking on your own

Work in pairs as Student A and B. Speak for about one minute.

3 The prisoners escaped and made _____ the railway station.
4 Please make the cheque _____ to me.
5 She put a lot of _____ on her face.
6 After their quarrel, they kissed and made _____ .

B Use *make* to say these things in another way.

1 see clearly
2 write someone's name on a cheque
3 cosmetics, such as lipstick or eye-shadow
4 invent in order to deceive
5 forget your differences or anger
6 go towards

How many different ways did you use *make up* and *make out*? Which example is not a phrasal verb but a noun related to a phrasal verb?

LANGUAGE STUDY

if or *whether* ➤ GS 6.6

A Complete these sentences with *if* or *whether*. Notice that sometimes both are possible.

1 I wonder _____ I should give her the money she wants.
2 I'll have to decide _____ to give it to her or not very soon.
3 I don't know _____ she is telling the truth.
4 It all depends on _____ she can prove it or not.
5 I phoned my boss and discussed _____ to see her again.
6 She said that I should go ahead _____ I thought the letters really were from Monroe.

B In which of the sentences above can we use either *if* or *whether*?

a, an or *some*? ➤ GS 3

C Complete the following sentences with *a, an* or *some*.

1 I am doing _____ research into Monroe's death.
2 I have told my boss that I have already made _____ progress.
3 I've got _____ job to do.
4 I've got _____ work to do, too.
5 Here's _____ interesting bit of news.
6 And now I've got _____ bad news for you, too.
7 There's _____ luggage in front of the door.
8 Let me give you _____ advice.
9 Here's _____ piece of advice for you.
10 I have _____ difficult homework to do this evening.

VOCABULARY

A Complete the table showing which words can be made by adding *-less* or *-ful*.

careless	care	_careful_
	awe	_awful_
	beauty	
_____	pain	_____
_____	help	_____
_____	harm	_____
_____	hope	_____
_____	end	_____
_____	rest	_____
_____	use	

B Complete the following text by adding *-ful* or *-less* to the words below. An example is given.

Norma Jean Baker was born in 1926. She was deeply unhappy at home, and always had (0) _painful_ memories of her (1)_____ childhood.

She started her career as a model, and because she was so (2)_____ she was quickly hired by Ben Lyon of Twentieth Century Fox, one of the most (3)_____ producers in Hollywood, who changed her name to Marilyn Monroe. Her first few films were not particularly good as she was often cast as a dumb blonde and had no chance to show what a (4)_____ actress she was.

In the 50s, however, she signed a new contract, and made a number of (5)_____ movies including *Some Like it Hot* and *The Prince and the Showgirl*. Her films were immensely (6)_____ and she became the most famous star of her generation.

In her personal life, however, she never found the affection she needed. She remained (7)_____ and her two marriages failed. She took pills to get her through her (8)_____ nights and she began to drink heavily. At work she became (9)_____ and difficult to work with, and her reputation began to suffer. In the end, she was abandoned by most of her friends, and on August 5 1962, she was found dead from an overdose of sleeping pills.

0	PAIN	5	WONDER
1	LOVE	6	SUCCESS
2	BEAUTY	7	CHILD
3	POWER	8	SLEEP
4	SKILL	9	CARE

USE OF ENGLISH

The following passage also comes from the novel *The Dark Side of the Street*. Fill each of the numbered spaces with one word.

'You had better decide quickly (1)_____ you want the letters or not,' she said.

I took another sip of my champagne and said nothing.

'$100,000 is nothing to pay for them. They're Marilyn's letters! Marilyn Monroe's! I (2)_____ prove that she wrote them !' Her voice (3)_____ becoming louder and louder. She seemed to have forgotten her fear that someone might be listening to us.

I thought about (4)_____ she had said. If the letters really were Monroe's, they could be worth (5)_____ much money or even more. It all depended (6)_____ what was in them, of course.

I told her I (7)_____ have to see the letters first and that I wanted a handwriting expert to examine them as well.

'All right,' she answered. I waited (8)_____ her to continue. She did.

'But only on one condition.'

'What's that?' I asked.

'I want $10,000 in advance, before anyone else sees (9)_____ letters.'

'I'll (10)_____ to think about that,' I said.

She got up to go. She had only taken a few mouthfuls of the salmon she had ordered.

'All right. I'll get (11)_____ touch with you tomorrow at your hotel. If you haven't made (12)_____ your mind by then, the letters go to someone else.'

When she had left, I asked the waiter (13)_____ he knew her name.

'Didn't she tell you?' he asked.

'I wouldn't be asking if she (14)_____,' I answered.

'Really? Then obviously she didn't want you (15)_____ know, did she?' he said, casually putting the bill in front of me.

LISTENING 📷

Listen to another scene from the radio play you heard earlier. Choose the best answer, A, B or C.

1 The woman says that she wants
   A a cheque for $10,000.
   B to be paid before he sees the letters.
   C $100,000 in cash in advance.

2 The woman says he can keep the letters
   A so that they can be examined.
   B if he pays a further $90,000.
   C until the day after tomorrow.

3 The woman says that the expert
   A can take copies of the letters.
   B should meet her at her hotel.
   C will have enough time to see if the letters are genuine.

4 The man says he needs time
   A to make a decision.
   B to find someone to examine the letters.
   C to find the money.

VOCABULARY

A What do the following words have in common?

bite   sip   chew   gulp   lick   swallow

Which of these words means:

1 pass the tongue over something lightly?
2 cut with the teeth?
3 use the teeth to make food into smaller pieces?
4 eat or drink quickly in large mouthfuls?
5 drink a very small quantity of something?
6 get something down the throat?

FOCUS THREE

B Use one of the words from A to complete the following sentences. You may have to change the form of the word.

1 Remember to _____ your food carefully.
2 The spy put the poison into her mouth and _____ it before anyone could stop her.
3 Instead of drinking the wine so quickly, you should _____ it slowly.
4 I _____ the postage stamp and put it on the letter.
5 Don't be afraid of the dog. He won't _____.
6 The reason you have such terrible problems with your food is that you _____ instead of _____ it.

Which word did you use in both sentence 1 and sentence 6? How did the form of this word change and why?

LANGUAGE STUDY

had better (not) ➤ GS 15.1.3

A Is there any difference?
a) You had better decide quickly.
b) If I were you, I would decide quickly.
c) I think you should decide quickly.

1 Which two examples sound most like simple advice, such as one friend might give another?
2 Which example suggests most strongly that there is very little time and that something bad may happen if you don't decide quickly?

B Complete the following sentences with an appropriate verb.

Example: The train is going to leave soon, so we'd better *get* on it.

1 Your cough sounds terrible. You had better _____ a doctor about it.
2 It might rain today. I think you'd better _____ this umbrella with you.
3 You'd better not _____ any more. You have to drive home.
4 The exam will start at exactly nine o'clock, so you'd better not _____ late.

What do you notice about the form of verbs you have used?

C Use *had/'d better* or *had/'d better not* in these situations.

Example: Your friend wants to drive home. He has drunk a bottle of wine.

➤ *You'd better get a taxi.*

1 It is getting cold. Your friend hasn't even got a sweater on.
2 You and your friend have to catch a train in a few minutes. Your friend is still drinking coffee in the restaurant.
3 You and your friend are walking in a dangerous part of a strange city. Your friend starts walking into a very dark street.
4 You and your friend are in a foreign country. Your friend is about to drink some unboiled water. You know this is dangerous.

WRITING

Transactional letter 5

In the transactional letter, you may be asked to write a reply based on two or more texts. You should look at all the texts carefully to find the relevant information. You must then organize your letter.

A Sample task

You are in charge of booking a weekend break with some friends at a small family-run hotel. Read the extracts below and write a suitable letter to the hotel.

A *For us:*
2 single rooms
Arriving Friday 5 p.m.

B *Unfortunately we won't be able to get there until Saturday morning, but we still think it would be worth coming. A double room would be fine, but could you just check that they can do vegetarian food for Jenny?*
See you soon, Jack

C *Friday afternoon would be fine for us. As regards the room, a double or twin room would be fine. Harry can sleep in a cot in our room. We can bring one if we have to but it'd be better if they could provide one. Could you find out for me?*
Love, Anna

D When you send the £50 deposit, please let us know when you will be arriving and what bedrooms you will need. If you have any special requirements, we would appreciate it if you could give us details in advance so that we can make the necessary arrangements.

Yours sincerely, P K Monkton Manager

B Read these two sample answers. Which one is better? Why?

Dear Mr Monkton

Thank you for your letter of 18 June.

There will be a total of six adults and one child in our party. Four of us and the child will be arriving on Friday afternoon, and the other two adults will be arriving on Saturday morning.

As far as the rooms are concerned, we require two singles and one twin-bedded or double room with a cot for Friday and Saturday night. Could you please let me know if you can provide a cot, or whether we should bring one? We will require an additional double room on Saturday night.

Could you also confirm that you serve vegetarian food, as one of the members of the party is a vegetarian.

I look forward to hearing from you and enclose the deposit of £50.

Dear Mr Monkton,

I will require a single room, and I will be arriving on Friday afternoon.

We have no particular special requirements, but one of the people in our group is a vegetarian. There will be four of us and the child on Friday. I enclose the deposit of £50.

We also require a twin or double room with a cot. Please let me know if we need to bring one or whether you will provide one. By the way, thank you for your letter. That is for two nights.

We require another single room, again for two nights, but we only need another double room on Saturday.

I look forward to hearing from you.

C Writing Task

Read the extract from the head teacher below, together with the students' comments, on which you have made some notes. Then write a letter to the head teacher, suggesting improvements to facilities at the college.

As the budget is limited to £1000, please find out from students what facilities are most in need of improvement.
P Higgs, Head teacher

I think we could really do with somewhere to keep milk for coffee, because it's always going off. Otherwise, things are okay, though lots of the books in the library are torn and we could do with some new ones. Yes

I hate the furniture in the students' room. It looks terrible. And another thing, why don't we get some class sets of books? I hate all these photocopies.

I'm getting tired of crisps and sandwiches every day. It would be so much better if we could make meals ourselves.
Suggest small cooker and fridge

D Base your reply on these notes.

1 Refer to the letter and say what you have done.
2 Discuss problems relating to the kitchen. Then discuss the students' room. Finally, discuss problems relating to books.
3 End the letter in a suitable way.

REVISION AND EXTENSION

A Complete the passage with the best option, A, B, C or D.

A surgeon flying from Hong Kong to London on a jumbo jet (1)_____ a fellow passenger's life by operating on her with a pair of scissors, a coat hanger, and a bottle of brandy.

Pauline Dixon was involved in a motorcycle (2)_____ on the way to Hong Kong airport, but she didn't want to see a doctor (3)_____ she missed her flight. Soon after boarding the plane, she complained about a pain in her arm. The pilot asked (4)_____ or not there were any doctors on board, and Professor Wallace and Dr Tom Wong came forward.

At first they thought her arm was broken, but within minutes they saw that her condition was (5)_____ worse. They realized that one of her lungs (6)_____ have collapsed and was filling up with liquid. Professor Wallace said 'I felt we had (7)_____ operate as soon as we could, but of course we didn't have (8)_____ right equipment, so we had to use what was there. I cut a hole in her chest with a pair of scissors and then we had to find something to push a tube into the lung. One of the cabin crew (9)_____ using a coat hanger, which worked well, and we (10)_____ to get the tube in quite easily.

Normally it is not a complicated operation (11)_____ you have the right equipment, but we had to be very (12)_____. We sterilized everything with five star brandy. When the operation was over, I had a few (13)_____ myself. I can tell you, I needed it.'

After the plane landed safely in London, Miss Dixon went to hospital to recover. Although the operation had been very (14)_____, she was very grateful to the doctors for saving her life, and was full of (15)_____ for what they had done.

1. **A** rescued **B** recovered **C** saved **D** freed
2. **A** accident **B** disaster **C** emergency **D** breakdown
3. **A** in case **B** unless **C** except **D** without
4. **A** for **B** about **C** if **D** whether
5. **A** changing **B** getting **C** turning **D** growing
6. **A** must **B** should **C** may **D** would
7. **A** sooner **B** greater **C** rather **D** better
8. **A** a **B** some **C** the **D** any
9. **A** advised **B** persuaded **C** suggested **D** convinced
10. **A** succeeded **B** managed **C** arrived **D** could
11. **A** if **B** unless **C** in case **D** except
12. **A** carefree **B** careless **C** caring **D** careful
13. **A** bites **B** sips **C** swallows **D** licks
14. **A** painful **B** harmful **C** hurtful **D** aching
15. **A** friendship **B** dedication **C** admiration **D** liking

B Rewrite the second sentence in each pair. Use no more than five words including the word in bold. Do NOT change this word.

1. It is essential that you make a decision quickly.
   better You _____ up quickly.
2. Take the spare key, because I might be out when you get back.
   case Take the spare key _____ when you get back.
3. I don't know if she's lying or telling the truth.
   not I don't know _____ she is telling the truth.
4. You won't feel any pain in the operation, and you'll be able to go home tonight.
   be The operation _____, and you'll be able to go home tonight.
5. Remember, going to the police would be a big mistake.
   had Remember, you _____ to the police.
6. Whose name should I write on the cheque?
   make Who should I _____ to?

LISTENING

Listen to the radio interview in which an interior designer talks about stencilling. Then choose the best answer, A, B or C.

1. According to the designer, the best stencils
   A are in the shape of leaves.
   B are clear and simple.
   C are more than one colour.
2. The designer says she uses spray paints if she
   A can't buy stencilling paints.
   B is in a hurry.
   C is painting furniture.
3. The designer says one disadvantage of spray paints is that
   A it is difficult to get the colours right.
   B they dry more slowly.
   C they are hard to find in the shops.
4. According to the designer, the main advantage of stencilling is that
   A it is very cheap.
   B it is easier to use than wallpaper.
   C you can use your own design.
5. The designer mentions that stencils can be used
   A on furniture.
   B instead of having curtains.
   C on carpets and floors.
6. According to the speaker, a beginner should begin stencilling on fabrics because
   A fabric paint is easier to use.
   B mistakes can be washed out.
   C you can practise more easily.

LEAVING HOME

SPEAKING

A Talking on your own

Work in pairs as Student A and B. Speak for about one minute.

Student A: Describe and compare what the people are doing in both pictures, and then say whether you have ever been in a similar situation.

Student B: Describe and compare what the people might be thinking in both pictures, and then say how you would feel in a similar situation.

B Discussion

1 What kinds of problems are there when people leave home for the first time?

2 If you left home to go to university, would you rather live in a university hall of residence, with a landlady or share a flat? Give reasons.

3 Describe the different things you would take with you if you were going on a trip to a foreign country for a week or longer.

4 At what age in your country do people first leave home for a period of more than a few days? Describe some of the reasons they have for leaving home and where they go.

READING

When I told my mother, she looked at me as if I had slapped her face.

'What? Live in London?' she said.

'I just feel it's time that I saw a little more of the world. After all, mum, I'm twenty-two!'

Just then, my father came downstairs, looking relaxed as he always did after his Sunday afternoon nap. I had chosen the moment carefully.

'Clive wants to leave home. He doesn't want to live with us any more,' she told him in a trembling voice.

My father's expression changed.

'What? You aren't serious, are you, son?' he asked. He sat down at the table opposite me.

Perhaps my parents wouldn't have reacted in this way if they hadn't spent all their lives in a small village in Wales. And perhaps my mother in particular wouldn't have been so possessive if her only other child hadn't died as a baby. I tried to explain to them that the bank I worked for had offered me a chance to take a job in their head office. But I didn't dare tell them I had already accepted the job.

'London's a long way away. We'll hardly see you any more,' my father said.

'I can come back at weekends, dad.'

'I don't know son, I don't know.'

FOCUS ONE

He shook his head and then got up and walked out into the garden.

My mother and I sat there at the table. In the silence, I could hear the old clock ticking away in the hall. There were tears in my mother's eyes. I knew she was going to put pressure on me to give up the idea, and I wondered if I could stand up to it. I even began to wonder if it was wrong of me to want to leave my family, the village and the people I had known all my life to live among the English in their cold, strange capital.

She put her hand over mine.

'Your father hasn't been well lately. Neither have I. You know that. But we won't stand in your way if it's really what you want,' she said.

A Choose the best answer, A, B, C or D.

1 When the writer's mother told his father the news, she
   A looked angry.
   B looked shocked.
   C sounded frightened.
   D sounded upset.

2 The writer told his parents that
   A he did not want to spend his whole life in a village.
   B he had accepted a job in London.
   C he had been offered another job.
   D he wanted to live in London.

3 The father was upset because he felt that
   A he would not be able to go to London regularly.
   B he would hardly ever see his son.
   C he would only see his son at weekends.
   D he would not see his son again.

4 After his father left, the writer
   A had an argument with his mother.
   B had doubts about his decision to leave.
   C explained to his mother why he wanted to leave.
   D tried to comfort his mother.

5 The mother's final words suggest that she
   A wanted to make him feel guilty and stay.
   B was happy for him to go.
   C would look after his father by herself.
   D would try and persuade the father to let him go.

6 The passage as a whole shows that the writer
   A doesn't really want to leave home.
   B wanted to leave at first but then changed his mind.
   C may find it difficult to do what he wants to do.
   D is very determined to leave despite the problems.

B Explain and describe.

1 Imagine the writer's house. Describe what it looks like.
2 How do you think the writer's parents felt?
3 The writer describes his mother as possessive. What sort of things do you think she did to make him say that?
4 Why do you think the writer wanted to leave home?
5 What do you think his father meant when he said, 'I don't know, son, I don't know'?
6 In what ways do you think the writer's mother would try and put pressure on her son to stay?

LANGUAGE STUDY

Cause and result in conditional sentences
➤ GS 4.3

A Each sentence below expresses both a cause and a result. Which part expresses the cause? Which part expresses the result?

a) My parents reacted in this way because they had spent all their lives in a small village.
b) If my parents hadn't spent all their lives in a small village, they wouldn't have reacted in this way.
c) My mother was very possessive because her only other child had died as a baby.
d) My mother wouldn't have been so possessive if her only other child hadn't died as a baby.

Now compare sentences a) and c) with sentences b) and d). What is the difference in the way cause and result are expressed?

B Rephrase the following sentences using *if.*

Example: I didn't go out yesterday because the weather was so bad.
➤ *If the weather hadn't been so bad yesterday, I would have gone out.*

1 Mary was shy with boys because her father didn't let her meet them.
2 She was attracted to Tom because he seemed so pleasant.
3 Tom wanted to marry her because she was rich.
4 Her father liked him because he thought Tom was a prince.
5 Mary believed his story because she had so little experience of men.
6 She married him because she thought he really loved her.
7 She shot him because he was so terrible to her.
8 All this happened because her father was so foolish.

A Read the advertisement below and choose the best answer, A, B, C or D to fill the spaces.

If only we'd known about
Young Contacts
before!

Thousands of young people come to London every month to (1)_____ love, romance and adventure. A few (2)_____ in finding what they are looking for, but most never do. It turns out to be far more (3)_____ than you imagined to meet people in London, (4)_____ the sort of people you want to meet. But now there is a new scientific way – YOUNG CONTACTS.

Q How does it work?

First, we (5)_____ you a scientific personality test, using the very (6)_____ computer techniques. Then we match you with someone whose tastes and interests are (7)_____ to yours, and who also has the characteristics you are looking for in your (8)_____ partner or companion.

Q Who can belong to Young Contacts?

We are the first organization in this country to (9)_____ in matching people between the ages of 17 and 29. But, (10)_____ from that, anyone can join. We have people from all walks of life. But they all have one thing in (11)_____. They're tired of feeling lonely and think it's time they did something (12)_____ it. And that's why they come to us.

Q How do I actually meet people?

Just come to one of our centres, with its special club-like atmosphere, and we'll do the rest. A (13)_____ of our friendly staff will (14)_____ to you and then arrange for you to meet just the sort of people you will get on with. For a list of centres and further (15)_____ , simply fill in the form and send it off today!

1 A make   B have   C find   D get
2 A manage   B are able   C succeed
   D achieve
3 A heavy   B hard   C difficult   D impossible
4 A particularly   B exactly   C precisely
   D additionally
5 A ask   B pass   C do   D give
6 A last   B recent   C modern   D latest
7 A alike   B similar   C same   D equal
8 A ideal   B best   C last   D absolute
9 A specialize   B focus   C concentrate
   D centre
10 A apart   B besides   C except   D without
11 A common   B usual   C normal   D everyday
12 A with   B about   C for   D to
13 A person   B member   C worker
   D representative
14 A discuss   B interview   C question   D talk
15 A facts   B information   C knowledge
   D news

SPEAKING

As part of a TV programme, you have agreed to go on a blind date with one of three people. You must make your choice by asking them each the same 15 questions, and selecting your partner by what they say.

Work in pairs or small groups. Think of a further ten questions you would ask to find out which person would suit you best. Look at these examples:

1 Where do you live?
2 Do you smoke?
3 What religion are you?
4 Would you like to have children one day?
5 What do you do?

When you have finished, compare your answers with another pair or group. Can you agree on ten final questions that ask all the most important things about a person?

FOCUS TWO

VOCABULARY

A Work in pairs. Can you match the phrasal verbs to their meanings?

get over something	• depress
get together	• have a good relationship
get something back	• escape being punished
get out of something	• meet together
get round to something	• explain what you mean
get up	• recover from
get on/along with someone	• regain possession of
get something across	• find time to do something
get someone down	• get out of bed
get away with something	• escape or avoid something

B Complete the following sentences with these phrasal verbs, in a suitable form.

1 Let's _____ next Tuesday at 8.30 and see a film.
2 She's upset, but she'll _____ it soon.
3 I find London so depressing. It really _____ me _____ .
4 I've got to _____ at 6.30 tomorrow to catch a plane.
5 He _____ going to work by saying he was ill.
6 I really like Tom. We _____ each other well.
7 The thief stole a lot of money, but he _____ it because the police couldn't find any proof.
8 If you repeat the main points in your speech, that will help you _____ your message _____ .
9 When are you going to _____ doing your homework?
10 I paid £40 to _____ my car _____ after the police towed it away.

between or *among*? ➤ GS 10.1, 10.3

C Complete each sentence with *between* or *among*.

1 The woman was _____ the ages of 25 and 30.
2 She entered the crowded restaurant and sat down _____ the people there.
3 _____ all the things in her handbag there was a photograph of a man.
4 When she looked up, the same man was standing _____ her and the door.
5 'Are you the woman that I am supposed to meet here _____ 3 o'clock and 3.15?' he asked.
6 _____ the many things they discussed that afternoon were the subjects of love and marriage.
7 Until that moment the man had only been a name _____ a lot of other names on a list.
8 What else do you think happened _____ the beginning of this story and their wedding day five months later?

• Which word, *between* or *among*, do we use when talking about only two people, things or points?
• Which word do you use for *more than* two people, things or points?

LANGUAGE STUDY

it's time

A Which sentence (a or b) suggests most clearly that the speaker has let some time go by without doing anything about the problem?

a) I should do something about this problem.
b) It's time I did something about this problem.

B Which sentence (c or d) really means 'You've been lying in bed too long'?

c) It's time to get up.
d) It's time you got up.

C Rephrase the following sentences using *It's time I/you/we. . .*

Example: You ought to get a haircut.

➤ *It's time you got a haircut.*

1 You ought to find a job.
2 I ought to get out of bed.
3 We ought to have a talk about this problem.
4 You really ought to get married.
5 I should have a holiday.
6 We should get down to work.
7 You should buy some new clothes.
8 The government should do something about this problem.

D How would you use *It's time. . .* in these situations?

1 Your 14-year-old son still doesn't know how to tie his shoelaces. What do you say to him?
2 You have a friend who says his shower at home is broken. He is beginning to smell a bit.
3 The brakes on your car have needed repairing for several weeks. What do you say to yourself?
4 You have just received reminders for a number of bills you got several weeks ago. What do you say to yourself?
5 A friend has an important exam soon, but has spent the last few weeks going out with friends every evening.

Diana P

AGE 25

JOB teaches art and music in secondary school

LIKES going to classical concerts, cinema and eating out – especially Italian, Thai and Chinese food, arguing about politics, driving her sports car; at home enjoys reading, listening to classical music

IDEAL PARTNER a man with a good sense of humour and intelligence who 'will allow me to develop my own career and interests but who is better than I am at managing money'

CHILDREN wants at least two, but 'not for a while'

OTHER non-smoker, 'can't stand men who get into fights or who have tattoos'

Adam

AGE 27

JOB financial journalist

LIKES good food, good films, all kinds of music, especially jazz and Bach

IDEAL PARTNER a woman who is a good companion but who 'is independent and will give me some time alone'

CHILDREN perhaps in the future; 'it all depends'

OTHER non-smoker, doesn't like driving

Bert W

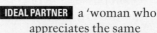

AGE 28

JOB owner of a small sportswear shop

LIKES football, 'going to the pub, eating good old-fashioned food like fish and chips and roast beef with lots of mustard'

IDEAL PARTNER a 'woman who appreciates the same things as me'. Can't stand 'career women' or women 'who talk too much'.

CHILDREN 'Not a bad idea, as long as I don't have to change the nappies and things like that.'

OTHER heavy smoker, divorced 3 years ago; was recently arrested in Berlin after Germany beat England 3–0

Charles K

AGE 29

JOB research scientist with government

LIKES hiking, cycling, mountain climbing; at home, prefers gardening, reading, playing the guitar and cooking exotic meals

IDEAL PARTNER an intelligent woman who wants children

CHILDREN wants them 'as soon as possible'

OTHER doesn't smoke or drink; hates 'wasting money' on things like food, cinemas etc.

SPEAKING

A Problem solving
In small groups, decide who would be the best person for Diana to choose as a partner. Then decide what kind of woman would suit the other two men.

B Now answer the questions (1–16) by writing:
A (Adam), B (Bert), C (Charles) or D (Diana).

Who likes staying in and watching soccer?	1
Who enjoys being in the open air?	2
Who likes listening to classical CDs?	3
Who dislikes spending money on entertainment?	4
Who is the youngest?	5
Who is unsure about wanting children?	6
Who dislikes taking care of babies?	7
Who has had trouble with the police?	8
Who enjoys foreign restaurants?	9
Who smokes a great deal?	10
Who works at a school?	11
Who say they want an intelligent partner?	12 13
Who has already been married?	14
Who plays a musical instrument?	15
Who is self-employed?	16

FOCUS THREE

LISTENING 😐

You will hear five people (1–5) talking about living in London. Match the five speakers with the sentences (A–F). There is one sentence you do not need. Which speaker:

A has always lived in London [1][ ]

B thinks it is not too hard for outsiders to make friends [2][ ]

C prefers village life to life in London [3][ ]

D feels freer in London to do what they want [4][ ]

E has met very few people from London [5][ ]

F feels partly responsible for their lack of real friends

SPEAKING

Discussion

1 If you were in London for a one-month course, which speaker would you prefer to show you around? Why?
2 How would you enjoy living in London?
3 How easy or difficult is it to make friends in a big city? What are the best ways of meeting people?
4 What would it be like for a foreigner to come and live where you live?
5 Would you rather live anywhere other than where you live now? Why?

VOCABULARY

Prefixes

A Study the words in Columns A and B. What is the same about them? What is different? What has changed the meaning?

A	B
personal	impersonal
friendly	unfriendly
satisfied	dissatisfied
satisfactory	unsatisfactory
tolerant	intolerant
religious	irreligious

B What do you need to add to each of the following words to give it the opposite meaning? An example is given.

0	capable	*incapable*
1	able	_____
2	accurate	_____
3	possible	_____
4	polite	_____
5	resistible	_____
6	regular	_____
7	loyal	_____
8	orderly	_____
9	lucky	_____
10	happy	_____
11	sensitive	_____
12	reasonable	_____
13	willing	_____
14	pleased	_____
15	pleasant	_____
16	convenient	_____
17	correct	_____
18	certain	_____

LISTENING 😐

Listen to a reporter interviewing a director of *Young Contacts*. Complete the notes below. Question 0 has been done for you.

Number of members is [0] *42,000*

Biggest group (aged 21–25) = [1]

Group aged 26–29 = [2]

Membership fee is [3]

On joining, members are given

[4]

Computer selects [5]

New members can choose [6]

Meetings are [7]

About eighty per cent of members are

[8]

Fifteen per cent of its members said

[9]

WRITING

Story 3

It is important that the sequence or order of events in a story or narrative is clear and easy to follow.

A **The paragraphs in this narrative (1–4) are in the correct order, but the sentences (a–s) are mixed up. Read the complete story. Give each sentence a number from 1 to 19, to indicate its correct order in the story.**

Paragraph 1

a) This one is about a man who worked in an American bank.

b) There are many stories about people who have taken large amounts of money from companies by using computers.

c) He was a brilliant programmer, and got a job in their computer department.

Paragraph 2

d) He realized that if he could use it during the night and return it the next morning, nobody would know.

e) After working in the bank for several months, he had a good idea.

f) These were kept at the bank overnight.

g) He noticed that at closing time, the bank had large sums of money in the computer.

h) The following morning, the money would be transferred to the bank's investment department.

Paragraph 3

i) His program instructed the computer to send the money to Switzerland every evening.

j) The next morning, before the bank opened, the money (less the interest that it had earned) was sent back to America.

k) The first stage in his plan was to write a special program.

l) He had opened this account the previous month.

m) It all stayed overnight in a secret Swiss account he had, where it earned interest for him.

Paragraph 4

n) When he arrived there, he bought millions of pounds' worth of diamonds.

o) This still left him with a fortune, which he started to spend.

p) Finally, his crime was discovered, but only because he was so proud of it that he had talked about it.

q) One day he left the bank and travelled to Switzerland.

r) Back home he sold them at a profit and secretly returned all the interest that he had earned.

s) Afterwards he flew back to America with them hidden in his suitcase.

B **The story in A used different ways of making the sequence of events clear. Can you find examples of the following?**

1 Link words such as: *first of all, then, next, finally*

2 Time expressions, such as: *one day, a few hours later, the following day, three months previously*

3 The past perfect (GS 13.2.4)

Example: *After/When we had seen the play, we went out to dinner.*

4 The *Before/After* + *-ing* form (GS 5.4)

Example: *After seeing the play, we went out to dinner.*

C **Read this passage and choose the best word or words, A, B, C or D.**

(1)_____ William Hall left university in 1989, he moved to London. He got a job in the same year with an insurance company that his grandfather had started exactly 80 years (2)_____, in 1909. (3)_____ working there for two years, he was promoted and (4)_____ the assistant manager of the Edinburgh office in 1991. (5)_____ this time, he was already engaged to Janet Simpson. They had met the (6)_____ year, while he was (7)_____ working in London. She also moved to Edinburgh. They got married a year (8)_____ and in the (9)_____ year their son, Henry, (10)_____ born.

1 **A** While **B** During **C** When **D** If

2 **A** ago **B** earlier **C** sooner **D** recently

3 **A** Until **B** By **C** While **D** After

4 **A** is becoming **B** has become **C** became **D** had become

5 **A** Until **B** From **C** By **D** After

6 **A** previous **B** last **C** late **D** recent

7 **A** still **B** already **C** yet **D** just

8 **A** after **B** later **C** following **D** next

9 **A** after **B** later **C** following **D** coming

10 **A** was **B** is **C** has been **D** had been

D Writing task

Your teacher has asked you to write a life history. It can be about yourself, or you can pretend to be someone you know well or a famous person.

E Use these notes to help you.

1 Before you write, make some notes with important dates and events in the life story you are relating.

2 Divide the notes up into paragraphs, so that the different life stages are clear.

3 As you write, try to use a variety of the techniques in B to make the sequence of the story clear.

FOCUS FOUR

REVISION AND EXTENSION

if, unless, when or in case? ➤ GS 6.6

A Complete the following sentences.

1 The sun was shining _____ I got up this morning.
2 However, I saw a few dark clouds, so I said, 'Hmm, I'd better take an umbrella to work _____ it rains.'
3 _____ I had known it was going to be such a beautiful day, I wouldn't have taken that umbrella at all.
4 I don't like carrying an umbrella _____ it's absolutely necessary.
5 I'm going to Spain for my holiday this year. I'll send you a postcard _____ I get there.
6 It hardly ever rains there at this time of the year, but I'm taking some books to read just _____ it does.
7 More people would spend their holidays in England _____ the weather weren't so unpredictable.
8 Look. The sun is shining now. We can have a picnic in the forest this afternoon, _____ it rains, of course. But somehow I don't think it will.

Conditional 3 ➤ GS 4.3

B Complete the following conversation with the correct form of each verb in brackets.

A What's wrong? Why are you looking so angry?
B I've just failed my driving test. I'm sure I (pass) it if I (have) a different examiner.
A So you think it was all the examiner's fault?
B No, it wasn't only the examiner's fault. A pedestrian suddenly ran into the middle of the road. If I (see) him, I (stop).
A What? Do you mean you didn't stop and you ran over a pedestrian?
B No, no. Of course I stopped. I mean, if I (stop) sooner, I (be able) to avoid hitting that lamppost.
A Just a moment. Are you saying you ran over a pedestrian and then hit a lamppost?
B No! Uh. . . I mean yes. I mean, if I (not use) the brakes, I (run over) the pedestrian.
A The brakes? You mean your brakes caused the accident?
B No, not exactly. I mean, if I (not use) the brakes, the car (not go) out of control.
A The car went out of control?
B You see, when I saw him, I used the brakes, but because I was going a little too fast, I lost control of the car. I tried to explain all this to the examiner. If he (listen) to me, he (understand) it wasn't my fault. It's clear, isn't it? I (not use) the brakes at all if the pedestrian (not run) into the road so suddenly. So, I'm going to make an official complaint about the driving examiner.

C Rewrite the pairs of sentences as one sentence only. Begin each one with If.

Example: The driver used the brakes suddenly. That's why he lost control of the car.
➤ If the driver hadn't used the brakes suddenly, he wouldn't have lost control of the car.

1 You were careless. That's why you had an accident.
2 You had an accident. That's why you failed the test.
3 You tried to kill the driving examiner. That's why the police arrested you.
4 The police arrested you. That's why you lost your job.
5 You were careless. That's why all the other things happened.

Mixed conditional forms

D Now rewrite these pairs in the same way. Make sure that you change the form of each conditional clause so that it is clear whether the cause or result are in the past or the present.

Past Cause: The driver tried to kill the examiner.
Present Result: He is in prison now.
➤ If the driver hadn't tried to kill the examiner, he wouldn't be in prison now.

1 The driver failed his exam yesterday. He is very angry now.
2 It rained very hard last night. The streets are wet now.
3 Bill is such a terrible driver. That's why he has had so many accidents.
4 People drive too fast. That's why there have been so many accidents lately.
5 We didn't have enough rain last winter. That's why there is a water shortage now.

Other mixed forms

E Complete these sentences with the correct form of the verb in brackets.

1 It's nearly midnight. It's time we (go) home.
2 I wish I (not go) to that party yesterday.
3 If I (not go) to that party yesterday, I (not feel) so terrible now.
4 Look! You've broken the vase. If only you (be) more careful.
5 You (not break) so many things if you (be) more careful.
6 This terrible weather has been going on for weeks. I wish it (get) better.
7 If the weather (be) better lately, I (not be) so depressed now.
8 It's time you (realize) that we (not have) any water to drink in the future unless it (rain) soon.
9 It's time you (have) a break. You (not be able) to sleep this evening unless you (stop) doing these exercises now.

SPEAKING

This image was found in an ancient temple in Mexico. One writer thinks the picture shows a man in a spaceship. In pairs, discuss one of the questions below.

1 What can you see in the picture that might make some people believe that this is a picture of a man in a spaceship?

2 Try to identify parts of the 'spaceship', such as the controls, the engine, etc.

READING

A Five paragraphs have been removed from the text below. Choose from paragraphs (A–F) on the next page the one which fits each gap (0–4). Gap 0 has already been done for you. There is one paragraph you do not need.

0 | *E*

Very little was known about this ancient civilization at the time, but Catherwood's drawings in the book revealed incredible cities with temples, pyramids and other buildings as impressive as those of their northern neighbours, the Aztecs. These cities, however, were deserted. The people had vanished.

1 |

When he wrote this, Stephens had already realized that these places were not cities in the European sense. They were, in fact, sacred gathering places for the farmers in the surrounding areas, consisting of a huge central square with various religious buildings around it. The people would journey there for the great religious festivals, and at other times the vast buildings would be empty except for the priests and some of the nobles.

2 |

In spite of the violence of their religion, the Mayas' civilization was very advanced. Their engineers were capable of moving huge blocks of stone long distances and cutting them into precise shapes and sizes. They also had a highly-developed system of government and of agriculture, as well as an incredibly accurate system for measuring time.

3 |

A more traditional explanation is that they developed their skills over more than a thousand years, and most archaeologists believe that the process of development began as long ago as 500 BC. The Mayas first began building their great cities in 250 AD, and developed a strong and stable society that lasted for centuries.

4 |

Some people believe that the end of the Mayas may have been brought about because of diseases or epidemics. Others think that it may have been caused by sudden environmental changes. The real reasons for the sudden collapse of their civilization may never be discovered. All we really know is that when the first Europeans arrived in 1517, this great and mysterious culture was only a memory.

FOCUS ONE

A At some stage however, Mayan civilization collapsed. Their society was suddenly and totally destroyed, and by the year 1200, their last great capital, Chichen Itza was deserted. All over the Yucatan, the great temples and pyramids were abandoned and allowed to fall into decay as the jungle grew back around them.

B The discovery of the cities was an experience that most archaeologists could only dream of. As Stephens wrote in his book 'We lived in the ruined palaces of their kings; we went up to their desolate temples and fallen altars, and wherever we moved was saw evidence of their taste, their skill in arts, their wealth and power. As we stood in the desolation and ruin, we looked back to the past and imagined every building perfect, with its terraces and pyramids and its sculptured and painted ornaments.'

C The Mayas were the only early civilization on the American continent to develop a form of writing that could express all types of thought and language. They used a combination of signs and symbols, and in recent years, considerable progress has been made in understanding these texts.

D These scientific achievements are particularly remarkable because there is no evidence that the Mayas had any contact with any other ancient cultures. Indeed, one writer has tried to prove that the Mayas must have been visited by aliens from outer space, and that their gods were astronauts.

E In 1841, a book was published that astonished the world. It was called *Incidents of Travel in Central America, Chiapas and Yucatan*. The author, John Lloyd Stephens, had just returned from a long, difficult and dangerous journey through the thick rainforests of southern Mexico and Guatemala. He had gone there with Frederick Catherwood, an architect and artist, to search for the remains of a lost civilization called the Mayas.

F The Mayan ceremonies that were held here were terrifying occasions, because the Mayas believed in gods that demanded human sacrifice. Sometimes the believers would offer their own blood to please the gods, and would cut themselves by passing a rope of thorns through their mouth. At other times, they would sacrifice prisoners or children, and Mayan paintings show how they would tear a victim's heart out and then cut off his head.

B In pairs or groups, go through paragraphs A–F again and say why you think they fit the gaps. For example, paragraph E, which fills gap 0, contains information you need to answer these two questions.

- Which 'ancient civilization' is the text about?
- Who was 'Catherwood'?

You would expect to have this information before reading the first paragraph on page 154.

VOCABULARY

Which is the word in each group that does not belong?

1 jungle desert forest woods
2 deserted abandoned inhabited empty
3 disappear vanish destroy leave
4 incredible astonishing unbelievable plain
5 exact general accurate precise
6 mysterious unusual ordinary strange
7 collapse develop decay fall
8 disprove demonstrate show confirm

LANGUAGE STUDY

Review of phrasal verbs

In each sentence, an important word is missing. Can you work out which word you need?

1 For some mysterious reason, the Mayan system of government suddenly _____ down.
2 Nobody knows what brought this collapse _____.
3 But when it happened, it was as if a candle had suddenly gone _____.
4 No doubt the Mayas had gone _____ some difficult times before.
5 Perhaps the Kings found they could no longer count _____ the support of the people.
6 Perhaps important supplies of food and minerals were suddenly _____ off.
7 Perhaps the people _____ down with strange diseases.
8 Writers will probably continue _____ for an explanation.
9 But I doubt if they will ever _____ up with a satisfactory answer.
10 It is one of the biggest problems historians have ever _____ up against.
11 They'll just have to _____ up to the fact that they may never find an answer.
12 Do you think they should _____ up trying to find an answer?

LISTENING 📷

Part 1

A **You will hear a guide telling a group of visitors about Chichen Itza. Match the five places (A–E) in the picture with the following buildings.**

The Temple of Kukulcan	**1** ☐
The Observatory	**2** ☐
The Temple of the Warriors	**3** ☐
The Well of Sacrifice	**4** ☐
The Ball Court	**5** ☐

B **Listen again and decide which of the places in the picture (A–E) fits the description below. You do not need to use one of them.**

It may have been used to keep prisoners.	**6** ☐
It was used to decide who should be sacrificed.	**7** ☐
It was used for an important ceremony once a year.	**8** ☐
It was of scientific significance.	**9** ☐
It contains an image of a Mayan god.	**10** ☐
It was where the majority of the victims were killed.	**11** ☐

Part 2

Listen and complete the notes.

Built around **12** ☐

The length of the court is 137 metres and the height of the walls is **13** ☐

Ball courts found at **14** ☐

Game was probably **15** ☐

May also have had **16** ☐

Evidence for this comes from **17** ☐

Information about the game comes from **18** ☐

Played by between **19** ☐

Aim was to get the ball through **20** ☐

Players were not allowed to **21** ☐

Sometimes members of the losing team **22** ☐

Was played very seriously **23** ☐

At other times, was played for **24** ☐ which was used as **25** ☐

Winners also were given the clothes of **26** ☐ and **27** ☐

VOCABULARY

Read the text and choose the best answer, A, B, C or D.

In 1967, a research team from an American university **(1)**_____ out to explore the Well of Sacrifice at Chichen Itza. Unfortunately, however, the water in this well was so dark that is was impossible for divers to see, so the team had to use filters to clean it.

Just as this work was about to begin, some **(2)**_____ Indians told the team that the well was **(3)**_____ by the spirit of a rain god. The god was **(4)**_____ as Chac, and they warned the team that Chac would **(5)**_____ revenge if his home was disturbed. The team listened politely but **(6)**_____ these warnings and went on with their research.

(7)_____ the summer, pumps and filters were used, but it wasn't until **(8)**_____ months later that the water was clear enough for divers to go down into the well.

When they got **(9)**_____ to work they began to discover various objects at the **(10)**_____ of the well. **(11)**_____ the things they brought back to the surface were human bones, and by the time they had **(12)**_____, they had recovered more than 50 skeletons. This was **(13)**_____ that the well had indeed been used for human sacrifice.

Perhaps it would have been better if the team had **(14)**_____ to the warnings of the Indians, because within a year, several members of the team had been **(15)**_____ in mysterious accidents.

1 **A** put **B** broke **C** set **D** looked
2 **A** local **B** natural **C** near **D** close
3 **A** lived **B** housed **C** resided **D** inhabited
4 **A** named **B** called **C** told **D** known
5 **A** have **B** make **C** do **D** take
6 **A** ignored **B** refused **C** denied **D** rejected
7 **A** Along **B** Within **C** Throughout
   D Inside
8 **A** few **B** several **C** various **D** any
9 **A** down **B** through **C** about **D** at
10 **A** end **B** ground **C** depth **D** bottom
11 **A** Between **B** Around **C** Within **D** Among
12 **A** ended **B** finished **C** concluded
   D achieved
13 **A** clear **B** proof **C** evident **D** obvious
14 **A** listened **B** heard **C** noticed **D** watched
15 **A** died **B** wounded **C** killed **D** missed

LANGUAGE STUDY

General revision 1

Rewrite the following sentences using the word in bold.

1 Stephens really wanted to see the ruins.
   forward Stephens was really _____ _____ the ruins.

2 He said 'They're the most beautiful things I've ever seen!'
   never He said that _____ so beautiful before.

3 'Where have the people gone?' he asked.
   wondered He _____ gone.

4 Although he was ill, he visited other ruins.
   spite In _____ he visited other ruins.

5 Reaching the other cities wasn't easy.
   difficult The _____ reach.

6 They managed to return to New York.
   succeeded They _____ to New York.

7 Stephens wrote his book in three months.
   took It _____ write his book.

8 People were very interested in it at the time.
   found People _____ at the time.

9 The book was so good that everyone bought it.
   such It _____ that everyone bought it.

10 I haven't read it for ages, but I loved it.
   been It _____ I read it, but I loved it.

READING

A
Read extracts 1 and 2 below from a tourist brochure and underline all the words you think should not be there. An example is given.

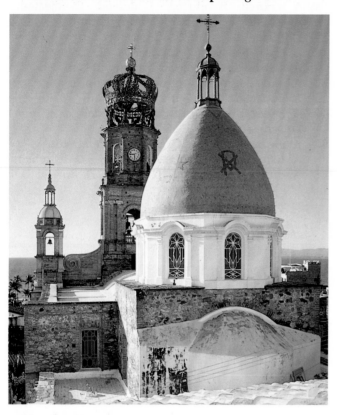

MEXICO EXCURSIONS

1 ROUGH GUIDE TO VALLARTA

One of the best ways _for_ to get to know Puerto Vallarta is to take this professionally-guided tour. A guide who he can speak English and Spanish will pick you up in the front of your hotel and deliver you back in time for a lunch. You will have a chance to walk through this Mexican charming small town and during the morning, you'll discover about its main plaza, and see its other attractions like as the Marina Pier and the cathedral. Afterwards, you will also be able to hunt out a few shopping bargains in the flea market.

2 SURF AND TURF

If you will want to see a different side of Mexico, this is a great opportunity to see the Vallarta's unspoilt coast and the countryside. You will be travel to the scenic south coast of Vallarta, and visit Mismaloya beach, where the movie 'Night of the Iguana' was filmed there. You'll be able to have swim in the sea or, if you would prefer, you can just relax yourself and have a drink on a beautiful white sandy beach. After then we'll go inland to one of the area's most best restaurants in a spectacular forest setting, and take an part in a guided walk of the forest.

B
In extracts 3 and 4 write the correct form of the words given below.

| 1 fascinate   2 wonder   3 civilize 4 see |
| 5 include   6 comfort   7 fly   8 impress |
| 9 enjoy   10 choose |

3 MEXICO CITY – 2 days/1 night

Spend a (1)_____ two days taking time out to visit the metropolis of this (2)_____ country, namely Mexico City. Fly with us to the land of the early Mayan and Aztec (3)_____, and experience this land of magnificent (4)_____, set against high snow-capped mountains. This all- (5)_____ tour covers a half day tour of the fascinating city, an overnight stay in a (6)_____ two-star hotel and all (7)_____. You will also have a full-day tour out to San Juan Teotihuacan, the City of the Gods, built around 100 BC. Visit the (8)_____ temples of the sun and the moon, and other remains of this ancient culture.

4 FIESTA MEXICANA

A thoroughly (9)_____ evening with the chance to experience a real Mexican party, which includes a (10)_____ of real Mexican drinks such as Margaritas, rum, tequila and beer! With a delicious Mexican-style buffet plus Mexican folk-dancing.

C
Now fill in the spaces in extracts 5 and 6 with one word only.

5 BACK TO NATURE BBQ CRUISE

Get away from it (1)_____ and leave the crowds (2)_____ as we sail north of Vallarta (3)_____ our own boat, _The Adventure_. We will stop at (4)_____ Marieta Islands, (5)_____ are uninhabited. Later we will call at the Hidden Paradise Beach, (6)_____ you will be able to swim, snorkel or simply sunbathe and imagine you (7)_____ Robinson Crusoe. The excursion costs £30, including a barbecue.(Note: no toilets (8)_____ restaurant facilities are available here.)

6 SAILING CHARTERS

If you really want a change (9)_____ the stresses and strains (10)_____ work, why not charter a sailing boat (11)_____ the day. You will be able to sail wherever you want, stop anywhere, and find secluded sandy beaches and complete privacy. The cost includes a free lunch as well (12)_____ free snorkelling equipment and windsurfers. With a maximum (13)_____ six people, you will have the boat (14)_____ yourselves, or alternatively, we can find sailing partners for you. Don't miss (15)_____ on this wonderful chance to cruise in complete tranquillity.

FOCUS THREE

D Read the texts again and answer the following questions. Match the numbers of the excursions (1 to 6) with the correct description (A–L).

A The beach lacks some important facilities.

B People who like to eat and drink a lot will really enjoy this excursion.

C It takes the longest.

D This one requires a certain number of people.

E This excursion goes to an island with no houses.

F You will enjoy excellent food and wonderful natural scenery.

G It supplies watersports equipment free.

H The price includes the cost of alcoholic drinks.

I This excursion only takes a morning.

J On this excursion, you go to an archaeological site.

K You will have a chance to buy souvenirs.

L This one involves staying in a different hotel.

SPEAKING

A Talking about yourself

1 Which of the excursions above would interest you if you were on holiday in Mexico? Explain why.

2 Which excursions would you not like to go on? Why?

B Problem solving
In pairs, plan a one-day excursion which you think would be of interest to a group of tourists coming to the area where you live. Include meals and decide what kind of transport you might use. When you have finished, compare your excursion with that of another pair of students.

C Discussion

1 What are the advantages and disadvantages of travelling in an organized group and travelling alone?

2 Some people say travel broadens the mind. Explain why you agree or disagree with this statement.

WRITING

When you have finished, work alone for a few minutes. Write out a short description of one excursion. Spend no more than five minutes doing this. Afterwards, compare what you have written with what your partners have written.

LANGUAGE STUDY

General revision 2

Rewrite the following sentences using the words in bold.

1 The subject of the guide's lecture was Uxmal.
talk The guide _____ Uxmal.

2 I spent an hour travelling to Mexico City.
took It _____ travel to Mexico City.

3 Could you take me back to my hotel?
lift Could you _____ back to my hotel?

4 The baby-sitter can look after the children.
take The baby-sitter can _____ the children.

5 We can organize everything for you.
arrangements We can _____ for you.

6 I once studied Mayan architecture.
course I once _____ Mayan architecture.

7 I enjoyed the excursion.
time I _____ the excursion.

8 I talked to the guide for a long time.
conversation I _____ the guide.

9 We have to decide what to do tomorrow.
make We have to _____ what to do tomorrow.

10 Would you like to see the photos I took?
have Would you like to _____ the photos I took?

11 Uxmal didn't impress me as much as Chichen Itza.
think I didn't _____ as Chichen Itza.

12 I'm so sorry we can't stay longer.
wish I _____ longer.

13 He was so tired he couldn't go on the excursion.
too He _____ on the excursion.

14 I paid someone to make this dress for me in Mexico.
made I _____ me in Mexico.

15 I've never stayed in such a good hotel.
ever This is the _____ stayed in.

16 Do ancient cities interest you or not?
find Do _____ or not?

17 Could you come back a bit later?
mind Would _____ a bit later?

18 She said to the tourists 'Please don't take photographs in the museum.'
asked She _____ take photographs in the museum.

19 'Don't take any more photographs!' she ordered.
stop She told them to _____ photographs.

20 I expect you don't want to revise any more for the exam.
tired I expect you _____ for the exam.

WRITING

Report 3

When you write a report, you should use language that is as simple and clear as possible. Above all, you must make sure that you answer the exam question fully.

A Sample task

A travel company has asked you to write a short report on the city or town you live in or near. They want to know if it is famous for anything that might attract tourists, what kind of tourist accommodation is available, which other major cities it is near, the quality of food in local restaurants and anything else that tourists might find interesting.

B Read the sample answer. Choose from list A–E the best heading for each paragraph (1–5).

1	

Dortmund is one of the most important cities in the north-western part of Germany. It is close to Essen, Dusseldorf, Cologne and other major cities in the Ruhr and Rhineland area. It used to be a centre of the coal mining and steel industries.

2	

Dortmund is famous for its beer. There are five breweries. It also has a theatre, a small opera house, a very large sports stadium and a well-known football team. The surrounding countryside is very attractive. In addition, a national garden exhibition takes place there each year.

3	

Dortmund has a wide range of hotels and other accommodation for tourists. Rail connections are particularly good. It also has a small airport with flights to most major German cities.

4	

Although Dortmund is not famous for its cuisine, there are many restaurants there that offer excellent value for money. Local pubs also serve excellent beer and light meals.

5	

I would recommend a stay of one or two days in Dortmund to tourists who are interested in visiting a typical, middle-sized German city.

> A Conclusion
>
> B Most important features
>
> C Travel and accommodation
>
> D Food and drink
>
> E Location and type of city

C Writing task

A travel company is arranging a 7–day tour of your country. You have been asked to write a report on the city or town you live in or near, saying why it should be included in the tour.

D Discussion

Before you write, discuss in pairs or groups what you can say about that city or town. As you talk, keep these questions in mind.

1 Where exactly is it? What else can you say about its size or location and the other places it is near?
2 Is it or has it ever been a centre of industry or commerce? If so, what kind of industry or commerce?
3 Is it famous for anything? If so, what?
4 Can you think of anything else that might interest tourists?
5 What about the surrounding countryside?
6 How could tourists get there?
7 What kind of accommodation is available?
8 What kind of food and drink is available in local restaurants?
9 What kind of tourists would you recommend it to?
10 How long should they stay?

E Now write your report, covering points 1–6 below.

1 A brief description of the city or town and where it is.

2 Information about the main attractions or places of interest; events there or nearby; the surrounding countryside.

3 How to get there; what kind of accommodation is available.

4 Information about where to eat.

5 At least one reason for recommending it and the kind of tourist you hope would find it worth visiting.

6 A typical length of stay for such a tourist.

REVISION AND EXTENSION

Complete the passage with the best word, A, B, C or D.

One of the most exciting archaeological discoveries in history was made in November 1922, when Howard Carter was working in the Valley of the Kings in Egypt. After many months of work, he finally (1)_____ across an unknown tomb.

Together with his friend Lord Carnarvon, who was providing the (2)_____ for the excavations, he entered the dark chamber. At first there was disappointment, because the tomb was (3)_____, and it was clear that it had been (4)_____ at some time in the past. However, one of the workers eventually uncovered a small stairway that (5)_____ down to another door that had not been opened.

Carter went down the dark staircase, walking (6)_____ in case there were any traps. As he opened the door, Lord Carnarvon (7)_____ if he could see anything. He replied 'Yes – wonderful things.' It was clear at once that they had discovered what they had been looking (8)_____. The tomb of the boy pharaoh Tutankhamun was full of treasures of great (9)_____. There were over 5,000 objects of silver, gold and precious stones which had (10)_____ there undiscovered for thousands of years.

Lord Carnarvon's pleasure at (11)_____ the treasures did not (12)_____ long. Many of the local people were afraid of disturbing the pharaohs' tombs, and believed that the pharaohs would (13)_____ revenge on anyone who entered them. Lord Carnarvon had (14)_____ little attention to these warnings, but only a few weeks later, he suddenly fell ill and died; at the exact time of his death, all the lights in Cairo suddenly (15)_____ out, and far away in England, his dog also died.

1   **A** came   **B** arrived   **C** got   **D** found
2   **A** salary   **B** money   **C** currency   **D** wage
3   **A** deserted   **B** abandoned   **C** left   **D** empty
4   **A** taken   **B** robbed   **C** stolen   **D** broken
5   **A** took   **B** brought   **C** led   **D** conducted
6   **A** accurately   **B** carefully   **C** carelessly   **D** precisely
7   **A** demanded   **B** requested   **C** questioned   **D** asked
8   **A** into   **B** after   **C** up   **D** for
9   **A** expense   **B** price   **C** cost   **D** value
10 **A** lied   **B** laid   **C** lain   **D** lying
11 **A** discovering   **B** inventing   **C** learning   **D** searching
12 **A** stay   **B** take   **C** make   **D** last
13 **A** have   **B** take   **C** make   **D** bring
14 **A** sent   **B** paid   **C** taken   **D** made
15 **A** went   **B** passed   **C** gave   **D** ran

LANGUAGE STUDY

General revision 3

Rewrite the sentences, using the words in bold.

1   You'd better take some cash as the banks may be closed.
    are   You'd better take some cash _____ _____ closed.
2   It's almost certain that someone saw the thief leaving.
    must   Someone _____ leaving.
3   I made a lot of mistakes because I didn't concentrate.
    concentrated   If I _____ have made so many mistakes.
4   I haven't been able to relax for a long time.
    since   It's been a long time _____ to relax.
5   The computer she bought was very cheap.
    pay   She _____ the computer.
6   Mary doesn't just dance, she also sings.
    only   Not _____ but she also sings.
7   The child started walking three months ago.
    for   The child _____ three months.
8   'Please explain something to me,' I said to the teacher.
    asked   I _____ something to me.
9   I left the party because I was bored.
    not   I _____ the party if I hadn't been bored.
10 Someone ought to have done this job yesterday.
    should   This job _____ yesterday.
11 Something about the way you talk suggests that you know a lot about this subject.
    as   You talk _____ a lot about this subject.
12 We studied this last week. Have you forgotten?
    remember   Don't you _____ this last week?
13 'Is he telling the truth?' I asked myself.
    wondered   I _____ the truth.
14 'If you cause trouble, I'll arrest you,' the policeman told me.
    warned   The policeman _____ trouble
15 'Study harder,' our teacher said to us.
    urged   Our teacher _____ harder.
16 'Don't forget! Answer the exam questions fully,' the teacher said.
    remember   'I hope you'll _____ the exam questions fully,' the teacher told us.
17 I'd like to have more time to study, but I haven't.
    wish   I _____ to study.
18 You have used this book and we hope it has been enjoyable at least some of the time.
    enjoyed   We hope you have _____ least some of the time.

Grammar Summary

1 Adjectives

1.1 Order of adjectives

Several adjectives can be used before a noun in English. See p. 64 for a guide to the order in which they can be used. In general we put the more precise adjective nearest the noun but it is not always easy to decide which is the most precise; a possible order would be:

   (1)   (2)   (3)   (4)
determiner, your own opinions, dimensions (size, weight), age,
  (5)   (6)   (7)   (8)   (9)
shape, colour, place of origin, material, purpose.

Examples

- a Chinese silk wedding dress
- some short blue denim jeans
- an awful old stair carpet

1.2 Other points to notice about the order and use of adjectives

1 He is 1 metre 30 **tall**.

2 I don't like living **alone**.

3 It's **difficult** to read.
The instructions are **easy** to follow.

4a She was **worried** about him.
He's a **worried** man.

b It's all very **worrying**.
It's a **worrying** time for us all.

1 Adjectives describing measurement come after the measurement.

2 Some adjectives (e.g. *alone*, *afraid*, *alive*, *awake*) come after the verb, never before a noun.

3 Adjectives are often followed by an infinitive with *to*.

4a Adjectives ending in *-ed* come after a verb like *be*, *seem* or before a noun and describe a person's feelings.

b Adjectives ending in *-ing* come after a verb or before a noun and describe the person or thing that produces those feelings.

1.3 Comparative and superlative of adjectives   ▷ pp. 75, 87

1.3.1 Form

1a London is **bigger** than Edinburgh.

b This armchair is **more comfortable** than that wooden seat.

2a This is the **biggest** factory in the area.

b I have many old books but this is the **most interesting**.

We form the comparative by

1a adding *-er* to one-syllable adjectives and to two-syllable adjectives ending in *-y*

using *more* + two- and more than two-syllable adjectives + *than*

We form the superlative by

2a adding *-est* to one-syllable adjectives and to two-syllable adjectives ending in *-y*

using *most* + two- and more than two-syllable adjectives

3 He is **as** strong **as** a horse.
He isn't **as/so** clever **as** his sister.

3 We use *as* + adjective + *as* for positive comparisons or *not as/so* + adjective + *as* for negative comparisons.

1.3.2 Adjectives of one syllable

1 If the adjective ends in two consonants (e.g. *-ng*, *-rd*, *-rm*) just add *-er*, *-est* to the adjective:
long *longer* *longest*
hard *harder* *hardest*
warm *warmer* *warmest*

2 If the adjective ends in one vowel and one consonant (e.g. *-in*, *-at*, *-ot*) double the consonant and add *-er*, *-est* to the adjective:
thin *thinner* *thinnest*
fat *fatter* *fattest*
hot *hotter* *hottest*

3 If the adjective ends in *-e* add *-r*, *-st* to the adjective:
wide *wider* *widest*
rude *ruder* *rudest*

Exceptions

good	better	best
bad	worse	worst
much/many	more	most
far	farther	farthest

(used to describe distance but can also mean 'additional, extra' e.g. *further* details, *further* information)

old	older	oldest

(used to describe objects and people)

old	elder	eldest

Notice *elder*, *eldest* are used before a noun to talk about family relationships but after a verb only *older*, *oldest* are possible (e.g. My *older/elder* brother. My brother is *older* than I am.)

1.3.3 Adjectives of more than one syllable

1 I've never been **happier** than I am now.
Friday the 13th is the **unluckiest** day of the year in Britain.

2 Sally is **cleverer/more clever** than her brother.
The **commonest/most common** cause of road deaths is careless driving.

3 I find science **more interesting** than the arts.
He told me the **most extraordinary** story.

1 If the adjective ends in *y*, change the *y* to *i* and add *-er*, *-est* to the adjective.
Exception *friendly*, *more friendly*, *most friendly*

2 Some adjectives with two syllables can form their comparative and superlative in two ways: either by adding *-(e)r*, *-(e)st* or by using *more*, *most*.

3 If the adjective has three (or more) syllables use *more*, *most* + the adjective.

2 Adverbs

2.1 Form

1 quick   **quickly**
  slow   **slowly**

2 careful   **carefully**
  beautiful   **beautifully**

3 lucky   **luckily**
  funny   **funnily**

4 He greeted me **in a friendly way**.
She looked at me **with a silly expression on her face**.

1 Adverbs can be formed from adjectives by adding *-ly*.

2 The same rule applies to adjectives which end in *l*.

3 To form adverbs from adjectives ending in *y*, change the *y* to *i* and add *-ly*.

4 To form adverbs from adjectives ending in *-ly* we use a phrase *in a . . . way* etc.

5 We arrived **late**.
   Stand up **straight**.
   He works **very hard**.
   Don't walk so **fast**.

5 Some adjectives do not change when they become adverbs. **Notice** *lately* and *hardly* have a different meaning from *late* and *hard*: *lately* = recently, *hardly* = scarcely.

7 He reads his newspaper **quickly at the breakfast table every morning**.

7 Adverbs and adverb phrases which tell us 'how, where and when' usually come in that order in the sentence (e.g. how = *quickly*, where = *at the breakfast table*, when = *every morning*).

2.2 Comparative and superlative of adverbs

1 She drives **more carefully** than her husband.
   This is the **most efficiently** run office in the area.

2 We arrived **later** than you.
   He walked the **fastest**.

1 We usually form the comparative and superlative by using *more*, *most* + adverb.

2 Adverbs with the same form as adjectives form their comparative and superlative with *-er*, *-est*.

   Notice some exceptions to these two rules
well	better	best
badly	worse	worst
little	less	least
much	more	most

2.3 Position of adverbs and adverb phrases in sentences

1 He plays the piano **well**.
   She sings **beautifully**.

2a She's **very** clever.
   I can **hardly** read it.
   I don't **quite** understand.

b I have **enough** money.
   He's not tall **enough** to join the police force.
   They don't work hard **enough**.

3a He's coming **tomorrow**.

b **Yesterday** he was in Paris.
   Today he's in Rome.

4a The magazine comes out **weekly**.
   We are paid **monthly**.

b **Every Saturday** we go out.

5a He **never** buys cigarettes.
   He **always** makes his own.

b She is **always** late.

c They have **never** offered to help.
   We are **often** being asked for information of this kind.

6 Sit down **there**.
   He went **to the cinema in the High Street in town**.
   Put the book **on the table in the dining room**.

1 Adverbs which tell us 'how' usually come in the end position.

2a Adverbs which tell us 'to what extent or to what degree' usually come in the middle position.

b **Notice** *enough* comes before a noun and after an adjective or adverb.

3a Adverbs which tell us 'when' usually come in the end position.

b They can come at the beginning for special emphasis.

4a Adverbs which tell us 'how often' usually come in the end position.

b Phrases like *every week*, *every Saturday* can also come at the beginning of a sentence.

5a Adverbs which 'do not tell us exactly when' usually come before a one-word verb.

b If the verb is *be* they always follow the verb.

c If it is a two- (or more) word verb they come after the first part of the verb.

6 Adverbs and adverb phrases which tell us 'where' usually come in the end position with the direction (*to the cinema*) mentioned first and the places second (smaller places come before larger ones).

2.4 Adverb or adjective?

That **smells good**, but it **tastes awful**.

Notice If the verb is *seem*, *appear*, *look*, *sound*, *feel*, *smell* or *taste* we use an adjective not an adverb.

3 Articles

3.1 Indefinite article (*a/an*)

1 You will need **a** pen and **an** exercise book.

2 There was **a** terrible storm last night. The storm swept across the whole country.

3 **A** million people received our help last year. **A** few, however, were not so lucky.

4 We come to classes twice **a** week.

5 She's **a** lorry-driver.
   He's **an** old-age pensioner.

Use with singular countable nouns

1 for more general meaning (it doesn't matter which pen). **Notice** *an* is used before a word that begins with a vowel sound (e.g. *an hour, an heir, an MP* **but** *a university*).

2 for a noun mentioned for the first time. **Notice** we use *the* for the second mention.

3 with numbers (e.g. *a hundred, a thousand, a million*) and fractions (e.g. *a half, a quarter* etc.).
   Notice
   a few (people) = some
   a little (help) = some
   but
   Ø *few* (people) = not many
   Ø *little* (help) = not much

4 to mean 'every' with expressions of time (e.g. *once a year*)

5 to describe a person's job or situation

3.2 Definite article (*the*)

1 Jane: A man phoned last night.
   Peter: Well, what did **the** man want?

2 Last night I read **the** book you recommended.

3 **The** sun rises in **the** east and sets in **the** west.

Use with most nouns for more specific meaning

1 to refer back to something already mentioned

2 when we know which one we are talking about

3 when we refer to only one of its kind

164

4 **The** computer has revolutionized office systems.

5 You can buy **the** best pizzas in town at Paulo's.

6 **The** British and **the** French agreed to build a channel tunnel. **The** strong should help **the** weak.

7 I live in **the** United States/**the** Netherlands/**the** Falklands/**the** West Indies/**the** Philippines/**the** USSR.

8 Paris lies on **the** Seine. **The** Atlantic separates Britain from America. It's very hot in **the** Mediterranean at the moment.

3.3 No article (∅)

1a ∅ Museums are interesting ∅ places.

b ∅ Sound travels very fast in ∅ water.

2a I live in ∅ Rome/∅ Percy Road/ ∅ China/∅ Jersey/near ∅ Lake Windermere.

b I shop at ∅ Harrods.

c I read ∅ *Punch*.

d The Queen lives in ∅ Buckingham Palace.

e He went to ∅ Sheffield University.

3a ∅ MAN FOUND DEAD ON ∅ TUBE

b Send ∅ representative immediately.

c ∅ Dinner in ∅ oven.

4 You will need a knife and ∅ fork. Take a bucket and ∅ spade to the beach.

Notice these other uses of *the*

4 with singular countable nouns when they stand for an invention or a species

5 with a superlative (*the* first, *the* most enjoyable)

6 with adjectives as plural nouns

7 with the names of countries or groups of islands which are plural. **Notice these exceptions** *The* United Kingdom, *The* Yemen

8 with names of rivers, oceans and seas

We do not use an article

1a with plural countable nouns and

b with uncountable nouns when speaking about the noun in general (e.g. food, music, love, etc.). **Compare** I hate *the* sound of a drill (a particular sound). **Notice** a few uncountable nouns (e.g. advice, news, luggage, information, research) require a phrase like *a/the bit of* or *a/the piece of* to refer to a particular example of that noun: *a bit of advice*, *the piece of news*

2 with the names of most

a towns/cities, streets, countries, single/individual islands, lakes

b shops

c magazines. **Notice these exceptions** *The Economist*, *The Listener* and most newspapers (*The Times*, *The Daily Mail*)

d named buildings

e named institutions (e.g. universities, schools, churches, etc.)

3a for newspaper headlines

b for telexes (where the message should be as short as possible)

c for personal, informal messages

4 before a second noun in a linked pair of nouns

3.4 Changes of meaning

Sometimes the use (or omission ∅) of the article changes the meaning of what we say.

3.4.1 Meals

1 **A** dinner was held last night at the Savoy. **The** dinner we had last night was marvellous.

2 Come to ∅ dinner next Saturday. What time do you have ∅ breakfast?

1 *a/an* or *the* for particular meals

2 no article (∅) for mealtimes in general

3.4.2 Transport

1 I hailed **a** taxi but it didn't stop. **The** six o'clock train was ten minutes early.

2 I always travel by ∅ bus. I came here on ∅ foot.

1 *a/an* or *the* for particular forms of transport

2 no article (∅) for the form of transport in general

3.4.3 Places

1 The meeting was held in **a** school. The workmen are busy in **the** church repairing the roof.

2 He's at ∅ university (studying). She's in ∅ hospital (receiving treatment). He's in ∅ prison (serving a sentence).

1 *a/an* or *the* to refer to a particular or known place or building

2 no article (∅) to refer to the normal activity which goes on at a place or building

4 Conditional sentences

Both *if* and *unless* (= *if . . . not*) can be used to introduce conditional sentences. The if-clause can come before or after the main (or 'result') clause. Notice we often use a comma when the if-clause comes first.

4.1 Conditional 1   ▷ pp. 51, 57

1a If you **take** drugs regularly, you **become** addicted to them.

b If you **mix** the colours blue and red, you **get** purple.

2 If you **work** hard, you'**ll get** a good job. **Unless** you **study**, you **won't pass** your exams. I'**ll explain** it again if you **don't understand**.

Use

1a for general facts that do not change

b for scientific facts. **Notice** the verbs in both parts of the sentences are in the present.

2 mainly for future possibilities. **Notice** the verbs after *if* and *unless* are in the present **but** the verbs in the 'result' part of the sentence are in the future.

4.2 Conditional 2 ▷ pp. 51, 57

1a If I **had** a million pounds, I **would buy** a yacht.
If he **knew** the answer, he **wouldn't tell** me.
If Mary **were** here now, she **would drive** me home.

b If I **were** you, I **wouldn't marry** him.

Use

1a for 'unreal' or improbable conditions in the present or future

b for giving advice and suggestions.
Notice the verbs after *if* are in the past but the verbs in the 'result' part of the sentence are in the present conditional.

4.3 Conditional 3 ▷ p. 147

1a We **would have gone** abroad for our holidays **if we hadn't bought** a new car.

b If we **hadn't set out** late, we **wouldn't have been caught** in that traffic jam.

c If you **had listened** to your father, you **wouldn't have made** so many mistakes.

Use

would + p.p. → Past P

1a for 'unreal' or impossible conditions in the past

b to imply regret   *Past P → Pres Perfec Passiv*

c to imply criticism.
Notice the verbs after *if* are in the past perfect but the verbs in *Past Perf →* the 'result' part of the sentence are in the perfect conditional. *would + Pres Perf √*

5 Gerunds and infinitives ▷ pp. 85, 89

5.1 Verbs followed by the gerund (or *-ing* form)

I **can't stand waiting** in queues.
We **considered buying** a house in the countryside, but we **enjoy being** in the town too much.
I **miss living** abroad.

Some verbs are followed by the *-ing* form. Here are some of the most common:

appreciate	keep (on)
avoid	look forward to
can't help	mention
can't stand	mind
consider	miss
deny	object to
dislike	practise
enjoy	put off
feel like	risk
finish	suggest
give up	be/get used to
imagine	be worth

5.2 Verbs followed by the infinitive

5.2.1 Verb + infinitive with *to*

We **can't afford to have** a holiday this year.
We **decided to get** married.
I **managed to find** another glass to replace the one I broke.

Some verbs are followed by the infinitive with *to*. Here are some of the most common:

afford	forget
appear	happen
arrange	hope
decide	intend
fail	learn
manage	promise
mean	refuse
offer	seem
plan	threaten
prepare	

5.2.2 Verb + direct object + infinitive **with** *to*

He **advised** me **to take** the exam.
They **persuaded** me **to stay** for a few days.

Some verbs have a direct object before the infinitive **with** *to*. Here are some of the most common:

advise	persuade
allow	remind
encourage	teach
force	tell
invite	warn
order	

5.2.3 Verb + direct object + infinitive **without** *to*

I **heard** him **sing** *Figaro*.
He **let** me **borrow** his car.
He **made** her **tell** him the truth.

Some verbs have a direct object before the infinitive **without** *to*. Here are some of the most common:

feel	let
hear	make
see	

Notice *hear* and *see* can be followed by the *-ing* form to express hearing or seeing only part of an action (e.g. compare *I heard him singing in the bath*.)

5.3 Verbs followed by either the *-ing* form or the infinitive ▷ p. 89

1 He **continued working/to work** after everybody else had left the office.

2a I **like going** to the cinema.
She **loves dancing**.

b I **like to go** to the cinema once a week.
She **would love to dance** the samba with you.

3a I **began studying/to study** in 1984.
I **started writing/to write** when I was very young.

b I **began to see** that something was wrong.
I **started to realize** what he had done for me.

Some verbs take either the *-ing* form or the infinitive.

1 Sometimes there is very little difference in meaning.

2a When verbs like *can't bear*, *like*, *love*, *hate*, *prefer* are followed by the *-ing* form, they tend to refer to a general activity

b **but** when these verbs are followed by the infinitive, they tend to refer to particular occasions.

3a *begin* and *start* can take either the *-ing* form or the infinitive

b **but** before a verb expressing understanding (*see*, *realize*) these verbs are followed by the infinitive.

4a He **stopped smoking** last week.
He **remembers going** to the seaside when he was a child.
He'll **never forget eating** raw fish for the first time.

b He **stopped** the car **to pick up** a hitch-hiker.
He **remembered to post** the letters.

5a I **tried to phone** you several times but I couldn't get through.

b I **tried working** in a shop, but it didn't interest me.

6 Your hair **needs cutting**.
The garden **wants weeding**.

4 With verbs like *stop, remember, not forget, regret*

a the *-ing* form refers to what happens/happened before the main verb e.g. first he smoked, then he stopped; first he went to the seaside, now he remembers the event; first he ate the raw fish, now he remembers the event (*never forget = always remember*)

b the infinitive refers to what happens/happened after the main verb e.g. first he stopped the car, then he picked up a hitch-hiker; first he remembered about the letters, then he posted them

5 *try* can take either the *-ing* form or the infinitive **but**

a it is followed by an infinitive when we mean 'to attempt to do something'

b it is followed by the *-ing* form when we mean 'to experiment'

6 *need* and *want* can be followed by either the *-ing* form or the infinitive **but** when they are followed by the *-ing* form the meaning is always passive.

5.4 Other uses of the *-ing* form

1 **Walking** is good for you.

2 After **walking** to work, I'm ready to sit at my desk all day.

3 I'm afraid of **missing** the train. He's good at **telling** others what to do.

The *-ing* form is also used

1 as the subject of a clause or sentence

2 following time words like *after, before, when, since, while*

3 after certain adjectives + prepositions. Here are some of the most common:

afraid of	good at
bad at	keen on
bored with	interested in
clever at	tired of
fond of	worried about

5.5 Other uses of the infinitive

1 I came here **to study** English.

2 She doesn't know what **to do** next.
Can you explain how **to do** it?

The infinitive is also used

1 to express purpose
▷ GS 6.3

2 after *who, what, where, how, whether* and verbs like *know, explain, wonder*. **Notice** the infinitive is not used in this way after *why*.

6 Link words

6.1 Words expressing result

1a He was **so** tired **that** he went to bed early.
He spoke Russian **so** well **that** everyone thought he was Russian.

b It was **such** a difficult exam **(that)** he knew he wouldn't pass it.

2 It was late, **so** he decided to take a taxi home.

3a We have invested too much money in this project. **Consequently**, we are in financial difficulties.

b His wife left him **and, as a result,** he became very depressed.

4 We feel, **therefore**, that a decision must be made.

1a *so* + adjective/adverb + *that* + clause

b *such* + noun + *that* + clause
Notice *that* can be left out in informal speech.

2 *so* + clause

3a *as a result, consequently,* can begin a new sentence.

b *and, as a result,* is used in the middle of a sentence.

4 *therefore* often comes in the middle of a sentence (it can also come at the beginning or the end).

6.2 Words expressing reason

1 **Seeing that/Since/As** we arrived late, all the best seats had been taken.

2 We couldn't find a good seat **because** all the best ones had been taken.

3 We were unable to go by train **because of** the rail strike.
Many of the deaths of older people are **due to** heart attacks.

1 *since, as, seeing that* + clause often come before the main clause.

2 *because* + clause usually comes after the main clause.

3 *because of, as a result of, owing to* and *due to* are followed by a noun or noun phrase.
Notice *due to* means 'caused by' or 'resulting from'.

6.3 Words expressing purpose

1 We came to the countryside **to** find some peace and quiet. Handle the flowers carefully **in order not to** damage them.

2 He chose this university **so that/in order that** he could study Physics.

1 We can use the infinitives *to (do), in order (not) to (do), so as (not) to (do)* to express purpose.
Notice *in order to, so as to* are more formal.

2 *so that, in order that* + clause (often with the verbs *can, could, might, would* in the clause)

6.4 Words expressing contrast

1 **Although/Even if/Even though** the car is old, it is still reliable.

2a **Despite/In spite of** the rain, I went for a walk.

b We enjoyed our walking holiday **despite/in spite of the fact that** it was tiring.

1 *although, even if, even though* + clause can come before or after the main clause.
Notice *even though* is more informal.

2a *despite, in spite of* + a noun or noun phrase or *-ing* form

b *despite the fact that, in spite of the fact that* + clause

3a Buying a house is expensive. It is, **however**, a good investment.

b It's a big decision to make, **though**.

4 John is very rich **but/while/whereas** his friends are extremely poor.

5 **On the one hand** these computers are expensive. **On the other hand** they are exactly what we want.

3a *however* can come at the beginning, in the middle or at the end of a sentence.

b *though* is more informal and comes at the end of a sentence.

4 *but*, *while*, *whereas* are usually placed in the middle of two main clauses expressing contrasting ideas.

5 *on the one hand* and *on the other hand* can be used at the beginning, in the middle or at the end of two sentences expressing contrasting ideas. **Notice** *on the other hand* is often used at the beginning of the second sentence.

6.5 Words expressing time

1 **When/While/As** I was driving along the road, I saw a terrible accident.
He went out **after** he'd finished work.

2 **Whenever/Every time** I see him, he's driving a different car.

3 **First** he closed all the windows, **then** he locked the doors. **Later** he came back to check that everything was all right.

4 **During/All through** the summer we get a lot of visitors.
It rained heavily **throughout** the night.

1 *when*, *while*, *as* and *after* + clause can come before or after the main clause.   ▷ GS 5.4

2 *whenever*, *every time* + clause often come before the main clause for added emphasis.

3 *first*, *then*, *later*, etc. can be used to introduce a chain of events.

4 *during*, *all through* and *throughout* are followed by a noun or a noun phrase.

6.6 Words expressing condition
▷ p. 153 and GS 4

1 **Even if** you are born rich, life is still difficult.
You can borrow the car **as long as** you're careful with it!
You can't come with me **unless** you promise to keep quiet.

2 I don't know **whether** you have met him or not.

a They **discussed whether** they should attend the Games.

b It depends **on whether** the government takes any action.
The organizers will decide **whether to impose** fines.

3 Take this umbrella **in case** it rains.
In case of emergency, break the glass.

1 *even if*, *as long as* and *unless* + clause can be used before or after the main clause.
Notice *unless* means *if . . . not*

2 *whether* + clause usually comes after the main clause and is often used in indirect questions with *. . . or not*.

a Certain verbs (e.g. *discuss*) can be followed by *whether* but not *if*.

b After prepositions and before *to* infinitives use *whether* but not *if*.   ▷ GS 12.4

3 *in case* + clause usually comes after the main clause.
Notice *in case of* + noun (often used in formal written notices)

6.7 Words expressing additional information or reinforcing a point

1a I don't really want to go out tonight. **Besides**, there's a good film on TV.
We are still waiting for the goods we ordered three months ago. **Furthermore**, we have been overcharged for our last order.

b This theory about the origins of the universe is new. It is, **moreover**, extremely interesting.

2a The painting is **not only** valuable **but also** a work of art.
She **not only** writes novels **but** (she) lectures **as well**.
The house was **not only** large **but** (was/it was) **also** modern.

b **Not only** *is the restaurant superb* **but** it is **also** expensive.

3 They robbed a bank **as well as** a post office.
As well as being sent to prison, they were fined £2,000.

4 They like Indian food. I like Indian food **too/as well**.
They aren't very generous people. They have**n't** got any friends **either**.

1a *besides*, *in addition (to that)* and *furthermore* can be used at the beginning of the sentence following the first statement made. **Notice** *besides* is less formal, *furthermore* is more formal.

b *moreover* can be used at the beginning or in the middle of the sentence which gives additional information.

2a *not only . . . but also/as well* can link two sentences, phrases or words to give additional information. **Notice** *but also* are used together when there is no subject pronoun and verb in the second part of the sentence. *but . . . also* are separated when there is a verb in the second part of the sentence.

b *Not only* can come at the beginning of the first part of the sentence to emphasize what the speaker is saying. In this case it is necessary to change the order of the subject and verb. In sentences like these the subject pronoun and verb in the second part of the sentence are usually mentioned and *but . . . also* are separated.

3 *as well as* can be followed by a single word, a phrase or *. . .-ing*.

4 *too*, *as well* and *not either* are informal and usually come at the end of the sentence which gives additional information.

7 Modals   ▷ p. 137

will, shall, would, should, may, might, can, could, must, have (got) to, ought to, need

7.1 *will*

1 It'**ll** be raining tomorrow.

2 Nothing on TV. I'**ll** go to the cinema instead.

3 **Will** you sit down, please?
I **won't** go with you.

4 I'**ll** take you to the cinema.

5 Could you lend me £1?
Of course I **will**.

6 You **will** start work at 8 on Monday.

7 I **will not** be treated in this way.

will is used to express.

1 a prediction about the future   ▷ GS 13.3

2 a decision made while you are speaking

3 a request or a refusal

4 a promise

5 willingness

6 an order

7 determination

7.2 shall

1 We **shall** send you the information as soon as possible.

2 **Shall** we go out for a meal tonight?

3 **Shall** I carry that case for you?

4 No pupil **shall** enter the library without the permission of a teacher.

shall is used to express

1 the future (in the same way as *will* but only with *I* and *we*)

2 a suggestion

3 an offer

4 **Notice** *shall* is occasionally used in very formal (written) orders.

7.3 would

1 I**'d** like to go now.
I wish you **wouldn't** smoke so much.

2 I **would** move house if I had the money.

3 **Would** you type this for me, please?

4 I**'d** rather have tea than coffee.

5 Will you ring me?
He asked if I **would** ring him.

6 He **would** sing at the top of his voice in the shower.

would is used to express

1 a wish (sometimes suggesting annoyance or disapproval)
▷ GS 14.1

2 the 'result' part of a conditional sentence ▷ GS 4.2–4.3

3 a polite request

4 a preference with *rather*
▷ GS 14.2

5 the reporting of *will*
▷ GS 12.1.1

6 a habit in the past
▷ GS 13.2.2

7.4 should

1 I **should** really help my mother with the dishes (but I won't).

2 You **should** study harder.

3 We **should** be taking off in a few minutes.

4 I/We **should** be most grateful if you could send us a copy of the agreement.

5 I **should** have told you but I forgot.

should is used to express

1 an obligation (which you may not carry out)

2 advice

3 something that will almost certainly happen as long as nothing unexpected prevents it

4 conditional sentences in more formal/written style with *I* and *we*

5 (with the perfect infinitive) an obligation which was not carried out

7.5 may and might

1 He **may/might** be the new teacher.

2 He **may/might** be late this evening.

3 **May/Might** I ask a question?

4 They **may/might** have been held up in the traffic.

may and *might* are used to express

1 a possibility now

2 a possibility in the future.
Notice *might* is rather less certain than *may* in meaning.

3 asking for permission.
Notice *may* is more common than *might* here and *can* is often used instead of *may*.

4 (with the perfect infinitive) a possible explanation for something in the past

7.6 can

1 I **can** ski/drive a car.

2 I'm free tomorrow. I **can** drive you to the airport.

3 **Can** I go now?

4 **Can** you come to the party?

5 You **can't** be tired! You've been asleep all morning.

6 You **can't** have been pleased when you realized what he had done!

can is used to express

1 knowing how to do something

2 being able to do something

3 asking for permission (used informally instead of *may*)

4 a possibility

5 an unlikely explanation for something now: *It's impossible for you to be tired.*

6 (with the perfect infinitive) an unlikely explanation for something in the past: *It wasn't possible for you to be pleased.*

7.7 could

1 When I was six I **could** play the piano.

2 When I was younger I **could** drive for hours without a break.

3 **Could** I use your phone?

4 **Could** he be right?

5 They **couldn't** have phoned her. She hasn't got a phone!

could is used to express

1 knowing how to do something in the past

2 being able to do something in the past

3 asking for permission (used informally instead of *may* but rather more polite than *can*)

4 a possibility (rather less strong than *can*)

5 (with the perfect infinitive) an unlikely explanation for something in the past: *It wasn't possible for them to phone her.*

7.8 must ▷ pp. 13, 133

1 I **must** wash my hair tonight.

2 The work **must** be done before tomorrow.

3 You **must** not smoke in here.

4 You **must** be exhausted after all that work.

5 You **must** have been surprised when she said she was getting married.

must is used to express

1 a personal obligation

2 what you consider to be someone else's obligation

3 (with *not*) what is not allowed

4 a reasonable conclusion made about something now

5 (with the perfect infinitive) a reasonable conclusion about something in the past

7.9 have (got) to

I**'ve got to/have to** be on time tomorrow.
We **haven't got to/don't have to** do it if we don't want to.

have (got) to is used to express what is or isn't necessary
▷ GS 15.1.1

7.10 *ought to*

1 I really **ought to** go and see her.
2 I **ought to** have gone to see her but I was busy.

ought to is used to express

1 an obligation (which you may or may not carry out)
2 (with the perfect infinitive) an obligation which you did not carry out.
   Notice *ought to* is rather stronger than *should*.

7.11 *need*

1 You **needn't** shout. I can hear you.
   You **needn't** bring anything to the party.
2 **Need** I take anything to the party?
   Need you ask that question?
3 You **needn't** have phoned. I already knew you were coming.

1 *needn't* is used here as a modal verb.
2 There is also a question form, constructed in the same way as questions with *can*, *must* and other modals.
3 *needn't* with the perfect infinitive expresses the idea that something in the past was not necessary but it was done.

   Compare the ordinary verb *need*:
   You don't need to shout. I can hear you.
   Do I need to take anything to the party?
   You didn't need to phone. I already knew you were coming.

8 The passive   ▷ p. 131

8.1 Most common forms

It	is has been will be was	done seen reported

This toy **is made** in Japan.
A strange object **has been seen** in the night sky.
Further information **will be given** in our next news bulletin.
This report **was prepared by** a team of experts.

The passive is formed by using a form of *be* (*is, has been, will be, was*, etc.) + the past participle of the verb (*made, seen, given, prepared*).

Notice when the person or thing responsible for the action (the agent) is mentioned, use the preposition *by*.

8.2 Use

1 Five policemen **have been killed** in Northern Ireland.
   The water **was heated** and a solution of chemicals **was prepared**.

The passive is used

1 when the agent is unknown (we may not know who killed the policemen) or not important.
   Notice the passive is often used in newspaper reports and in scientific experiments or processes.

2 A description of the gunman **was issued** by the police.
3 A charity record **has been made** by many famous names in the world of pop music.

2 to make the object of the active verb more important (attention is drawn to the description of the gunman rather than who issued it)
3 when the description of the agent is very long (*many famous names in the world of pop music*)

8.3 Points to remember

1 The painting **should be finished** by next week.
2 The decorating **would have been finished** but I ran out of paint.
3 Mother Teresa **was awarded** the Nobel Peace Prize.
   The Nobel Peace Prize **was awarded** to Mother Teresa.
4 I **got stuck** in a traffic jam.
   She is **getting married** next month.
5a It **is thought** that he started the fire deliberately.
b He **is thought** to have started the fire deliberately.
6a He **had/got** his hair **cut** yesterday.
b He **had** his car **stolen**.
7 This job **needs/wants doing**.

1 Use *be* + past participle after *should* and other modals.
   ▷ GS 7
2 Use *been* + past participle after *would have*, *should have*, etc.
   ▷ GS 7
3 Verbs with two objects which can form two types of active sentence can also form two types of passive sentence.
4 *get* + past participle is sometimes used instead of *be* with passive meaning. Expressions with *get* are often used in informal English.
5 The passive is used in constructions with verbs like *think, believe, say, consider, feel, find, know, understand*
a after the introductory *it*
b before an infinitive
6 *have/get something done* expresses the idea of
a arranging for or paying for somebody to do something for you. **Notice** *get* is more informal.
   ▷ GS 15.1.1
b experiencing something
7 After *need, want* the *-ing* form can be used with passive meaning.   ▷ GS 5.3

9 Phrasal verbs

9.1 What is a phrasal verb?

1 A phrasal verb consists of a verb plus one or two words like *on, up, into*, etc.
2 The words which come after the verb are usually adverbs, although sometimes a phrasal verb can consist of verb + adverb + preposition.
3 When an ordinary verb is followed by a preposition, the meaning of the verb will usually be clear from the meanings of the individual parts of the verb. In the case of a phrasal verb, however, the parts of the phrasal verb together have one basic meaning which may be completely different from their individual meanings.

Ordinary verbs + prepositions	Phrasal verbs
I looked into the mirror.	The police *are looking into* the murder.
She ran out of the room crying.	We *ran out* of money on holiday. **Notice** these verbs change their meaning when adverbs and prepositions are added e.g. *look into* (a murder) = investigate; *run out of* (money) = have none left.

9.2 Phrasal verbs which **can** be separated

9.2.1 Verb + adverb + object

1 He **looked** a word **up** in the dictionary.
  He **looked up** a word in the dictionary.
2 He **looked** it **up**.

1 If the object is a noun it can come before or after the adverb.
2 If the object is a pronoun (e.g. *it*) it must come **before** the adverb.

9.3 Phrasal verbs which **cannot** be separated

9.3.1 Verb + adverb (no object)

They **called in** to see us.
The plans **fell through**.
They **turned up** unexpectedly.

You cannot separate the two parts of the verb. **You cannot say** 'They called to see us in'.

9.3.2 Verb + adverb + preposition + object

We **dropped in on** the Smiths.
We **dropped in on** them.

Even when the object is a pronoun it must come **after** the adverb + preposition.

9.4 Ordinary verbs + prepositions

The boy ran over the bridge.
He stepped over the puddle.
He stepped over it.

The object must come **after** the verb + preposition, even when it is a pronoun.

9.5 Verb check-list

9.5.1 Verbs which **can** be separated

Back
back . . . up — support
Break
break . . . off — bring to an end (talks, engagement)
break . . . up — smash to pieces

Bring
bring . . . about — cause
bring . . . back — return
bring . . . off — succeed in doing
bring . . . out — make clear
bring . . . round — help to regain consciousness
bring . . . up — raise (a family, a point)

Call
call . . . off — cancel
call . . . up — take people into the army
Carry
carry . . . out — finish, perform a duty
Check
check . . . in — present your ticket/luggage at an airport
check . . . out/ over — make sure everything is as it should be
Clear
clear . . . up — make tidy
Count
count . . . in — include
count . . . out — not include
count . . . up — add up
Cross
cross . . . out — put a line through
Cut
cut . . . off — disconnect (on the phone) — make unavailable
cut . . . out — remove with scissors
cut . . . up — divide into parts
Do
do . . . out of — cheat, stop from having
Draw
draw . . . out — take money (out of the bank)
Get
get . . . across — explain what you mean
get . . . back — regain possession of
get . . . down — write down — depress, make unhappy
Give
give . . . away — betray, reveal — not take money for
give . . . back — return
give . . . out — distribute
give . . . up — stop doing
Hand
hand . . . in — present something official
hand . . . out — distribute
hand . . . over — give up

Have
have . . . in/ round — receive as guests
Hold
hold . . . back — restrain
hold . . . up — delay — rob (a bank)
Keep
keep . . . back (from) — not tell something, keep secret
keep . . . down — retain in the stomach — control
keep . . . in — not allow out
Knock
knock . . . down/over — make fall
knock . . . out — make lose consciousness
Leave
leave . . . out — omit
Let
let . . . down — not keep a promise
let . . . in — allow to come in
let . . . off/out — allow to go free
Look
look . . . over — examine closely
look . . . up — search for and find in a book or list
Make
make . . . out — see clearly — write in certain details
make . . . up — invent in order to deceive — forget your differences/ anger
Pass
pass . . . off (as) — pretend to be
Pay
pay . . . back — return something borrowed
Pick
pick . . . up — go and collect — take hold of and lift
Pull
pull . . . down — demolish
pull . . . off — succeed in doing
Put
put . . . off — not do something at the proper time, delay

put . . . on – switch on / – dress in
put . . . out – switch off
put . . . through – connect people on the telephone
put . . . up – raise the price of

Ring
ring . . . back – phone again
ring . . . up – phone

Rub
rub . . . out – make disappear

Run
run . . . over – hit and knock down

See
see . . . off – say goodbye to

Send
send . . . in – present something/someone official
send . . . off – post
send . . . on – forward by post

Set
set . . . back – halt progress
set . . . up – organize, establish

Show
show . . . in – bring in
show . . . off – display / – boast about

Stick
stick . . . out – put up with

Take
take . . . away – remove / – subtract

take . . . back – withdraw what you said / – return an object
take . . . in – deceive / – absorb, understand
take . . . on – accept responsibility for
take . . . over – gain control of
take . . . up – start a hobby

Think
think . . . over – consider carefully

Throw
throw . . . out – get rid of

Try
try . . . on – check clothes for size
try . . . out – see if it works

Turn
turn . . . back – refuse someone entry
turn . . . down – reject an offer / – lower sound (of TV, radio, etc.)
turn . . . into – change into something different
turn . . . off – switch off
turn . . . on – switch on
turn . . . up – make louder

Wear
wear . . . out – make exhausted/useless

Work
work . . . out – solve a problem / – draw up a plan

9.5.2 Verbs which **cannot** be separated

Ask
ask after – inquire how someone is getting on
ask for – request

Back
back out of – withdraw from an agreement

Break
break down – stop working (e.g. a car) / – collapse emotionally or physically
break into – enter by force
break out – escape (e.g. from prison)
break up – separate (e.g. husband and wife)

Burst
burst in(to) – enter suddenly

Call
call for – require, demand / – pick someone up (at their home)
call (in) on – visit

Care
care about – take an interest in, love
care for – like, look after

Carry
carry on – continue

Catch
catch on – become fashionable

catch up with – reach the same level as

Check
check in – register at a hotel
check out – leave a hotel
check up (on) – make sure everything is correct

Clear
clear off – disappear quickly
clear up – stop raining

Come
come across – find by accident
come by – pass
come down – be reduced in price
come forward – appear / – present oneself
come off – succeed
come out – appear (sun, flowers)
come round – visit / – regain consciousness
come up against – face or meet a problem
come up with – produce, find

Count
count on – rely or depend on

Cut
cut down (on) – reduce expenses

Do
do away with – get rid of, abolish
do without – manage if you haven't got something

Draw
draw up – stop (e.g. cars etc.)

Drop
drop in (on) – visit without an arrangement
drop out – not take part in at the last minute

Face
face up to – confront problems

Fall
fall for – be very strongly attracted to / – be deceived by
fall in with – agree to
fall out – have an argument

fall through – not succeed (e.g. plans)

Feel
feel like – want to do
feel up to – be capable of

Get
get along (with) – have a good relationship with
get away – escape
get away with – not be punished for
get by – survive, manage
get in(to)/out – enter/leave a car
get off/on – board/leave a train/bus
get on with – continue doing / – have a good relationship with
get out of – escape or avoid (work, a meeting, etc.)
get over – recover from (an illness, surprise, etc.)
get round to – find the time to do something
get through – succeed in doing / – spend, reach the end of / – manage to live through
get together – meet
get up – get out of bed

Give
give in – surrender

Go
go after – pursue, follow
go down – fall (prices)
go down with – become ill with
go in for – take up an interest / – enter competitions
go off – become bad (e.g. food)
go on – continue
go out – stop burning, shining (of light)
go out with – go to a theatre/cinema/restaurant, etc. with a boy/girlfriend
go over/through – examine
go through – suffer, endure
go up – rise, increase
go with – match (e.g. colours)

Hang

hang about/ around	– stand about doing nothing
hang back	– hesitate
hang on	– wait
hang onto	– keep a grip on something
hang up	– put the telephone receiver down (in anger)

Hold

hold on	– wait
hold onto	– not let go

Join

join in	– take part in
join up	– enter armed forces

Keep

keep back	– stay away from (danger)
keep off	– stay away from
keep on	– do something more than once
keep up	– maintain, not allow to end or fall
keep up (with)	– go at the same speed or pace

Live

live on	– support oneself by means of
live through	– survive a difficult period
live up to	– do what is expected of you

Look

look after	– take care of
look around	– inspect, survey
look for	– search for
look in on	– visit unexpectedly
look into	– investigate
look out (for)	– take care
look through	– examine, inspect
look up to	– respect

Make

make for	– go towards
make up for	– compensate for

Miss

miss out (on)	– not take the opportunity to do

Pass

pass away	– die
pass out	– lose consciousness

Pull

pull in/up	– stop (e.g. cars)
pull out	– move out (to overtake cars etc.)

Put

put in for	– apply for
put up with	– stand for, tolerate

Ring

ring off	– put the phone down

Run

run away/ off with	– elope – take something which does not belong to you
run into	– encounter, meet – collide with
run out (of)	– have no more
run over/ through	– read or examine quickly

See

see about/to	– arrange, attend to
see through	– not be deceived by

Send

send for	– ask to come and see

Set

set off/out	– depart/leave

Sit

sit for	– take an exam

Stand

stand back	– not come too near
stand by	– stick to what you say – give help, support
stand for	– mean – tolerate
stand in for	– act as a substitute for
stand out	– be noticeable
stand up for	– act in support of
stand up to	– resist

Stick

stick to	– not change course

Stop

stop off (at)	– break your journey
stop over	– spend the night

Take

take after	– resemble
take down	– write down
take off	– leave the ground
take to	– like straight away
take up	– occupy (time or space) – begin (a hobby)

Think

think of	– have an opinion about – remember

Turn

turn back	– go back where you started from
turn out	– be the result in the end
turn up	– arrive unexpectedly

Wear

wear off	– disappear (effects of something)

Write

write away (for)	– send away (for) by post

10 Prepositions

10.1 *among* ▷ p. 149

1 Divide these sweets **among** the children.

2 The workers talked **among** themselves as they waited to see the boss.

3 He was the only one **among** all my friends who supported me.

Use for a group of things to express

1 'with a share for each of'

2 'with one another'

3 'in the group/company of'

10.2 *at*

1 The train left **at** midnight/8.30p.m.

2a I'll meet you **at** the corner of the street.

b The train stops **at** Birmingham. I studied **at** London.

3 Look **at** this new car. Aim **at** the centre.

Use to express

1 an exact point of time

2a an exact position or place

b with the name of a city, town or village if we are interested in a particular point or activity in it rather than the whole place

3 'in the direction of'

Useful expressions

at all costs/ events	at hand	at peace/war	astonished at
at any rate	at home/the office	at present	bad at
at church/the hairdresser's/ school	at last	at sea	clever at
	at least	at a time (when)	good at
at Christmas/ Easter	at a loss/a profit	at the same time (as)	shocked at
at ease	at lunch	at times	shoot at
at first (sight)	at night	at the weekend	shout at
	at once	at work	smile/laugh at
			surprised at

10.3 *between*   ▷ p. 149

	Use to express
1 The bank is **between** the post office and the baker's.	1 a position in the middle (with things or people on two sides)
2 The ferry sails **between** Dover and Ostend. An agreement was made **between** the three super-powers.	2 bringing two or more things or people together
3 Just **between** you and me, I think he's awful.	3 sharing something together (a secret)
4 I can't choose **between** these three dresses.	4 either one thing or another

10.4 *beyond*

	Use to express
1 The farm lies **beyond** that field.	1 'further than' (distance)
2 His story is **beyond** belief. She is **beyond** help.	2 'outside the understanding or the reach of'
3 The success of the plan was **beyond** anything we had hoped for.	3 'more or better than'

10.5 *by*

	Use to express
1 This book was written **by** Charles Dickens.	1 who does/did/will do an action
2 This model was made **by** hand.	2 how something is/was/will be done
3 The bank is just **by** the Post Office.	3 closeness or nearness to
4 **By** next year I'll have finished this book.	4 'not later than'

Useful expressions

by accident	*by* all means	*by* post	amazed *by**
by air/bus/car/	*by* chance	*by* sight	astonished *by**
plane/sea/	*by* day/night	*by* surprise	impressed *by*
ship/train (and	*by* (doing)	*by* yourself	surprised *by**
other means	*by* far	(alone)	upset *by*
of transport)	*by* mistake		
			* = or at

10.6 *except*

	Use to express
1 All the boys had pens **except** one.	1 'excluding'
2 The holiday was excellent, **except** for the rain.	2 'apart from' + noun
3 He's a good student, **except** that he's always late.	3 'apart from the fact that' + clause

10.7 *for*

	Use to express
1 This is **for** you.	1 'intended to belong to'
2 We've lived here **for** three years.	2 length of time ▷ GS 13.1.3
3 We walked **for** several miles.	3 distance
4 Are you **for** or against nuclear weapons?	4 'in favour of'
5 What did you do that **for**?	5 reason
6 Let's go out **for** a meal.	6 purpose (+ noun)
7 They left **for** America this morning.	7 movement towards

Useful expressions

for ever	once and	anxious *for*	pay *for*
for goodness'	*for* all	as *for*	reason *for*
sake	*for* a while/	ask *for*	responsible *for*
for heaven's	time	care *for*	search *for*
sake			

10.8 *from*

	Use to express
1 We travelled **from** Vienna to Paris by train.	1 place of origin
2 He works **from** 9 till 5.	2 a starting point in time
3 Prices start **from** £5.	3 a starting point in quantity
4 I can't tell one **from** the other.	4 separation

Useful expressions

from A to Z	*from* morning to	away *from*	prevent *from*
from beginning	night	apart *from*	(doing)
to end	*from* time to	hear *from*	suffer *from*
from head to toe	time		

10.9 *in*

	Use to express
1 They're **in** the kitchen.	1 place
2 We got married **in** March/winter/1985.	2 a point during a longer period of time – weeks, months, seasons, years and centuries
3 I'll be back **in** an hour.	3 'within a certain time'
4 He's **in** banking/the local police force/a mess.	4 a job/profession/situation

Useful expressions

in all	*in* general	*in* particular	*in* time
in any case	*in* half	*in* prison	*in* turn
in bed	*in* a hurry	*in* private	*in* a way
in common	*in* ink/pencil	*in* public	*in* a sense
in danger	*in* love	*in* secret	dressed *in*
in debt	*in* a loud voice	*in* sight	get *in*
in difficulties	*in* the morning	*in* spite of	interested *in*
in the end	*in* my opinion	*in* stock	succeed *in*
in fact	*in* other words	*in* tears	take part *in*

10.10 *into*

They came **into** the room.

Use to express movement towards

Useful expressions

bump *into*	jump *into*
crash *into*	run *into*
get *into* (trouble)	throw *into*
go *into*	walk *into*

10.11 *of*

1 The cover **of** this book is attractive.

2 He's one **of** my best friends.

3 a ton ⎫
   a pint ⎬ **of** ⎧ bricks
   a pound ⎭ ⎨ milk
            ⎩ butter

4 He died **of** starvation.

5 a man **of** 40/the City **of** London/made **of** gold

Use to express

1 'belonging to'

2 'from among'

3 measure

4 cause

5 description

Useful expressions

ahead *of*	enough *of*	in front *of*	proof *of*
because *of*	everyone *of*	instead *of*	remind someone
by means *of*	example *of*	lack *of*	*of*
cure someone *of*	explanation *of*	on account *of*	several *of*
die *of*	hundreds *of*	on behalf *of*	think *of*
dozens *of*	in case *of*	out *of*	typical *of*

10.12 *off*

1 A tile has come **off** the roof.

2 Our house is **off** the High Street.

Use to express

1 movement away from

2 'at a distance from'

Useful expressions

off duty	get *off* (the bus)
off limits	take *off* (your coat)
off work	

10.13 *on*

1 The book is **on** the table.

2 I'll see you **on** Saturday morning/Christmas Day/your birthday.

3 What's **on** TV tonight? There's a good film **on** at the cinema.

4 He's written a book **on** insects.

Use to express

1 contact (on the surface of)

2 time – a particular day

3 what entertainment is being offered

4 what something is about

Useful expressions

on business	*on* holiday	agree *on*	depend *on*
on duty	*on* purpose	congratulate	have an effect
on time	*on* sale	someone *on*	*on*
on foot	*on* the whole		
on the other hand			

10.14 *out of*

1 She ran **out of** the house.

2 Two **out of** five children have learning problems.

3 I copied the recipe **out of** the newspaper.

4 The dress was made **out of** a lace curtain.

Use to express

1 movement away from

2 'from among' (with ratios)

3 place of origin

4 the material something is made from

Useful expressions

out of breath	*out of* date	*out of* the	*out of* reach
out of control	*out of* order	question	*out of* stock
out of danger	*out of* practice	(impossible)	*out of* work

10.15 *since*

1 I hadn't seen him **since** 1978.

2 **Since** he had 'flu, he decided not to go to work.

Use to express

1 a starting point for actions and situations which continue up to the moment of speaking ▷ GS 13.1.3

2 'because' ▷ GS 6.2

10.16 *to*

1 We're going **to** Paris.

2 It's a quarter **to** 12.

3 We'll be in the office from 5 **to** 6.

4 He won by 2 games **to** 3. I prefer sleeping **to** working.

Use to express

1 'in the direction of'

2 before (in time)

3 'until'

4 comparison

Useful expressions

according *to*	in order *to*
in addition *to*	so as *to*
due *to*	
owing *to*	

10.17 *under*

1 The box is **under** the stairs.

2 Please don't sweep the dust **under** the carpet.

3 The bridge is **under** repair.

Use to express

1 'beneath'

2 'beneath' (with movement)

3 'in the process of'

Useful expressions

under control	*under* orders
underneath (preposition) = under	*under* oath (in a court of law)

10.18 *until/till*

1 I'll keep the ring **until** we meet again.

2 Stir the mixture **until** it thickens.

Use to express

1 up to a certain time

2 'up to the point or degree when'

10.19 up

Don't run **up** the stairs.
He went **up** to the next class.

Use to express movement to a higher place

Useful expressions

up-to-date (modern)
*up*hill

ups and downs (good times and
  bad ones)
fed *up* (bored or unhappy)

10.20 with/without

1 Be patient **with** the children.
2 He hit the burglar **with** a hammer.
3 You'll have to go **with/without** me.
4 A room **with/without** a view.

Use to express

1 'as regards'
2 instrument
3 accompanying/not accompanying
4 having/not having

Useful expressions

with best wishes	angry *with*	disgusted *with*	trembling *with*
with/without difficulty	do *without*	impressed *with*	(fear)
without any fuss	filled *with*	pleased *with*	(what's) wrong
with love	green *with* envy	shivering *with*	*with*(?)
with pleasure		(cold)	
agree *with*	have difficulty *with*		

11 Relative clauses

11.1 Defining relative clauses ▷ pp. 5, 99

Is that the man **who wants to buy your car**?

These clauses are necessary in order to complete the meaning of a sentence. They identify somebody or something. No commas are used.

11.1.1 Relative pronouns in defining clauses

1a The person **who deals with that** isn't here at the moment. The person **that interviewed me** was a nice sort of fellow.

b The person **who/whom/that you want** is out of the office.

c The man **whose address you've asked for** has left the firm.

2a The instructions **which come with this machine** are impossible to follow. The book **that you lent me** was very difficult to read.

These relative pronouns are used

1 for people
a *who/that* – as the **subject** of the verb in the clause
b *who/whom/that* – as the **object** of the verb in the clause (*whom* is more formal)
c *whose* – meaning 'belonging to'

2 for things
a *which/that* – as **subject or object** of the verb in the clause. **Notice** *what* can be used to express 'the thing which/that' (e.g. It was difficult to believe *what* you told me.)

11.1.2 Leaving out the relative pronoun in defining clauses

The man (*who/whom/that*) I was meeting was an important client.

The relative pronoun can be left out when it refers to the **object** of the verb in the clause. **Notice** the relative pronoun cannot be left out when it refers to the **subject** of the verb in the clause e.g. *The man who came to meet me was an important client.*

11.1.3 Prepositions used with relative pronouns in defining clauses

1 The man who/that I was talking **to** is my uncle.

2a The person **to** whom I was addressing my comments does not seem to be listening.

b The problem **about** which we had so much discussion has been solved.

1 The preposition comes at the **end** of the clause in informal speech and writing.

2a The preposition comes at the **beginning** of the clause in formal speech and writing.

b **Notice** the relative pronoun cannot be left out in sentences like these even though it is the object of the verb in the clause.

11.2 Non-defining relative clauses ▷ pp. 5, 86

I've just met Mr Watts, **who wants to buy your car.**

These clauses give further information, which could be left out, about the sentence. Commas are used.

11.2.1 Relative pronouns in non-defining clauses

1a The members of the expedition, **who had been away from home for six months**, said they were proud of their achievements.

b The candidates, **who/whom we met for the first time yesterday**, are all preparing their speeches for the debate tomorrow.

c A car manufacturer, **whose name I have forgotten**, has invented an electric car.

2a The report, **which was drawn up by a special committee**, states that more needs to be done in the inner city areas.

b He had been in prison, **which was a fact nobody had realized.**

These relative pronouns are used

1 for people
a *who* – as the **subject** of the verb in the clause
b *who/whom* – as the **object** of the verb in the clause
c *whose* – meaning 'belonging to'

2 for things
a *which* – as the **subject or object** of the verb in the clause
b *which* – to give further information about the whole main sentence

Notice the relative pronoun cannot be left out in non-defining clauses and *that* cannot be used to replace the relative pronoun.

11.2.2 Prepositions used with relative pronouns in non-defining clauses

The organization, **to** which we owe so much, has announced a further contribution to our appeal.

Prepositions usually come at the beginning of the clause as the use is rather formal.

11.3 Participle phrases

In participle phrases the relative pronouns and the auxiliary verb(s) are left out.

	These phrases can be
1 The boy **(who is) sitting in that corner** has been there all morning. The bricks **(which have been) used to build this church** were specially made.	1 defining or
2 Simone de Beauvoir, **(who was) well known for her fight for women's rights**, died in 1986.	2 non-defining

12 Reported speech ▷ pp. 29, 37, 54

9 a.m.

12 midday

12.1 Tenses

12.1.1 Changes

Verbs used in direct speech often change their tense in reported speech, especially when the 'reporting' verb is in the past (e.g. *said*).

Direct speech	Change	Reported speech
1 'I*'ll put* the letters in the post.'	1 *will* to *would*	1 He said he **would put** the letters in the post.
2 'I *work* for an insurance company.'	2 *work* to *worked*	2 She said she **worked** for an insurance company.
3 'We *can't* borrow any more from the bank.'	3 *can't* to *couldn't*	3 They said they **couldn't** borrow any more money from the bank.
4 'We*'ve moved* to a bigger house.'	4 *have moved* to *had moved*	4 They said they **had moved** to a bigger house.
5 'I *must* pay the gas bill.'	5 *must* to *had to*	5 She said she **had to** pay the gas bill.

12.1.2 No changes

Some verb tenses used in direct speech do **not** change in reported speech. The 'reporting' verb is often in the present tense.

Direct speech	Reported speech
The verbs do not normally change when	
1 reporting a present state of affairs e.g. 'The cost of living here *is* high.'	1 The reporter says/said that the cost of living here **is** high.
2 reporting things which are always true e.g. 'It*'s* always cold at this time of year.'	2 Mary says it**'s** always cold at this time of year.
3 reporting something which we believe (or someone believes) will happen e.g. 'They*'re going to sack* 300 workers next week.'	3 The union representative said they **are going to sack** 300 workers next week.
4 they are the modal structures *would*, *could*, *might*, *ought* and *should*, e.g. 'You *might* be mistaken.'	4 She said (that) he **might** be mistaken.

12.2 Reporting statements

12.2.1 Verb (+ *that*)

(e.g. *say, claim, admit, explain, insist, agree, complain, deny, reply*)

'I'm an art student.'	She **said** (that) she **was** an art student.
'I don't know you.'	He **claims** he **doesn't know** her.
'I was lying.'	She **admitted** she **had been lying**.
'I'm hot.'	He **explained** (that) he **was** hot.

Notice *admit* and *deny* can also be followed by the *-ing* form.

12.2.2 Verb + pronoun/noun (+ *that*)

(e.g. *tell*)

'I'm an art student.'	She **told** him (that) she **was** an art student.

12.2.3 Verb + infinitive

(e.g. *offer, refuse, agree, promise*)

'I'll take you to the dance.'	He **offered to take** her to the dance.

12.2.4 Verb + *for* + *-ing* form

(e.g. *apologize, thank*)

'I'm sorry I trod on your foot.'	She **apologized for treading** on his foot.
'Thank you for doing the shopping.'	He **thanked her for doing** the shopping.

12.3 Reporting requests and orders

'Close the door, please.'	He **asked me to close** the door.
'Please don't shout.'	She **asked them not to shout**.
'Sit, Rover.'	The boy **told his dog to sit**.
'Don't move.'	The policeman **ordered the burglar not to move**.
'Attack.'	The Captain **ordered his soldiers to attack**.

12.4 Reporting questions

Remember to change the word order in a reported question to subject followed by verb.

'What time is it?'	He asked what time **it was**.
'How much money do you need?'	She asked how much money **I needed**.

Remember to use *if* or *whether* if there is no question word.

'Are you tired?'	He asked **if** I was tired.
'Do you want the car or not?'	She wondered **whether** I wanted the car or not.

12.5 Reporting suggestions ▷ p.117

suggest can be followed by an *-ing* form or *that* + *should* + infinitive.

'Let's go home.'	He **suggested going** home.
	He **suggested that** they **should** go home.

12.6 Other points to notice about reported speech

Direct speech	Reported speech
1 The pronoun often changes e.g. '*I*'ve washed the dishes.'	1 **She** said **she** had washed the dishes.
2 Words like *tomorrow* change to words not directly related to present time e.g. 'I'll do it *tomorrow*.'	2 He said he would do it **the following day/the next day**.
a '*today*' →	a **the same day/that day**
b '*yesterday*' →	b **the day before/the previous day**
c '*next week/year*' etc. →	c **the following week/year etc.**
d '*last week/year*' etc. →	d **the previous week/year etc.**
e '*now*' →	e **then**
f '*here*' →	f **there**
g '*this*' (in time expressions) e.g. '*this week*' →	g **that** (e.g. **that week**)
3 Other changes are	
a '*this, these, that, those*' (as adjectives) →	3a **the**
b '*this, these, that, those*' (as pronouns)	b **it, they/them**
4 Some words like *please* and *now* disappear e.g. '*Please* come in.' '*Now* what do you want to talk to me about?'	4 He asked her to come in. She asked him what he wanted to talk to her about.

13 Tense forms

13.1 Present forms

13.1.1 Present simple

1 We **go out** every Saturday night.
He never **gives** me presents.

2 He **lives** in Greece.
The earth **travels** round the sun.

3 Jane: I **don't like** big cities.
They **smell** of cars.
Peter: I **know** what you **mean**.

4 First you **check** the gears and handbrake, then you **switch on** the engine.

5 A gorilla **goes** into a bar and **asks** for a drink. . . .
The Pope **visits** Tokyo today.

Use

1 for something which happens regularly or which is a habit (often with adverbs of time e.g. *always*, *usually*, etc.)

2 for something which remains true for a long time or for a scientific fact

3 with verbs not normally used in any of the progressive forms (*believe, understand, imagine, suppose, hear, see, taste, love, hate, need, want, prefer, seem, appear, belong, deserve*).
Notice *feel* can be used either in the simple or progressive forms e.g. *I feel ill/am feeling ill*.

4 to give instructions (more friendly and personal than the imperative *Check, switch on . . .*)

5 to describe events in jokes, stories or news items to make them seem more dramatic
▷ GS 13.3 for the future use of the present simple

13.1.2 Present progressive

1 Look, they**'re coming** out of the cinema now.
The standard of living in this country **is** slowly **rising**.

2 She**'s always borrowing** money from me.
It**'s always raining** here.

3 A man **is standing** on the pavement when suddenly a spaceship lands.

Use

1 for an event in progress at the present time.

2 with *always* to show surprise or disapproval when an action is repeated

3 to set the scene in a joke or a story and describe events which have already begun but which are not complete

▷ GS 13.3 for the future use of the present progressive

13.1.3 Present perfect ▷ pp. 41, 53

1 I**'ve seen** that film.
  I**'ve just seen** him.
  I **haven't finished yet.**
  I**'ve never been** there.

2 She**'s been** a widow for about six months/since last year.

3a I can't write because I**'ve broken** my arm.

  b Look at the mess you**'ve made.**

4 This is the third time he**'s taken** his driving test.
  This is the worst film I**'ve ever seen.**

Use

1 for an event which happened at an indefinite time in the past. **Compare** I saw that film last week where the time reference is definite.
  Notice adverbs which express indefinite times are often used: already, just, yet, often, never, so far, still, etc.

2 for an event which began in the past and is still going on now.
  Notice we use for to talk about the length of time ▷ GS 10.7; we use since to talk about when the event started ▷ GS 10.15

3 for an event which

  a is finished but which still affects the present (e.g. **compare** The President died **and** The President has died (so we must make various arrangements)

  b has a result which can be seen in the present (e.g. **compare** What have I drawn? **and** What did I draw?)

4 after expressions like

  $\left.\begin{array}{l}This \\ That \\ It\end{array}\right\}$ is the $\left\{\begin{array}{l}first, second \dots \\ best, worst \dots \\ most\ interesting \\ \dots \\ only \dots\end{array}\right.$

13.1.4 Present perfect progressive ▷ p. 53

1a We**'ve been living** here for six years/since 1981.

  b We**'ve been standing** at this bus stop for half an hour in the pouring rain.

2 I**'ve been staying** with my cousin for the last week.

3 Look at the mess you're in! What on earth **have you been doing**? I can see that you**'ve been decorating.** The house looks lovely!

Use

1a for an activity which began in the past and is still going on (to emphasize the length of time taken by the activity)

  b (**Notice** it often shows anger, surprise, etc.)

2 to describe a temporary arrangement which may still be going on or which may just have finished

3 for an activity which was going on, which has now finished and the **result** of which is still evident. (This, too, often shows anger, surprise, etc.)

13.2 Past forms

13.2.1 Past simple ▷ pp. 41, 53

1 Last night I **went** to a concert. The last time I **saw** Maria was three years ago.

2 Jane: **Did** you **have** a nice time in Paris?
  Peter: Yes, we **did.**

3 The thief **went** into the bank, **pulled out** a gun and **pointed** it at the cashier.

4 When I was at school, I **got up** every day at seven o'clock.

Use

1 when a definite point in time is mentioned when talking about the past

2 when the event took place at a time the speaker is aware of but does not mention

3 for a number of events which took place one after another in the past

4 to describe a past habit ▷ GS 13.2.2.

13.2.2 used to and would

1a I **used to** smoke cigars but now I prefer cigarettes.
  He **used to** be very fat but he's lost a lot of weight.

  b I **didn't use to** go to the theatre but I try and go about once a month now.
  I **never used to** like him but I do now.

  c **Did** you **use to** do sport at school?
  Didn't you **use to** be much thinner?

2 He **would** keep telling me what to do!

used to only exists in the past form. Use it to express

1a a habit or a state in the past ▷ GS 13.2.1

  b something which did not happen in the past but which has now become a habit or state. **Notice** the negative form (e.g. I used not to go to the theatre) is becoming less common in speech but is still found in formal or written English.

  c an inquiry about a habit or state in the past

  Compare the expressions be/get used to:
  I'm used to getting up early.
  I was used to getting up early.
  You'll soon get used to drinking tea!
  I soon got used to working so hard.
  Notice after be/get used to we use the verb + -ing

Use would

2 for a habit or repeated event in the past which is now finished and which shows the speaker's attitude to the event (anger, irritation, etc.) ▷ GS 7.3

13.2.3 Past progressive

1a I **was driving** along the motorway when I had a puncture.

b It was six o'clock and darkness **was falling**.

2 I **was digging** the garden while John **was painting** the kitchen.

3 He **was coming** to dinner but he had to go away on business.

Use

1a for an event which was in progress when another event happened

b to set the scene and provide the background for a story

2 for two (or more) events which were in progress at the same time in the past

3 for an event which had been arranged but which did not happen

13.2.4 Past perfect

1 I went back home because I'**d forgotten** my keys.
I was sure I **hadn't seen** him before.
By 1986 Bob Geldof **had raised** millions of pounds for charity.

2 I **had scarcely/hardly put** the phone down **when** the bell rang.
No sooner had I left the house **than** it started to rain.

Use

1 for an event which happened before another in the past (first I forgot my keys, later I went back home)

2 with *scarcely/hardly + when* or *no sooner + than*. **Notice** these words (*scarcely, hardly, no sooner*) are often put at the beginning of the sentence to emphasize that one event happened almost immediately after the other (notice the word order).

13.2.5 Past perfect progressive

They'**d been studying** for hours when they suddenly realized it was midnight.
He knew they **hadn't been paying** attention during the lesson.

Use

to emphasize the continuous nature of an action or activity which happened before another in the past

13.3 Talking about the future

I'**m going to wash** my hair.
It'**s going to snow**.

I'**ll see** you tomorrow.

Term **starts** on Monday.

I'**m meeting** the boss at 10.

This time tomorrow I'**ll be sitting** my exam.

I'**ll have finished** it by 4 o'clock.

We'**ll have been living** here for ten years next spring.

They'**re about to announce** the election results.
He'**s on the point of changing** his job.

be going to

future simple

present simple

present progressive

future progressive

future perfect

future perfect progressive

be about to or *be on the point of*

1a I'**m going to write** some letters.

b Look at those black clouds. I think it'**s going to rain**.
The work **is not going to be** easy.

2 Tomorrow **will be** fine and sunny.
We **shall expect** you next week.

3 Easter **is** early this year.
The match **begins** at 3.30.
When he **comes**, I'll tell you.

4 We'**re flying** to Spain next week.
I'**m taking** my driving test tomorrow.

5 This time next week I'**ll be swimming** in the Mediterranean.

6 They'**ll have done** their homework by tomorrow.

7 He'**ll have been working** for the bank for 30 years next summer.

8 The plane **is on the point of taking off**.
Nick **was just about to put** the money in his pocket.

---

1 Use *be going to* for

a an intention

b an indication that something is probable

2 Use future simple (*will/shall*) to make a prediction about the future. ▷ GS 7.1
Notice *shall* is only used for *I* and *we*. ▷ GS 7.2

3 Use present simple for future events on a timetable or a fixed programme. **Notice** *when* can be used with the present simple for an event in the future.

4 Use present progressive for a definite arrangement, plan or appointment.

5 Use future progressive for an event which will be in progress at a certain time in the future.

6 Use future perfect for an event which will be over not later than a certain time in the future.

7 Use future perfect progressive for something still in progress but which will be complete not later than a certain time in the future (often used to emphasize the length of time involved).

8 Use *be about to* or *be on the point of* for an event which is or was just going to take place.

14 Wishes, regrets and preferences

14.1 Wishes and regrets ▷ pp. 43, 47

1 I **wish** I **were** rich!
If only we **could see** each other more often!
I **wish** we **didn't live** in this terrible place.

2 I **wish** you **wouldn't make** so much noise!
If only they **would stop** that terrible noise!
I **wish** it **would stop** raining!

3 I **wish** I **had** never **married** him.
If only I **had studied** harder at school.
I **wish** you **hadn't told** me your secret.

1 These examples express wishes (often suggesting that the speaker is sorry about something – *I'm sorry I'm not rich*).
Notice the 'past' form of the verbs (*were, could see, didn't live*) after *I wish* and *if only* as with conditional 2. ▷ GS 4.2

2 These examples express wishes for a change in the future and often suggest that the speaker is angry or dissatisfied about (or tired of) the present situation. ▷ GS 7.3.

3 These examples express wishes or regrets about the past (*I wish I had studied harder but I didn't!*).
Notice the past perfect is used in the same way as conditional 3 sentences. ▷ GS 4.3

14.2 Preferences

1a I **like** the summer **better than** the winter.

b I **prefer** soft drinks **to** alcohol.

2a I'**d rather have** a snack **than** a take-away meal.

b I'**d rather not go** to the football match, if you don't mind.

3 I **would rather** you **stayed** at home tonight. I think it's going to snow.
I'**d rather** you **didn't see** him again.

1a *like . . . better than . . . and*

b *prefer . . . to . . . express general preferences.*

2a '*d rather* + infinitive without *to . . . than . . .* expresses either a general preference or a preference for a particular occasion ('this is what I usually prefer' or 'this is what I would like now').
Notice '*d prefer* expresses a preference for a particular occasion (e.g. *I'd prefer (to have) a glass of wine now*).

b '*d rather not* + infinitive without *to* expresses the fact that you would prefer not to do something which has been suggested.

3 *would rather* + (*you* etc.) + past tense suggests that you would be happier if someone did or didn't do something.
Notice the 'unreal' present is expressed by a 'past' form of the verbs *stayed, didn't see*.
▷ GS 4.2

15 Words that cause difficulties

have, make and *do*

15.1 *have*

15.1.1 Three basic uses of *have*

1 She **has** bought a new car.
He said he **had** seen the film.

2 I **have** (got) **to** be ready at 6.30.
You **don't have to** (**haven't got to**) do it if you don't want to.
Do I have to (Have I got to) go?

3 They'**re having** the house **decorated**.
Did he **have** his hair **cut** yesterday?
I **didn't have** the curtains **made**. I made them myself.

4 I'**ve got** a headache.
Have you **got** a big family?
I **haven't got** any brothers or sisters.

have can be used

1 as an auxiliary verb

2 to express what is or isn't necessary. **Notice** *have got to* can be used to express the same idea as *have to*.
▷ GS 7.9

3 to express the idea of arranging for or paying somebody to do something for you. **Notice** the object of the sentence comes between *have* and the past participle. ▷ GS 8.3

4 with *got* to express a condition or state (less common in the past tense and often suggesting the idea of 'possession').
Notice *have got* is now more common in statements than the rather formal *I have four brothers*, **but** question forms and negatives with *do* and *have* are commonly used (e.g. *Do you have a big family? I don't have any brothers or sisters*).

15.1.2 Other expressions using *have*

1 I'll **have** the chicken/some tea, please.

2 He'**s having** a shower/bath/rest.

3 She'**s** just **had** a little girl.

4 She **had** an enormous hat on.

5 We'**ve had** a marvellous holiday.
We **didn't have** any trouble with the car.

6 **Have** a try!
Did they **have** a quarrel?

have in these examples means

1 'eat' or 'drink'

2 'take'

3 'give birth to'

4 'wear'

5 'experience'

6 In these examples and others like them, *have* means the same as the word it is used with (e.g. 'try', 'quarrel').

15.1.3 *had better*

You **had better** decide quickly.
You'**d better not** have any more to drink!

had better is used to give strong advice (= *ought* ▷ GS 7.10)

15.2 *do* and *make*

15.2.1 Meanings of *do* and *make*

1 What are you **doing**?
I'm **doing** a puzzle.

2a I'm **making** a cake.
This firm **makes** TV sets.

b The car journey **made** him sick.

c They **made** him work very hard.

1 *do* can mean 'perform an action in general' and 'solve or put together'.

2 *make* can mean

a 'create' or 'construct'

b 'cause to happen'

c 'force'

15.2.2 Other expressions using *do* and *make*

DO		MAKE	
– a course	– History, Maths, Science (as subjects)	– arrangements	– money
– a favour		– an attempt	– a noise
– homework		– the beds	– an offer
– military service	– work or jobs in general (the cleaning/ gardening etc.)	– a decision	– a phone call
– something/ nothing/ anything		– an effort	– a profit
		– an excuse	– a speech
		– love	– a suggestion
		– a mistake	– trouble

Notice there are many phrasal verbs with *do* and *make*. ▷ GS 9.5

1) Форма ЛБ + квитанция 50 руб. И всё-таки что нужно?

2) Medecal assesment for Андрюшки Sen? and me?
   How we can obtain all paperwork

3) Internal passport (Is it possible or not